PROBLEMS OF THE MODERN ECONOMY

The Crisis of the Regulatory Commissions

PROBLEMS OF THE MODERN ECONOMY
General Editor: EDMUND S. PHELPS, *Columbia University*

Each volume in this series presents
prominent positions in the debate of
an important issue of economic policy

The Crisis
of the Regulatory
Commissions

AN INTRODUCTION TO A CURRENT
ISSUE OF PUBLIC POLICY

Edited by
PAUL W. MAC AVOY
MASSACHUSETTS INSTITUTE OF TECHNOLOGY

NEW YORK
W · W · NORTON & COMPANY · INC ·

Contents

Introduction

WHEN FACED WITH a single source of supply of transportation or energy or communications services, the consumer has reacted by going to the legislature for protection against arbitrary price behavior. This has been the almost habitual response for more than three quarters of a century, beginning with Grangers' and shopkeepers' appeals to State legislatures for maximum intrastate railroad rates in the 1870's, and culminating in the general farmers and merchants movement for formation of the Interstate Commerce Commission in 1887 to control railroad rate discrimination. The regulatory commissions so founded have developed habitual procedures for reviewing the behavior of companies in their industries—procedures which emphasize ceilings on prices that allow a "reasonable rate of return" on the investments of the regulated companies. Regulation has become "bureaucratized", with consequent effects on production, prices, and technical progress throughout American industry. Indeed, the regulatory process may have become frozen in the last half century, while the regulated industries themselves grew and developed around the commissions.

The regulatory commissions showed enough vigor and inspiration in the 1960s to forestall the impression that they were frozen into repetitive and largely ineffective application of court rules. The Federal Communications Commission and the Civil Aeronautics Board were reorganized early in the Kennedy administration. The Interstate Commerce Commission largely reorganized itself so as to begin to write its own opinions in cases and to provide consistent standards for deciding issues relating to a national transportation policy. The Federal Power Commission broke through years of case backlog in setting natural gas field prices by constructing new "area price ceilings" for hundreds of cases involving gas in one or the other particular producing field. There was some hope that these regulatory agencies would begin to formulate policy for setting prices and product quality in the public utility industries—even more, that new policies would fos-

ter efficient use of resources and new technology in these industries.

By the end of the 1960s it had become clear that these hopes
were not justified. Little more was accomplished in the decade.
There were many reasons for this state of affairs, but new research has suggested that the hopes were fundamentally un-
sound. The basic problem seems to be not a lack of high quality
leadership in the regulatory commissions, or the lack of commission activity, but rather that the *methods* of regulation themselves cause inefficient operations in the public utility industries.
There were instances where this was readily apparent—regulations prohibiting entry into a market had led to shortages, and
regulations prohibiting price increases in periods of substantial
general price inflation had also led to shortages. There was also
more substantial and general evidence, however. Economic research in the universities, the commissions, and the regulated
companies had led to the accumulation of substantial quantitative findings on the general effects of regulation. These findings,
when brought together from such diverse sources, lead to the
very general conclusion that regulation has imposed considerable
costs on public utility company operations without providing
compensating benefits.

This conclusion has created a crisis for regulation in the
United States. The findings seem not to be explainable on
grounds of the commissions' laxity or ineptitude, but rather to
follow from the basic procedures for setting "just and reasonable
rates." Unless these procedures are changed—perhaps even
done away with entirely—administrative reform cannot lead to
greater efficiency and growth in the regulated industries. The
crisis is not in *regulation,* but rather of the *need for regulation as
it now exists,* in comparison with totally new techniques or no
regulation at all.

The crisis and some possible remedies are the subject of this
volume. To begin, the methods now generally used for setting
regulated prices have to be understood. The classic review in
Part One of these methods by the late Justice Felix Frankfurter
and Henry M. Hart, Jr. not only elucidates the procedures for
setting "just and reasonable prices" but shows the prolonged
controversy in the courts over half a century on the appropriate-
ness of the most widely used procedures. The controversy, as

the authors indicate, strengthened procedures using judgmental rates of return on original investment as the basis for setting final prices. Professor Abba Lerner, in the second article, assesses the theoretical efficiency of this kind of regulation as compared to alternatives. Both articles provide the *rationale for regulation* of natural monopolies in the United States and point to ways of carrying out this regulation.

Part Two contains representative or leading assessments of the economic effects from present forms of regulation. Richard Posner's article outlines the possible and probable inefficiencies generated by "rate of return" regulation. In a broadly realistic approach, Posner shows the likely reactions of the public utility company to the impositions of controls, the important part played by possibilities for evasion of these controls, and the effects on full use of resources where the controls cannot be evaded. George Stigler and Claire Friedland show that the presence of a regulatory commission in a state has little effect upon electricity prices there, and they go on to speculate that the effects of competition across markets and the opportunities for evasion overwhelm the power to regulate price. This is one of the first statistical analyses of price differences between regulated and unregulated utilities, and has been an important source of ideas and approaches in quantitative analysis of commission behavior in the later 1960s. Ronald Coase, in the "Comment" at the end of Part Two, surveys some of the later work. He finds that regulation has not been an obvious success, and that the reasons include both "government failure" and "economists' failure," where the latter consists of the inability of economic analysts to solve important contemporary economic problems. This review holds out little hope for improvement: the techniques for showing the effects of present regulation are so limited that the ways to improve on these effects are obscure.

These general reviews provide an effective framework for examining the present economic status of industries regulated by a national commission. The transportation industries under the aegis of the Interstate Commerce Commission are examined in Part Three, and television broadcasting under the Federal Communications Commission is reviewed in Part Four. Air transport regulation, and natural gas field price regulation, are analyzed in Parts Five and Six respectively.

The studies of regulation in the transportation industries in Part Three show strong adverse effects from regulation, and also demonstrate that economy-wide gains can be made by reducing the control of rates by the Interstate Commerce Commission. George Wilson shows that regulation of some carriers but not others "imposes an artificial restraint and higher costs upon those subject to ICC jurisdiction and thus occasions a relative over-expansion of unregulated carriage." The cost to the economy in over-use of resources is not negligible. Merton J. Peck shows that expenditures on freight transport would be reduced by more than $400 million per annum by relaxing rate controls so that the shipper used the low-cost transporter. Not all of this amount consists of transportation costs, so that not all would be savings in resources; yet, as the author suggests, savings of part of this amount here and in other industries from changes in regulation cannot be ignored.

The assessment of regulation in radio and television broadcasting is adverse and close to unanimous, but the proposals for reform are more controversial. There is agreement—in the Coase, Steiner, and White articles in Part Four—that present broadcast services do not meet the demands of an educated (and thus articulate) minority. They could be served by changing market institutions, and these changes could be brought about by the regulatory authorities or Congress acting on the authorities. But there is no agreement on the exact nature of the required changes. Coase proposes a new mixture of market and regulatory incentives, while Peter Steiner prefers a subtle criterion for regulatory agency allocation of television bandwidth to increase the diversity of programming. To some extent, the two new Ford and Carnegie Foundation proposals borrow strategies from both of these. Stephen White outlines the new ways the two foundations propose to build "public television," shows the differences in promised services, and the degree of reliance on the mechanisms of the Federal Communications Commission. By implication, the success of the Carnegie proposal shows the disregard for this commission as the means for solving communications problems.

Part Five contains the broadest assessment possible of the behavior and effects of the Civil Aeronautics Board. Richard Caves defines the goals of the Board, and treats the decisions of this agency in terms of its adequacy for achieving these goals. As a most valuable additional step, the author analyzes the additions to air service costs that result from commission pursuit of its political aims and aspirations. He concludes that "reasonable men may surely doubt that these goals are worth the cost" and he offers a feasible plan for deregulation of air transportation.

Price regulation in the natural gas field has been an experiment over the last two decades quite unlike regulation elsewhere. The requirement that the Federal Power Commission set prices of gas producers in sales to pipelines is quite recent—imposed not by new statutes in the mid-1950s, but by a surprising and controversial interpretation of a 1938 statute by the Supreme Court. Also, the procedures evolved over very few years from traditional "rate of return" regulation to price ceilings on all transactions in predesignated geographical regions. The reasons for the advent and evolution of controls, and the results for exploration and development of new gas reserves, are assessed in Part Six. The first paper approaches the problems created by reasons and results with the tools of economic and statistical analysis, while the second uses the tools of both economist and legal analyst to judge long term trends in industry behavior. Even given the differences in approach, there is much agreement in the two final assessments. The two papers make the strongest possible case for reversal of history—for new legislation for FPC procedures which remove controls over field prices.

Given the general case against traditional regulation in Part Two and the subsequent particular industry problems from commission rules in Parts Three to Six, should new and better policy approaches to the public utility be devised? The answer, as given by William Baumol in the first essay in Part Seven, is found in evaluation of the alternatives. This author offers simple and flexible rules which do not differ in kind from those now in affect, but differ—in emphasis on the timing and economic content of regulatory reviews—enough that they might well produce higher rates of technical progress and lower prices in the "natural monopoly" industries. E. W. Clemens and Edward Renshaw offer more revolutionary alternatives. Clemens proposes a set of decision rules which remove the net profits which cause distortions under the traditional rules, Renshaw a change in the

profit motivations of regulated firms. None of these new approaches has been tried; but an a priori case can be made for
experimentation on the basis of the evidence that poor results
are now being achieved with traditional procedures. None of
these or other approaches will be attempted until there is general recognition of the need for regulatory reform. The achievement of recognition is the purpose of research and teaching in
economic analysis, and the final justification for books such as
the one that you are now reading.

Part One   The Reasons and
Methods of Regulation

Rate Regulation

FELIX FRANKFURTER AND HENRY M. HART, JR.

The authors contributed this essay to the Encyclopaedia of the
Social Sciences *when both were professors of law at the Harvard
School. Subsequently, Mr. Frankfurter became an Associate Justice of the Supreme Court, while Professor Hart continued fundamental research on the Federal judicial system. The essay remains
as basic now as when published, more than twenty-five years ago.*

RATE REGULATION in the common usage of the term in the United
States is concerned with the fixing of prices to be charged by
public utilities. Usually these are enterprises furnishing transportation, communication, heat, light, power, water, and the
like, and it is with such businesses that this article deals.

The English common law, perhaps continuing familiar church
doctrine regarding the just price, gave ample recognition to the
power of the state generally to control prices in the public interest. As late as the eighteenth century virtually any calling
which a man pursued for profit was considered a common calling
and treated as public in a sense akin to the modern. All such
callings were under duty to serve the public at reasonable rates,
and from time to time they were subjected to price fixing either
by Parliament directly or through the delegated authority of the
justices of the peace. English example crossed the Atlantic. Statutes in colonial America established prices for many of the
staple commodities and services. As the economics of Adam
Smith won its way in the congenial mental climate of the nine-
teenth century American law, however, this long experience

was discredited when not forgotten, and the assumptions upon which it rested were in great part repudiated. Ultimately this reversal of opinion was written into state and federal constitutions by the lawyers and judges of the latter part of the century. The resultant contemporary separation of industry into businesses that are "public," and hence susceptible to manifold forms of control, of which price supervision is one aspect, and all other businesses, which are private, is thus a break with history. But it has built itself into the structure of American thought and law; and while the line of division is a shifting one and incapable of withstanding the stress of economic dislocation, its existence in the last half century made possible, within a selected field, a degree of experimentation in governmental direction of economic activity of vast import and beyond any historical parallel.

The survival of a few of the traditional common callings provided the nucleus from which developed by enlargement the modern category of public utilities. Chief among them was the common carrier, given new form and acquiring new importance with the perfection of the steam engine. The growth of railroads compelled legislative protection of the public against extortionate tolls. This purpose was commonly given effect in conditions attached to the grant of the privilege of incorporation, following the method employed in the case of the familiar bridge, canal, and turnpike companies. Thus the charter itself frequently fixed specific tolls or reserved power in the legislature to change those fixed by the carrier or, often, provided limitations upon net earnings. But such methods of control were at once too tenuous and too inflexible to meet the exigencies of a transportation system fast out-growing all possible anticipations of the incorporating legislatures. Even before the Civil War several states paved the way to subsequent development by experimenting with rudimentary forms of continuous administrative supervision. After the war both agrarian and industrial pressures made the problem of control acute. In the 1870s legislation growing out of the Granger movement and in 1887 the creation of the Interstate Commerce Commission served to establish beyond controversy the principle of railroad rate regulation and to fix the administrative as the normal method of giving effect to it, definitely superseding rate fixing by charter or statute.

Other utilities from another beginning took a different course to a similar end. Water companies and light companies, first gas and then electricity, requiring franchises for the use of city streets, were originally regulated through franchise grants. Since their activities were confined in the beginning to individual communities, regulation by such localities sufficed. Gradually, however, the extension of the area of service by the utilities, their growing importance in economic life and the enormous power both economic and political which they exerted combined to create the necessity and the demand for more effective regulation. Meanwhile new forms of analogous public services, like pipe lines and electric power, patently beyond the reach of any but state authority, were coming under legislative scrutiny. Under these conditions the movement to establish public service commissions with state wide authority over all classes of utilities grew into one of the most significant legislative developments of the twentieth century. The issues were early made vivid by Theodore Roosevelt in the nation and such men as La Follette of Wisconsin, Hughes of New York, and Dolliver of Iowa in the states. In 1907 Wisconsin and New York led the way in adopting legislation. Today tribunals of like character exist in all the states but Delaware, commonly exercising over the utilities broad powers with respect to rates, accounts, conditions of service, finance, and management.

The legal conception of a public utility was established and applied to an ever-widening group of services in the face of powerful currents of both thought and action, tending to the insulation of business from government. In a society committed to the general principle of free competition, the economic justification of rate regulation in particular industries has naturally been framed in terms of the exceptional conditions prevailing in those businesses. Public utilities as a class lend themselves readily to such an analysis. On the affirmative side the argument of free competition as the automatic price regulator and public protector has not even doctrinaire validity; on the negative side, the practical difficulties which ordinarily surround the enterprise of governmental price fixing are of greatly diminished force. The factors limiting the effectiveness of competition as a normal regulator of prices are cumulative. Fundamental is the peculiarly functional relationship which the utilities characteristically bear to the economic order as a whole. Transportation, communication, light, and power are the keystones of an integrated industrial structure, control of which is attended by extraordinary economic power. Such power lends itself to abuse and tends to be concentrated in relatively few hands. For the utilities as a group are either enterprises which move toward monopoly or those whose highest efficiency may be reached under monopolistic operation. This characteristic may be due to a variety of reasons, such as the necessity of unitary management for adequate service, as in the case of telephones and telegraphs, or the limited capacity of city streets, as in the case of most municipal utilities. Most strikingly and most generally it grows out of the huge investment in plant required in proportion to current income, the operation of that plant largely at joint cost, and the consequent necessity of a large and steady volume of traffic to maintain the investment. These circumstances render complete competitive duplication of facilities improbable or impossible and make duplication, so far as it exists, wasteful and uneconomic. New competitors are slow to enter and old ones slow to leave an industry in which participation involves so large a stake. Monopoly once secured thus tends to perpetuate itself; while competition, if it exists, offers only the alternatives of combination or of destructive price cutting, designed to maintain volume at any cost. The experience of a century with railroads, and for shorter lengths of time with other utilities, attests the abuses of instability and waste, of alternating high rates and ruthless price cutting, of inadequate service and discrimination, which follow from a regime of unregulated competition.

Similar factors create conditions especially favorable for regulation. Competitors are few; and heavy expenditure together with the usual necessity of governmental permission to engage in the business prevents mobility of entrance and exit from it. The problem of supervision and control of investment is thus simplified. Because the businesses consist typically in the dispensing of services which are not, like tangible goods, susceptible either of being withheld from the market or of flooding it, private manipulation of prices through control of supply is difficult or impossible. Hence an area is marked out in which governmental price fixing may operate effectively even in the context of an economy basically laissez faire.

Some such economic considerations underlie the decisions of

the Supreme Court on the constitutional power of the states and the federal government to regulate rates, but the reasoning has seldom been explicit. This is due partly to the relative novelty of the problem. The earliest decision upholding a state's power to regulate rates under appropriate circumstances is scarcely more than half a century old; and the legal basis for denying it under any circumstances is only eight years older. In 1876, when the potential breadth of impact of the Fourteenth Amendment upon restrictive state legislation was as yet scarcely imagined, statutes of middle western states regulating the rates of grain elevators and of railroads were attacked under the due process clause [Munn v. Illinois; Chicago, B. & Q. R.R.Co. v. Iowa; Peik v. Chicago & Northwestern Ry. Co., 94 U.S. 113, 155, 164 (1876)]. Chief Justice Waite's judgments sustaining the measures rested heavily upon the practical circumstances of monopoly and the inadequacy of normal competition to protect the public; in none of the cases did he make serious effort to mark out the limitations upon state power. But in justifying a conclusion otherwise arrived at he quoted a passage from Lord Chief Justice Hale's essay on the ports of the sea: "Looking then," Waite said, "to the common law, from whence came the right which the Constitution protects, we find that when private property is 'affected with a public interest, it ceases to be *juris privati* only.'" By reading into this colorless statement a negative principle justified neither by history nor by the context, decisions of the last twenty years have made Waite's opinion serve a purpose for which it plainly was not intended, have authoritatively set up the verbal canon of affectation with a public interest as determining legislative power to fix prices in a particular business. The history of this development is traced by Justice Brandeis in his dissenting opinion in the New State Ice Company v. Liebmann [285 U.S. 262 (1932)].

The words themselves are palpably empty. Chief Justice Taft essayed definition by classifying types of enterprise within their ambit: first, businesses "carried on under the authority of a public grant of privileges which either expressly or impliedly imposes the affirmative duty of rendering a public service demanded by any member of the public"; secondly, "certain occupations, regarded as exceptional, the public interest attaching to which, recognized from earliest times, has survived the period of arbitrary laws by Parliament or Colonial legislatures for regulating all trades and callings"; and, finally, as a catchall, "businesses which though not public at their inception may be fairly said to have risen to be such and have become subject in consequence to some government regulation" [Wolff Packing Co. v. Court of Industrial Relations, 262 U.S. 522 (1923)]. Into the third category the court has received the businesses of insurance and of livestock and insurance brokers; it has in specific instances excluded that of vendors of gasoline, of theater ticket brokers, and of employment agencies, as not then "affected with a public interest" [Tagg Bros. v. United States, 280 U.S. 420 (1930)]. The category is still open; nor may it be expected soon to become closed. For in essence the futile efforts at dogmatic statement of doctrine cover a clash of opinion on a far reaching issue; namely, to what degree free competition is so complete a protection to the public interest as to render arbitrary any governmental departure from it. That issue remains open and will call for continuing accommodation so long as our politico-economic system is based on individualism.

The controversy over new admissions into the magic circle of public utilities is an aspect of the general problem of price regulation. Within the circle the critical issues are different. Like every other aspect of expanding governmental activity in the United States, rate regulation has presented for preliminary determination manifold questions involving the harmonious adjustment of power within the federal system. The most intricate of these have been concerned with railroads, for their development most palpably transcended arbitrary state lines and abstract conceptions of state and national authority. Here too, where experience has been longest and pressure for effective action most insistent, the adjustment has been worked out in greatest detail. Originally the Supreme Court appeared to sanction state regulation of interstate rates in the absence of congressional action [Peik v. Chicago, Northwestern Ry. Co., 94 U.S. 164 (1876)]. In 1886 by repudiating this construction of its decision (Wabash, St. L. & P. Ry. Co. v. Illinois, 118 U.S. 557, 567, 569) it gave effective impetus to the passage of the Interstate Commerce Act of 1887. The movement finally culminated in the curtailment of state power even over intrastate rates. The court began by upholding in sweeping terms the states' authority to establish intrastate rates in the absence of federal action [Minnesota Rate Cases, 230 U.S. 352 (1912)]. But thereafter it upheld successively the power of the commission, under the original act, to set aside such rates if they discriminated unduly against particular persons or places in interstate commerce [Shreveport Rate Cases, 234 U.S. 342 (1914)] and the extension of its authority in 1920 to prescribe intrastate rates in lieu of existing ones discriminating against interstate or foreign commerce generally [Wisconsin Rate Case, 257 U.S. 563 (1922)]. The ultimate adjustment, however, has been achieved, not by the general terms of congressional legislation or in occasional explosions of litigation before the court but by the day to day work of the commission, which on the whole has exercised its plenary power with statesmanlike regard, on the one hand, for the necessities of a national transportation system and, on the other, for the desirability of harmonious cooperation between the Interstate Commerce Commission and state regulatory bodies, with a minimum of encroachment upon the latter's authority.

Effective collaborative action between federal and state administrative agencies is still unrealized in other fields. Particularly in respect to interstate power, where the situation is of comparable gravity, the utilities have for some time eluded control. The jurisdiction of the receiving state over retail distribution has apparently been recognized [Pennsylvania Gas Co. v. Public Serv. Comm., 252 U.S. 23 (1920); compare East Ohio Gas Co. v. Ohio Tax Comm., 283 U.S. 465 (1931)], but over wholesale distribution it has been definitely denied [Public Utilities Comm. v. Attleboro Steam & Elec. Co., 273 U.S. 83 (1927); Missouri v. Kansas Natural Gas Co., 265 U.S. 298 (1924)]. Meanwhile effective exercise of authority has been hampered by multifarious difficulties in obtaining adequate information and enforcing decisions, arising especially from confusion of intercorporate relations. In Smith v. Illinois Bell Tel. Co. [282 U.S. 133 (1930)], however, the court indicated how intercorporate interests might be divided for the purpose of bringing them under different regulative authorities. Control by the Federal Power Commission reorganized in 1930 is confined to licensees of federal power sites, and the provisions of the act of 1920 looking toward federal and state cooperation have yet to bear substantial fruit in action. Legislation is bound to enter this field with more comprehensive control.

Of a wholly different nature from problems of jurisdiction but of no less moment are the issues of constitutionality centering around procedural and substantive aspects of the rate fixing process itself. These are issues of conformity to whatever may be the requirement drawn from the due process clauses of the Fifth and Fourteenth amendments and they exist only because of the decisions of the Supreme Court. The earliest of these decisions disclaimed all concern with such questions. If the rate "has been improperly fixed," said Chief Justice Waite, in first sustaining railroad rate regulation, "the legislature, not the courts, must be appealed to for the change" (Peik v. Chicago, Northwestern Ry. Co). But this judicial self-abnegation did not long survive the pressure of distrustful property-holding groups soliciting protection from unrestrained legislative action. There were several warnings of a different view, and in 1890 the court definitely adopted the position that "if the company is deprived of the power of charging reasonable rates for the use of its property, and such deprivation takes place in the absence of investigation by judicial machinery, it is deprived of the lawful use of its property, and, thus, in substance and effect, of the property itself, without due process of law. . ." (Chicago, M. & St. P. Ry. Co. v. Minnesota, 134 U.S. 418).

This step was scarcely less important in procedural than in substantive law. The court did not stipulate, and it never has stipulated directly, any particular procedure in the fixing of a rate as an essential of due process. But it was indispensable to the success of the administrative method that the party demanding "investigation by judicial machinery" should not be able to compel every step in the administrative process to be retraced afresh in court. Questions of law must be re-examined by a judicial tribunal. Questions of face, the Supreme Court holds, needs not be so re-examined if, but only if, the administrative procedure conforms to elementary fairness, without which judgment becomes arbitrary. The tribunal must grant a proper hearing to the parties affected: it must decide upon the evidence presented at the hearing, and there must be evidence in the record to support its findings. In the enforcement of these standards the court—primarily the Supreme Court—have at once strengthened the essential administrative arm of government and protected private individuals against its arbitrary conduct, besides having evolved empirically a body of administrative law relevant in other fields of governmental activity. In one important group of cases, however, the court seized for the judiciary power that plainly belongs to the administrative experts, if they have any *raison d'être*. In Ohio Valley Water Company *v.* Ben Avon Borough [253 U.S. 287 (1920)] it decided that in rate controversies involving the issue of confiscation, due process of law required that administrative findings of fact be open to independent re-examination in a court. This doctrine may be accounted for by judicial distrust of the non-judicial determination, even indirectly, of issues of constitutional right; by the extent to which in rate proceedings questions of law turn upon questions of fact; and above all by the vast interests that are at stake and the distrust of governmental curbs to big business at the time a divided court rendered the decision. In practise, a genuinely independent judgment by the court is almost impossible by reason of the multitudinous details and their recondite significance; yet the Ben Avon case remains a sword of Damocles hanging over the regulatory systems, especially those of the states.

But it is in giving content to the substantive limitation announced in the early Minnesota rate cases that the Supreme Court has most decisively influenced the course of rate regulation. By that decision the court projected into every rate proceeding, state or federal, a potential issue of the denial of due process of law as guaranteed by the Fifth and Fourteenth amendments. The issue was of a character unfamiliar to the courts; save for the simple and scarcely adequate concept of reasonableness, the common law furnished no canons for determining when the rates which a utility was permitted to charge had been reduced to the point of confiscation. The opinion in the famous case of Smyth *v.* Ames [169 U.S. 466 (1898)] gave the first indication of how the court was going to attack the task of formulating such canons. The court undertook to measure the reasonableness of rates to be charged by a utility by inquiring into the return which they yielded; and it set out to determine the fairness of the return by inquiring into the value of the property which was used to earn it. Later decisions have brought into sharper focus another element of the decision, have made clear that in speaking of "the fair value of the property being used for the convenience of the public" the court meant the present value of that property. Out of this effort to tie rate regulation, as a matter of constitutional right, to a perennially shifting and inherently unstable rate base have flowed the most troublesome of the problems which ever since have beset the courts and the commissions. By a process of self-delusion not uncommon to judges when casting grave issues of public policy into the mold of law, the court seemed unaware that it was trying to formulate into legal principles and doctrines what were really determinations resting largely in opinion quite outside the orbit of judicial insight or experience.

Justice Brandeis, whose concurring opinion in the Southwestern Bell Telephone Company case [262 U.S. 276 (1923)] is the classic refutation of the doctrine of present value, explained its emergence in terms of the conditions following the panic of 1893. "Watered stock, reckless financing, and unconscionable construction contracts" had created fictitious capital values far in excess of those on which the shippers believed the railroads should be permitted to earn a return. At that time supervised accounting and financing had not yet been introduced to provide reliable proof of actual cost and investment. Accordingly, in Smyth v. Ames, William Jennings Bryan as counsel, representing shippers in agricultural communities, urged upon the court estimates of the present value of the railroad properties, which in a time of low prices were estimates of reproduction cost. A different explanation, however, must be sought for the Supreme Court's continued adherence to a rule thus established under conditions which no longer obtain. Basic was the conviction, rooted in attitudes toward the social justification of the stimulation of investment through its amplest protection, that utility investors should not be deprived of the benefit from appreciation of capital incident to investment in all other enterprises. The test of present value has been defended as a flexible instrument of accommodation to changes in the price level, doing equal justice to the public and the utility owners and making possible the attraction of new capital.

The determination of utility rates and the ascertainment of the rate base are essentially economic problems. But no judicial pronouncements upon matters fundamentally economic run so counter to the views of economists as do the predepression utterances of the Supreme Court upon present value. The theoretical unfairness of the doctrine has been repeatedly pointed out, for common stockholders benefit out of all proportion from increases in the price level appreciating the value of the entire property, whereas holders of bonds and preferred stock bear the risk of decreases without corresponding possibility of gain. Most conclusively, however, is the doctrine condemned by experience; the test of thirty-five years has powerfully demonstrated its unworkability. The Supreme Court itself has as yet been able to furnish no calculus of present value; and it becomes increasingly clear that none can be furnished, for uncertainty inheres in the standard.

The consequence has been, in every important rate-fixing proceeding, a preoccupation, lasting sometimes for years, with contention over fanciful elements in quest of a rate base; that is, a supposedly objective mathematical ascertainment, in fact illusory, of the amount on which the allowable rate of return must be fixed. This procedure has entailed an incredible waste of time and money and inevitably embittered relations between the utilities and the public. Thus in a leading valuation controversy in New York over telephone rates the litigation began before a commission in 1920 and went its snail-like pace through the federal court until 1930. Half a dozen estimates of value—by the commission, the master appointed by the court, the court itself and the company's experts, all purporting to apply the Supreme Court's formula—ranged between $366,000,000 and $615,000,-000. A similar case in Chicago was in the federal courts for more than ten years and had not been concluded at the end of 1933. In the latter case it cost $25,000 to print the record of the proceedings for review by the Supreme Court. The whole process is fundamentally an elaborate fiction. In the end rates are fixed which reflect no other reality than that of compromise, re-enforced partly by the superior advantage of the utilities in litigation.

Actual cost, capitalization, prudent investment, cost of reproduction either of the existing plant in present use or of a modern plant giving equivalent service, these and many other elements have been pressed for consideration in diverse cases involving rate bases, and in various situations the propriety of all of them has been recognized. Necessarily the formula depends upon particular conditions: the past, present, and probable future level of prices, the history of the company and the conditions of its property. No formula can survive serious changes in these elements of the problem.

Dominant effect, the court has indicated in a series of decisions antedating 1932, must normally be given to reproduction cost. To ascertain the expense of constructing a railroad, a power plant or a telephone system in the midst of a community which could have no existence without them is to operate on an unreal hypothesis and requires calculations upon assumptions foreign to human experience. It is not surprising therefore that the Supreme Court has never provided the commissions with workable intellectual tools for making the determination. The so-called rules constitute a maze; their operation in practise descends into a process of economic legerdemain whereby those who control utilities through narrow equities are enabled to seek constitutional sanction for speculative gains.

Nor has it proved to be true that the rule of present value provides a means of flexible adjustment to changing price levels. The process of valuation is too ponderous to permit flexibility under any circumstances. In practise, moreover, initiative in rate proceedings is more often taken on behalf of the utilities than of the public; the hands of the commissions are variously stayed in beginning actions for reduction, by lack of time, money, will, or authority. More important still, in times of depression the doctrine of present value will not bear a rigid application in favor of the public. A deflated price structure is not responsive to the assumptions of a theory sedulously cultivated by the utilities during high prices; it produces a theoretical base too low to permit fixed charges, assumed at higher levels, to be met —the more so because decreasing traffic raises operating costs and earnings shrink even under existing rates. Thus, while obedient to theory, rates may rise with prices when business prospers and profits swell with heavier traffic, under opposite conditions they fall less rapidly or not at all.

For all these reasons the practical result of the control evolved by the Supreme Court over rate regulation has been to put the constitution behind the right to earnings on utility investments, to an extent that contradicts the very basis on which governmental intervention rests. Indeed the judicial doctrine of valuation sanctions what the utilities themselves, as a matter of business, cannot practise. As a matter of "good business judgment," utilities commonly charge rates which, if established by the commissions and attacked in the courts, would be declared confiscatory and unconstitutional under the doctrine of a reasonable return on present value. On the other hand, as the point of confiscation drops with falling prices, utility rates habitually lag far above it, subject only to delayed and intermittent attacks by public authorities, the basis of which is liable to be destroyed at any time by price recovery. The depression which began in 1929 is replete with proof of this experience.

The difficulties with the method of determining the rate base, as developed under the rule of Smyth v. Ames, have their counterpart in the attempt to determine what is a reasonable rate of return. For by similar reasoning the utility is entitled to a return at a rate determined by the present condition of the money market, without regard to the price actually being paid for capital already invested. Hence common stock dividends, already swollen by inflated valuation, may benefit doubly from allowance of a higher rate of return. Similar uncertainty, too, beclouds the method of computation. Although the Supreme Court has indicated that the rate should be that generally ruling investments of comparable risk at the same time and place, the usual practise in rate cases is to submit opinion testimony by bankers or other persons as to the rate currently necessary to attract new capital, a test which in times of business stress may lead to an altogether different result. Since 1929, however, several federal district courts have upheld rate reductions ordered by commissions, holding that a fair return in times of depression should be calculated at a lower rate than in periods of prosperity.

Questions concerning the rate of return are, however, overshadowed in practise by controversies about valuation and the rate base, where the opportunity for inflated claims is greater. The reluctance of courts to recognize directly the necessity of a relatively high rate of return has contributed also to their willingness to permit adjustment of the rate base to serve in part the function of adjustment of the rate of return. The two problems are inextricable; a workable technique for computing fair return must await satisfactory determination of the elements to be considered in computing fair value.

The importance of the constitutional aspects of rate regulation is the greater because they in effect control proceedings not only in the courts but before the commissions. In theory the duty of a commission under the statute is to set a reasonable rate, and between the statutory standard of reasonableness and the constitutional one of confiscation there may well be a substantial margin. In practise, however, the line of confiscation is likely to be so high that the pressure of circumstances, and not least the desire not to run foul of the judiciary, will be to set the rate as near that line as possible.

But the problem of confiscation has only to do with the general level of rates. That level being fixed to allow a fair return on the property as a whole, administrative considerations have freer play in the determination of particular rates. It is here that rate regulation has achieved its most substantial accomplishment and has amply justified itself. Particularly in the case of railroad rates, which have been regulated far more minutely and effectively than those of other utilities, the most intricate problems concern the adjustment of tariffs for different commodities and hauls. In the making of these adjustments the Interstate Commerce Commission and the several state commissions exercise vast powers over the development of communities and industries. To a lesser degree similar problems and similar interests attend the adjustment of differentials in telephone and telegraph rates and rates for light and power. Joint costs being high and accurate allocation of costs to particular services impossible, the controlling considerations tend to be the assurance of adequate service throughout the area as a whole, without regard to loss at particular points, and the fullest possible promotion of the economic development of the entire community. Moreover the constitution cannot be invoked against state policy in treating a localized part of a larger system as the unit in determining the rate base [Wabash Valley Elec. Co. v. Young, 287 U.S. 488 (1933)]. In such conflicts among groups of consumers the inclination of the courts has been strongly toward accepting the administrative judgment. And while discrimination in rates was originally a dominant factor in the movement for regulation, particularly in respect to railroads, similar complaints are now of comparatively minor importance.

The adoption of the modern machinery of utility rate regulation during the decade prior to the [First] World War was accomplished upon a wave of popular enthusiasm. In the postwar
decade, however, skepticism and discouragement tended to
supplant the earlier feeling of hope. Particularly in the leading
industrial states criticism was voiced against the failure of utility
rates to reflect decreased operating costs due to technological
improvements, against the costly futility of rate proceedings and
against failure of the commissions to exercise skilled initiative in
the promotion of the public interest. Conviction has been gathering that the regulatory systems do not realize but even operate
to defeat the aims for which they were designed. This change of
temper is no doubt partly a reflex of the different price levels
obtaining before and after the war. When the commissions began to operate, rates were widely believed to be unreasonable;
some measure of success at first attended the efforts to secure
their reduction. With the great rise in prices after the war the
commissions became more often instruments for the increase of
utility rates than for their decrease. Dissatisfaction with the
workings of the system, however, has still deeper roots. In a
wide variety of concrete instances the machinery of utility regulation has shown increasing strain. Revealed shortcomings in administration and legislation and in the judicial doctrines to
which they are required to conform have been accentuated by
the stress of new economic forces and by the ingenuity of the
utilities in devising unanticipated means of eluding effective
control. Beyond question successful regulation cannot be
achieved upon a permanently unstable and incalculable rate
base.

The difficulties inherent in the methods imposed by the judiciary upon administrative agencies have been intensified by
the quality of their personnel. Almost everywhere the commissions have been inadequately staffed, overburdened by detail,
denied necessary technical aid, dependent on meager salaries,
and without security of tenure. The hope behind public utility
legislation during the era of Theodore Roosevelt was a body of
administrators intellectually as well equipped as the higher officials in the British Civil Service and exercising independence
and authority comparable with that enjoyed by judges in the
United States. A few men—like John M. Eshleman of California,

George W. Anderson and Joseph B. Eastman of Massachusetts, Milo R. Maltbie of New York, and David E. Lilienthal of Wisconsin—vindicated that hope. But in the main the public interest has suffered from too many mediocre lawyers appointed for political considerations, looking to the Public Service Commission not as a means for solving difficult problems of government but as a step toward political advancement or more profitable future association with the utilities. As a result there has been inequality in expertise, in will, and in imagination between the utilities and the regulatory bodies. Thus, with only a few notable exceptions, the utilities have commanded the services of the best of the engineering profession on those technical issues which are so central in valuation controversies.

Nor has legislation been adequately responsive to the shifting exigencies of the problem. Many commissions lack adequate authority in various directions: they cannot enforce proper accounting methods, initiate proceedings for rate regulations, compel disclosure of essential information, inquire into the hide-and-seek mysteries of intercorporate relations. Especially have the efflorescence of the holding company and the organization of auxiliary companies for management, construction, purchase, and finance created intricacies of technical ownership and practical control before which the investigating authority has often been helpless. Yet these very devices serve powerfully to sustain schemes for inflated values. These difficulties have been further enhanced by expansion of activity across state lines, so that effective legal control falls too frequently between the two stools of state and federal authority.

Pessimism as to the future of rate regulation, however, has nowhere been so profound as to suggest return to unregulated private enterprise; rather it has contributed to the impulse in quite the opposite direction, that of public ownership. To be sure, this development, even in the face of grave abuses and growing discontent, encounters the obdurate and stimulated traditions of the United States against government in business. On the other hand, government ownership as a yardstick gives every assurance of being powerfully promoted by the Tennessee Valley Authority. The reactive effect of this government enterprise upon electric rates of private companies has already made itself felt. To the extent that public opinion will not be won to public ownership strengthening of the existing regulatory system is plainly indicated. Another mode of accomplishing the old objectives of utility regulation is by contract arrangements between municipalities or states and grantees of public franchises. Whatever the forms of the attempted solutions, problems of utility rate regulation—so long as private enterprise survives—are at once the epitome of crucial and characteristic issues of contemporary government and the test of its resources. Not until those resources, as to both men and method, have been explored far more patiently, persistently, and imaginatively than they have been, will anything approximating a final verdict upon the undertaking be feasible.

Conflicting Principles of Public Utility Rate Regulation

ABBA P. LERNER

Abba Lerner is professor of economics at the University of California, Berkeley, and one of the leading economic theorists in the United States. His paper was originally presented to an American Telephone and Telegraph seminar at the University of Chicago which seeks each year to interest young economists in the problems of regulation. Subsequently published by the Journal of Law and Economics, *it provides a basic outline of a rationale for regulation for both lawyers and economics students.*

LOOKING THROUGH SOME LISTS of criteria that distinguish public utilities from other parts of the economy, I found them so varied and confusing that it seemed best to go behind them to consider the general social function of price in the economy before turning to the special situations we call public utilities.

There are two basic functions of price: to discourage the buyer of a commodity (or service) from using up too much of it, and to induce the supplier to produce enough. But what is the right amount? What is enough and not too much?

Any increase in the consumption of a commodity is a *benefit* to the consumer (not considering the utopian state where everybody has as much as he can use of every item). But every such expansion implies a withdrawal of resources from the provision of something else (not considering the "upside down" economy where the expansion would be provided entirely from unemployed resources). It therefore entails a *damage* to the would-be consumers of the alternative product. Whenever the benefit is greater than the damage, the output and consumption of the item in question should be expanded, and in the reverse case it should be contracted. The ideal position is reached when the two are just equal so that there would be no net gain either from expanding or from contracting the output. In more technical language, the ideal output is where marginal social benefit is

18

equal to marginal social cost.

The price paid by a buyer of anything is what it costs him to get an extra unit of it—but only if his buying does not increase the price. If it does, then the cost to him is equal to the price *plus* the increase in the price of all the other units he buys. If he does not think the price is significantly influenced by how much he buys, then as long as his benefit from another unit of the item is greater than the benefit he could get from using the price to buy other things, he will buy more, and he will buy less in the reverse case, until the difference has disappeared. The price of the item is then a measure of his private marginal benefit from it. If, furthermore, nobody else either benefits or is hurt by his use of an additional unit, his private benefit is also a measure of the marginal social benefit from having another unit of the item.

Similarly, if the seller of an item does not believe that the price is significantly affected by how much he sells, then the price is exactly what he gets from selling an extra unit, and as long as the damage to him or cost involved in giving up or making an extra unit is less than the damage from not getting the price (which is the same thing as the benefit from getting the price) he will sell more, and he will sell less in the reverse case, until the difference has disappeared. The price will then be the measure of the private marginal cost. If, furthermore, nobody else either benefits or is hurt by his effort or sacrifice in providing what he sells, the price will then also be a measure of the marginal social cost of providing another unit of the item.

If these conditions are satisfied throughout the economy—that is, if every buyer and every seller accepts the market prices as independent of the amount he buys or sells, and there are no "externalities" (no outsiders, but only the buyers and the sellers, are affected by the consumption or production of the commodities they buy or sell)—then the prices will have achieved perfectly their basic function of bringing about the "right" output of every item. Given the technical possibilities of production and the tastes and preferences of the consumers and producers, and accepting, for our present purposes, the distribution of income and wealth among the members of the economy, there will be neither too much nor too little produced or consumed by anybody of any item.

The next thing to observe is that this ideal is achieved automatically in a perfectly competitive economy where nobody has any power over any prices. All the prices are determined by the impersonal forces of supply and demand on the various markets. Such a perfectly competitive economy need not be completely (or even partially) run by private enterprise. A government-owned enterprise could conceivably behave just like a perfectly competitive private enterprise. Prices would still be carrying out perfectly their basic function of inducing the "right" production and consumption of everything by everybody.

A government-owned *industry* would, of course, be able to raise prices by selling less or buying more and to lower prices by selling more or buying less. By restricting output, it could cause the price to rise, say, one dollar; or it could set the price one dollar higher, recognizing that this would reduce the amount it could produce and sell. The amount produced and consumed would then be less than the "right" amount and the price mechanism would have failed to fulfill its basic function in an ideal manner. But this could happen just as well in an economy which consisted entirely of private enterprise even with perfect competition. The government could order the firms to pay it one dollar on every unit of the item that it sold. All the effects would then be exactly the same.

In that case, if four dollars were being paid for a unit of the item, we would say that only three of the dollars were performing the basic function of price. The fourth dollar was a *tax* which, whatever its justifications, interfered with the ideal functioning of the price mechanism. But this is just as true for the government-owned industry. That industry does not separate the fourth dollar from the other three to give it to the government because the whole business belongs to the government anyway, but the extra dollar charged disturbs the ideal output just the same. We are therefore justified in calling it a *tax*. Any excess of the price charged over the marginal cost is therefore in the nature of a tax, and we may define it as such. This is the basic distinction between a price and a tax. Similarly, the government could sell for a dollar less than the marginal cost, or, equivalently, it could *pay* perfectly competitive private producers a dollar for each unit sold. In both cases, we would have a subsidy or *negative tax* of one dollar per unit.

It is not only the government that can cause the customer to be charged more than the marginal cost. Whenever a seller discovers that he does have some influence over price, he is tempted to restrict output so as to benefit from the resulting higher price. In all such cases, we have not only interference with the ideal working of the price mechanism but "taxation without representation"—a charge in excess of the marginal cost imposed by private enterprise. This combination constitutes the essence of the objection to *monopoly* (the power of sellers over price, often standing also for *monopsony,* the power of buyers over price).

Where the restriction is due only to sellers or buyers getting together in order to create power over market prices, the appropriate medicine is some form of "trust-busting." But the large size of firms that gives them power over prices is often necessary for efficiency. Breaking up such firms would do more harm than good. How to retain the large firm for the sake of the efficiency while preventing its power over prices from interfering with the ideal working of the price system involves some kind of regulation, and this is the essence of the public utility price regulation problem.

When the government is sufficiently concerned about the excessiveness of the price charged for a commodity to feel that it must correct this, even though price regulation would be required, we have a public utility and the problem of how the price should be regulated. Most definitions of a public utility consist of reasons, of which there may be many, why the government should be sufficiently concerned about the excessiveness of the price for the commodity or service (or the inadequacy of the commodity or service for the price).

It is the failure to understand and apply the principles sketched above that leads to regulation being misdirected against bigness in the name of competition or against competition in the name of efficiency, and to the elevation of regulation by some into a good in itself, in the name of "order," or to its condemnation by others as a pure evil under the name of "regimentation." A more sober approach often leads to the idea that if monopolies could be made to behave as if they were perfectly competitive, we would be able to enjoy the benefits both of large-scale efficiency and of the perfectly working price mechanism. But here there is a danger of coming to regard *perfect com-*

petition as an end in itself, rather than as one way in which marginal social benefit may be brought into equality with marginal social cost so that the price mechanism can carry out its basic social function. Regarding perfect competition as an end in itself makes it difficult to separate those of its qualities that serve as means for our purposes from those that do not.

For a firm in perfect competition, there are four items which are all equal to each other: price, marginal revenue, average cost, and marginal cost. There are consequently six different possible equations between different pairs out of the four items. Which one or which ones of these should the regulator try to impose on the monopolist in the form of instructions to follow about the inputs and outputs that he can control? We may go through the six possibilities:

1. *The equality between price and marginal revenue* is not one that can be imposed. It is not but a description of the perfectly competitive state of the market in which there is no monopoly.

2. *The equality between marginal revenue and marginal cost* does not need to be imposed. It is reached automatically by the firm in maximizing its profit.

3. *The equality between average cost and marginal cost* is one that *can* be imposed by the regulator. The monopolist can be instructed to produce that output which brings about this equality. Furthermore, such an output is reached when the average cost is minimized, and that seems like a good idea. But what is really desirable is something that sounds like this but is really very different. What is really desirable is that the *right* output should be produced at the minimum average cost (and therefore at the minimum total cost)—not that a *different* output should be produced because the average cost would then be less. This is still not the regulation we are looking for.

4. *The equality between price and average cost* is a possible rule for regulating the monopolist's output. With a fair return on the capital included in the costs, this may be recognized as the well established rule as to what a public utility is entitled to earn.

There are two difficulties about this. The first difficulty is that there may be more than one output at which the average cost is equal to price. This is usually dealt with by dragging in an auxiliary principle, namely, that the largest of such outputs should be chosen. The second difficulty is that price may be below average cost for all outputs so that there is no output which would satisfy the rule, even though *some* output of the item is unquestionably desirable. This difficulty can be "solved" by the device of charging different prices to different groups of consumers, when that would make it possible for the *average price* to be equated to the average cost, some of the prices being above and some below the average cost. (The essential incompatibility of the price discrimination with the perfectly competitive model which the regulation is supposed to reproduce is obscured by calling both *price* and *average price* "average revenue.") Furthermore, there often are many sets of discriminatory prices that equate average price with average cost so that auxiliary principles still have to be dragged in, such as that the largest of these outputs should be chosen.

But even when all these difficulties have been "solved" by a patchwork of *ad hoc* auxiliary principles, the achievement of equality between average cost and price (or average price) still does not indicate the achievement of the socially desirable output that equates marginal social benefit to marginal social cost. It merely shows the result of freedom of entry into the industry, and it could be achieved with any degree of monopolistic restriction of output. Prices could even be raised very high (by monopolistic "taxes"), but the new firms attracted by the resulting profits would keep coming in. This would cut into the sales of each firm, raising the average cost as the firm's scale of operations became smaller and smaller, until the rising average cost had swallowed up all the profits. The consumers would still be paying the "tax," which would not even be enjoyed as profits by the firms charging the high price. It would all be wasted in the inefficiency of the high cost due to the reduced output per firm.

5. *The equality between price and marginal cost* is of course the significant one. In the absence of "externalities" (that is, of benefits or damages accruing to outsiders), it induces consumers to consume the "right" amount. Perfect competition is socially desirable only because this is one of its six equalities. It is consequently this equality that the regulator should try to impose

on the sellers to prevent them from succumbing to the temptation of raising the prices of what they sell by monopolistic restriction of their sales.

6. *The equality between average cost and marginal revenue* is the only one left. This is the mirror image of equality 5, which equates price (which is also the average revenue) to marginal cost. Equality 6 is analytically on a par with equality 5 and should be imposed by the regulator on *buyers* to prevent them from succumbing to the temptation of *lowering* the prices of what they *buy* by monopsonistic restriction of their *purchases*.

Monopsony is less pervasive than monopoly, and so it is customary for economists to treat only of monopoly, in terms of equality 5, and then to add a footnote saying that all of the monopoly analysis applies in symmetrical manner to monopsony too. A better way is to deal with both monopoly and monopsony at the same time, extracting the essence of both equalities in a rule that would direct producers to adjust all their outputs and inputs so as to bring about equality of the price of each marginal output to the price of the marginal input required for the marginal output. But this is only a spelling out of the implied inclusion of equality 6 in the language of equality 5.

The widespread acceptance of equality 4—that is, of the principle that price ought to be equal to *average cost* (including a fair return on the capital invested)—seems to be based on a fusion of the capitalistic (ideological and practical) antipathy to losses with the socialistic (purely ideological) antipathy to profits.

The argument for equality 4 in the case where marginal cost is above average cost is nowhere more eloquently expressed than by George Bernard Shaw in his *Intelligent Woman's Guide to Socialism*. He recommends that the profits and royalties from England's low-cost mines be used to cover the losses from selling all the coal, including the coal from the high-cost mines, at a price equal to the average cost of all the mines. Mrs. Blanco-White responded with a book called *The Socialist Woman's Guide to Intelligence*, where, with inferior literary skill but with better economics, she points out that such a reduction in the price of coal would lead to much more being used, even though the resources required to produce the extra coal (at high marginal cost) are able to produce other items much more useful to the coal consumers themselves.

Almost all economists agree with this criticism of Bernard Shaw's economics and would say that charging less than the marginal cost (and just covering the average cost) constitutes a *subsidization* of wasteful use of coal; and that this is not in any way altered by the consideration that the subsidy is financed out of the profits (or rents) that would emerge from charging a price equal to marginal cost. What is not so widely recognized is that exactly the same considerations apply for exactly the same reasons where the marginal cost happens to be *below* average cost. Charging more than marginal cost (in order to cover average cost) constitutes a wasteful *tax* or *negative subsidy* on the consumption of the item; and this is not in any way altered by the consideration that the tax is imposed in order to cover the losses (or negative rents) that would emerge from charging a price equal to the marginal cost.

The reason for the asymmetry seems to be that the case where marginal cost is above average cost is an *easy case* where the socially desirable policy of making price equal to marginal cost (equality 5) can be made to appear to satisfy the popularly acceptable policy of making price equal to average cost (equality 4). It is not too difficult to get the capitalist to charge a price equal to marginal cost and to keep the excess of this price over average cost even if such profits have to be called "rents." There are no losses to disturb him. The Socialist who, like Bernard Shaw, is uneasy about the profits being made is tranquilized by the confusing device of capitalizing the rents, calling them interest on the capital needed to buy the right to receive the rents, and claiming them as legitimate costs that ought to be covered. And the economist observes that the "right" price is resulting in the "right" output. Everybody can be fairly happy.

But where marginal cost is below average cost, we have a *hard case*. There are losses instead of profits. The rents are *negative rents*, and no capitalist is ready to absorb them. The optimum outputs can be achieved only if some arrangements can be made for the absorption of the negative rents, thus permitting the price to be equal to the low marginal cost. Since that is not in anybody's private interest, it cannot be achieved by private enterprise alone, but only by social action. Where marginal cost is below average cost, the right public utility price can be established only if the government steps in and takes the negative rent which nobody else wants.

This is normally called a government subsidy, but in the language used here, which is more logical if less familiar, this is *not* a subsidy. It does not unduly encourage the use of the item. It merely permits the proper price to be charged, namely, the marginal cost which provides just the right degree of incentive to consumers to hold down their consumption and to producers to extend their output. A true subsidy consists of making the price *less than the marginal cost.* Shaw's proposal was for a true subsidy, and an unjustifiable one, even though it called for no contribution of money by the government. True subsidies are justified only if there is an "externality" consisting of net benefits or net damages to outsiders from the consumption of the product by the buyers—as, for example, in vaccination, which reduces the dangers of infection to the unvaccinated too. In Shaw's proposal any externalities are certainly negative—in the harm done by the smoke to outsiders—so that a *tax,* which would make the price *greater* than the marginal cost, would be more justifiable.

In recent years, a more subtle objection has been raised on distributional grounds in favor of equating price to average cost as against the principle of marginal cost pricing. Some economists who accept equality 5 (with 6) as a proper principle for "right" outputs nevertheless argue that the reduction of a price from average cost to a lower marginal cost would result in an unjustified benefit to those who consume disproportionately large amounts of the cheapened item at the expense of those who use little or none of it, and this injustice must be counted against the increase in the efficiency of the economy as a whole. The net or combined result may be undesirable. This argument is perfectly sound. What is strange is that exactly the same argument can be applied, only in a stronger form, against the reverse change. Raising price from marginal cost to a higher average cost would result in an unjustified benefit to those who use little of the item at the expense of those who use much, and this injustice must be *added to* the decrease in the efficiency of the economy as a whole. The combined result is therefore doubly undesirable. Essentially the argument is against *any change,* even if it is a generally beneficial one, since some people would be hurt by the change. It is not an argument against using one rule rather than another if one is starting fresh, although it has some force if modified to suggest that it might be desirable for a change, even if it is for the better, not to be so fast as to grievously damage established legitimate expectations. But the legitimacy of expectations of continuing private benefits from social inefficiencies diminishes over time, and such arguments for gradualness must be very carefully watched if they are not to turn into apologies for never moving at all.

A kind of compromise often suggested, and indeed practiced, between the equality 4 and equality 5 for the *hard case* where price is below average cost for all outputs, is to resort to discriminating prices, making *average price* rather than *price* equal to average cost, but keeping *one price* equal to marginal cost. This is equivalent, as we have seen, to covering the loss from the sales at marginal cost by imposing taxes on other sales at higher prices, the "tax" being the excess of those prices over marginal cost. This raises three questions:

1. Are such taxes socially necessary? (The loss could be financed by a government deficit unless that would make total spending in the economy excessive and result in inflation.)

2. Is the public utility price regulator a proper authority for imposing such a tax—or indeed any tax?

3. If a tax is necessary (to prevent inflation), is this the best tax available to the economy?

Only if all three questions must be answered in the affirmative is this compromise the best solution to the conflicting principles.

In conclusion, I would like to say that I have found it illuminating to relate the concepts of public utility and public good. The latter has not suffered from the same falling between conflicting principles, but the stock criteria of what constitutes a public good are not very satisfactory either—like the unplausible suggestion that private corporations are unable to raise enough capital to supply the public goods, or tautologies like asserting "governmental functions." I did find interesting the suggestion that a public good is one from which all people "have equal use." Clearly, different people do not get the same *utility* from the provision of a public good. The elimination of malaria is certainly a public good, but there are those who are immune to malaria anyway. I take the expression "equal use" to mean that everyone is free to take as much as he wants to of the service or of the benefits from the service that constitutes the public good. This can be permitted where the marginal (social) cost of enjoying the service is zero. Since one can use as much of it as one wants to without using any of it *up* (no resources are consumed by my not contracting malaria), there is no need to induce consumers to economize in its use. No price should be charged. The appropriate price being zero, there is no room for the popular idea that price should equal average cost. The question as to whether a particular public good should be provided, and if so how much of it, can therefore be considered with less hindrance of analysis by ideology, and the clear principles emerge that the public good should be provided if the total benefit is greater than the total cost, and that its degree of provision should be extended as long as the total benefit from any extension is greater than the total cost of the extension.

I am not saying that the practical execution of these clear principles is easy, but estimates may be made by trying to find out how much different beneficiaries would be willing to pay for the benefits (if they had to) and comparing this with what they would be willing to pay for alternative products that could be made from the same productive resources. The former measures the benefit from the public good, and the latter measures the cost. The same principle can be applied to public utilities, even though the public good appears to be only a special case of the "*hard case*" of a public utility (where the marginal cost is below the average cost). The proper price calls for the absorption of a negative rent, and private enterprise, therefore, is not prepared to provide the item at the socially desirable price. A public good is the special case where the marginal cost is not merely below the average cost. It is all the way down to zero.

But the public good principle is just as applicable to the more general *hard case* of the public utility. A public utility should be provided (and any extension in the degree of its provision should be undertaken) whenever the negative rent is exceeded by the total benefit to the consumers from being able to buy the quantity they want to buy at a price equal to the marginal cost. The surprising extension of this proposition from the special to the more general case is valid because the argument can also be put in the reverse manner—just as, for example, one can indifferently deduce the three sides of a rectilinear figure from its having three angles or its three angles from its having three sides. The *opportunity* of buying a commodity at a price equal to its marginal cost can be called a public good, since *its* marginal cost is zero. It costs society nothing to produce an extra unit of the commodity if the price paid for it, being equal to the marginal cost, sets free just enough resources (those now not needed to produce the alternative products that would have been bought with money) to provide the extra unit of the item in question. This opportunity should be provided and extended just like any other public good if the total cost of providing or extending it is less than the total benefit. The total cost of providing the *opportunity*, the excess of the total cost of providing the commodity or service over the revenue collected by charging a price equal to the positive marginal cost, is the total negative rent. It is the excess of average cost over the marginal cost (the negative rent per unit), multiplied by the output.

In the *easy case* where marginal cost is *above* average cost, the positive rent constitutes a "negative cost" or "producer's benefit" which must be *added* to the "consumer's benefit" from being able to buy the commodity at marginal cost. This is why the existence of the industry is a good thing and why any restriction, monopolisitc or monopsonistic or any other kind, is socially harmful.

The public utility can therefore alternatively be considered as a special case of a public good (which by definition has a marginal cost of zero); the public good consisting of the *opportunity* of buying something at a price equal to the marginal cost. By starting from a consideration of the general basic social function of price, we can separate the appropriate equality 5 (and its mirror image 6) from the chaff of assorted equalities and irrelevant principles that grow together in conditions of perfect competition, and thereby achieve a complete integration of the theory of public utilities and the theory of public goods in the general field of welfare economics.

PART TWO Measuring the Success of Regulation in Terms of Its Economic Effects

Natural Monopoly and Its Regulation

RICHARD A. POSNER

Richard Posner is Associate Professor of Law, Stanford University. Shortly after leaving Federal government service as general counsel of the President's Task Force on Communications Policy, he began work on a general critical review of public utility rate regulation. The review was published under the title given above in the Stanford Law Review *of February, 1969. Only Part II of Professor Posner's review appears here.*

IT MAY be helpful at the outset to describe briefly the basic workings of the regulatory process, a process that is susceptible of generalization despite the many differences in detail and emphasis among the various public utility and common carrier statutes. The heart of the process is the determination of the overall revenue requirements of the regulated firm. A test year (ordinarily the most recent typical year of operations for which complete data are available) is selected and the firm is asked to submit its operating and other expenses for that year. The regulatory commission reviews the submission and may disallow expense items that either were imprudently incurred or are not properly expenses—for example, an excessive depreciation allowance constituting a disguised return to investors. The allowed cost of service includes an allowance for a "fair return" to stockholders and bondholders who have provided the capital used to render the regulated service. That allowance is computed by multiplying the company's rate base—either the depreciated original or the replacement cost of the assets used in rendering the service—by the "fair rate of return," a composite percentage made up of the interest the corporation must pay bondholders and the estimated cost of attracting and holding the necessary equity capital. The firm then files a tariff schedule designed to enable it to just cover its cost of service including the return allowance.

The determination of a company's costs and rate base and the ascertainment of a fair rate of return involve sufficient complications to discourage the most zealous regulatory agency from conducting such proceedings continuously or even frequently. Commonly, several years elapse between proceedings, and in the interim periods the firm's costs may change from those of the test year. If they decline the firm's profits will increase, because the rate schedule fixed in the last proceeding remains unchanged until the next proceeding. Ordinarily, the firm can retain such profits, even though they exceed the fair rate of return previously determined. If costs rise, the firm will seek and usually obtain the agency's permission to file revised tariffs.

Although the regulated firm normally enjoys substantial latitude in choosing a combination of rates for specific services that will just yield its overall revenue requirements, regulatory agencies do have comprehensive power over specific rates. An agency may disallow a rate if it is "unjust" or "unreasonable" or "unjustly discriminatory." If a competitor or customer of the regulated firm complains about a specific rate—that it is unjustly low (in the case of the competitor) or unjustly high (in the case of the customer)—the agency will hold hearings and, proceeding much like a court, decide whether the complaint has merit. If so, it will order the regulated firm to revise its rate structure.

A regulated firm may not initiate, extend, or abandon a service or construct additional facilities without first obtaining a certificate of public convenience and necessity from the commission. A new firm desiring to enter the regulated business is also subject to this requirement. In addition, regulatory agencies often have broad power over a variety of restrictive practices normally covered by the antitrust laws, for example, tying arrangements, service discriminations, and mergers. Frequently the power to prohibit such arrangements is coupled with the power to approve and, by approving, to immunize them from prosecution

under the antitrust laws. Regulatory agencies have additional
powers (over accounting practices, financing, intercarrier contracts, and so on), but they are mainly ancillary to the powers
mentioned above.

With the general picture now in mind, let us look more closely
at the specific regulatory controls.

THE EFFECTS OF REGULATORY CONTROLS

Limiting the Overall Profits of the Regulated Firm · Because
the core of the monopoly problem, as traditionally conceived, is
monopoly prices and profits, the determination of the overall
revenue requirements that will just cover the test-year costs of
the regulated firm is the heart of the regulatory process. Nonetheless, the social utility of this control is questionable. The case
for placing legal limits on monopoly profits, whether on grounds
of social justice or of economic efficiency, is not compelling. What
is more, it is questionable whether regulatory agencies in fact
exercise much effective control over the profits of the regulated
firms and, if they do, whether such control has, on balance,
good effects on performance.

One reason for questioning the efficacy of regulatory constraints on profit is the intermittent character of the regulatory
determination. As mentioned earlier, in the considerable intervals of "regulatory lag" the profits of the regulated firm will
pierce the ceiling imposed by the regulatory agency if, as has
frequently been the case in the regulated industries in recent
years, costs are falling rapidly. Furthermore, the determination
of a "fair rate of return" on equity capital presents formidable
difficulties. Conceptually there is no problem; it is the cost of
attracting and holding the equity capital necessary to provide
the regulated service. In deciding what the cost is, however, the
parties to the regulatory proceeding and the commission itself
are thrown back on very rough comparisons with other firms and
other industries. Frequently these comparisons are circular because they are to other regulated firms. When they are not
circular, they are misleading because they compare a regulated
firm with firms that are not monopolists and that are engaged
in dissimilar businesses. Assuming the company is usually given
the benefit of the doubt, the return allowance will often conceal

some monopoly profits.

A firm forbidden to raise rates or ordered to reduce them may react by reducing the quality of its product or service. Suppose that consumers will pay $12 for a widget that costs $10 to make and $10 for a slightly inferior widget that costs $8.50. The manufacturer is ordered to reduce his rate from $12 to $10; by substituting the inferior widget he can retain a substantial portion of his monopoly profits. In theory the agency can prevent a regulated firm from degrading the quality of its service but there are serious practical difficulties. To illustrate, if the waiting period for telephone installation lengthens, or the number of busy signals increases, or repairs are slower, the consumer may gain virtually nothing from a rate reduction; yet these changes in the level of service, unless gross, are difficult to detect, prove, or rectify.

Finally, there is a good deal of room for concealment of monopoly profits through adroit accounting. Many close questions of judgment arise in deciding which assets should be included in the rate base; in valuing those assets; in determining depreciation allowances; and in separating costs between regulated and nonregulated services and between different regulatory jurisdictions (some of which may be very lax). Moreover, where services involve joint or common costs a rational allocation is impossible even in theory. How much of the cost of a telephone handset is assignable to local and how much to interstate telephone service? There is no right answer. It is fair to assume that most doubtful cases are resolved in the company's favor, simply because a regulatory agency is naturally reluctant to displace corporate business judgments unless it seems reasonably clear that management is wrong. The result may be that substantial monopoly profits are obtained that never show up in the profit column of the ledger.

One should note that the foregoing factors are additive and, together, can easily emasculate the profit ceiling. To illustrate, suppose that in the test year the true depreciated original cost of public utility·X's assets is $100,000, the true cost of capital 5 percent, the proper depreciation rate 10 percent, and the true operating expenses (defined as all costs other than capital and depreciation) $30,000. On these assumptions, X's annual revenue requirements are $45,000. Suppose, however, that the regulatory agency, uncertain how to compute the capital cost and inclined to resolve doubts in favor of the company, in fact allows X 7.5 percent as a return allowance. Assume further that by exploiting the accounting vagaries associated with rate-base valuation X is able to inflate the rate base by 10 percent, and by judicious allocations of plant between regulated and non-regulated activities and between strict and lax jurisdictions is able to add another 10 percent to the rate base. As a result the allowed rate of return of 7.5 percent and the depreciation allowance of 10 percent are applied to $120,000, not $100,000. Suppose, moreover, that X is able to inflate its operating expenses by 10 percent, and suppose, finally, that at any particular moment in time its actual operating expenses are 5 percent less than its test-year expenses due to the combined effect of regulatory lag and either lower costs or degraded service. A little arithmetic indicates that X's true rate of return is not 5 percent, but 15.5 percent. And that rate is a composite of interest to the bondholders and return to stockholders. If we assume that the capital structure of the company is composed 50 percent of bonds and 50 percent of equity and that the interest rate is 4 percent, the return on stockholders' equity is 27 percent, even though the true cost of equity capital to the firm is only 6 percent.

This is doubtless an extreme example. The standard error in profit regulation is probably less than 450 percent. What is clear, however, is that relatively moderate errors, of the kind that regulatory agencies can scarcely avoid committing given the intractable problems involved in the computation of revenue requirements, can render profit regulation quite ineffectual; for while I do not believe that in fact public utilities are permitted to earn 27 percent for their stockholders, neither do I believe that many unregulated utilities would fix prices that returned them such profits. In all likelihood, either demand conditions would not warrant such high prices, or fear of inducing entry would lead the firm to charge somewhat lower prices. It is thus plausible to argue that profit regulation may have little actual effect on monopoly prices and profits.

Some readers may react by thinking, "Surely regulation must have *some* effect on the profits of regulated firms. Regulated firms *do* file rate increases that are disallowed, and commissions *do* on occasion order regulated firms to reduce their rates." These are not, however, convincing points. That regulated firms are from time to time forbidden to raise their rates may in some instances signify regulatory error—the agency refusing to allow the firm to cover unavoidably higher costs. In other instances it may simply be the prologue to a deterioration of service. Or it may mean that the firm habitually presents exaggerated requests, knowing the agency will not grant them in full. Regulation may be a ritual in which the participants make a noisy but empty show of adversity in order to reassure their respective constituencies of their zeal, and then compromise at a level not far different from what the free market would have dictated.

Orders to reduce rates present the same equivocal aspect. Even without regulatory prodding, a profit-maximizing monopolist would normally reduce rates whenever his costs were reduced (although not by the full amount of the cost reduction), in order to maximize profit under the new cost conditions. But will not shrewd management of a regulated company put up a show of resistance so that the regulatory agency can take credit for having ordered the rate reduction? That will enable the agency to flaunt its effectiveness without impairment of the firm's profits.

It is possible that regulatory control of profits is not so ineffectual as suggested. In that event, however, one would be concerned about its effects on the monopolist's incentives to operate efficiently. Suppose a case of perfect profit control. All costs are accurately determined, including the cost of equity capital; the rate base is accurately valued; and costs and valuation are continuously updated. The firm's overall revenue requirements are equated to its cost of service and continuously revised upward or downward with any rise or fall in that cost. There would be no monopoly profits under such a regime, but neither would there be any incentive on the part of the monopolist to improve his efficiency. Lacking either the "stick" of competitive pressure or the "carrot" of supracompetitive profits, the managers of the firm would have no reason to strive for better performance save their own pride or professionalism. While such factors should not be underestimated, so drastic an alteration of the structure of incentives operating on a monopolistic firm would be an exorbitant price to pay for the elimination of monopoly profits.

One can reply that the problem of incentives is solved by the accident of regulatory lag—and solved in a way that preserves a large measure of regulatory effectiveness in limiting the monopolist's profits. Rates are periodically, not continuously, equated with costs, and this procedure limits without absolutely foreclosing the monopolist's opportunity to extract supracompetitive profits; for in the periods between regulatory determinations the regulated firm has a profit incentive to become more efficient. Regulatory lag may not, however, be a complete answer to the incentive problem. In the first place, it is an inadvertent method of injecting a profit incentive. While it permits supranormal profits to be obtained, there is no express recognition that they are legitimate and acceptable as a method of encouraging a monopolist to better his performance. I have considerable doubt, however, whether this inexplicitness makes any practical difference. More important, one cannot be sure that the opportunity provided by regulatory lag to obtain monopoly profits is sufficient to avoid serious disincentive effects, albeit those effects might be even greater were there no lag. If the regulated firm achieves a technical breakthrough that enables it to reduce its costs and increase its profits substantially, the regulatory agency, if reasonably alert, will move with dispatch as the firm's rate of return begins to climb. The regulated firm will enjoy some profits in the interim, but they may be less than without regulation—conceivably so much less as to diminish the firm's interest in pursuing future breakthroughs. It is striking to observe that regulatory agencies appear not even to make a distinction between profits derived from the exploitation of a patented device or process and other monopoly profits. An effectively regulated firm, then, may be denied the minimum reward for inventive activity that a competitive firm would obtain and that society deems essential to elicit adequate innovation.

I do not argue that a monopolist's incentive to efficient and progressive operation is necessarily diminished by *any* curtailment of the amount of profits it can obtain from improved performance. But it would not follow that one could practicably limit the profits of a monopolist without impairing his incentives. There are two difficulties. First, it is no easy trick to determine the level at which one can be confident that there will be no significant disincentive effects. The difficulty is sufficiently indicated by asking, by way of analogy, whether a ceiling of $50,000 on individual incomes would have such effects. The second and, I think, critical point is that even a rather high ceiling on profits might well reduce a monopolist's *inventive* activity. Those who argue that competitive firms are likely to innovate more rapidly than monopolists point out that the competitive firm is motivated by a desire to obtain and exploit a monopoly, which the monopolist already has. I indicated earlier my view that this difference is probably unimportant, in part because the monopolist can obtain very large profits from a successful innovation, especially one that creates an improved or different product. If, however, regulation curtails the monopolist's ability to profit from innovation, it may impair his incentive to innovate. Given the cardinal importance of technological advance to economic welfare, and the fact that regulation includes no techniques for inducing a regulated firm to innovate at an optimal rate, this point argues strongly against profit controls.

One could argue that any disincentive effects of profit regulation are likely to be offset by the pressure that it may be thought to place on the regulated firm to keep its costs down in a period, such as the present, when costs generally are rising due to inflation. The regulatory agency may be reluctant to allow rate increases; or regulatory lag may operate to prevent the firm from placing new rates in effect promptly. It behooves the firm, therefore, to economize wherever possible. I am inclined to doubt the importance of this effect. First, I sense no general tendency of regulatory agencies to refuse justified rate increases. Moreover, commonly the firm is entitled to place a rate increase in effect after a brief suspension period, subject only to a duty to refund should the increase eventually be found to have been unwarranted. Second, a firm denied a justified rate increase usually has a simple remedy that does not require any economizing: to reduce the quality of its output. Third, the incentive effect that we are discussing is operative only when the cost trend in the regulated industry is upward. Even in highly inflationary periods, this condition will not always hold. Not all industries are equally affected by inflation, and in some technological progress or other factors may completely offset any inflationary pressures. Despite the general upward cost trend in the economy, costs have been falling throughout much of the regulated sector for many years.

Finally, even if it is true that regulation often prevents a regulated firm from automatically covering any cost increase by raising its rates, an unregulated monopolist is in a quite comparable position. A monopolist whose costs increase will raise his price, but not by the full amount of the increase; and at the new price his profits will be less than before the cost increase. Recall, too, our point that the current owners of a monopoly firm receive only normal profits, the monopoly profits being discounted in the current price of the firm's stock. If we join these two observations, we see that a cost increase will reduce an unregulated monopolist's profits and that the profit reduction will hurt. In sum, profit regulation reduces the reward to the monopolist of superior performance without, it would seem, materially increasing the penalty for failing to minimize costs.

What Can Regulators Regulate?
The Case of Electricity

GEORGE J. STIGLER and CLAIRE FRIEDLAND

This paper, originally published in the Journal of Law and Economics *in October 1962, brought forth many critics and imitators. Although many objections have been raised, substantive results to the contrary have not yet appeared. The position taken by Professor Stigler and Miss Friedland, both of the University of Chicago, remains relatively secure.*

THE LITERATURE OF public regulation is so vast that it must touch on everything, but it touches seldom and lightly on the most basic question one can ask about regulation: Does it make a difference in the behavior of an industry?

This impertinent question will strike anyone connected with a regulated industry as palpably trivial. Are not important prices regulated? Are not the routes of a trucker and an airline prescribed? Is not entry into public utility industries limited? Is not an endless procession of administrative proceedings aging entrepreneurs and enriching lawyers?

But the innumerable regulatory actions are conclusive proof, not of effective regulation, but of the desire to regulate. And if wishes were horses, one would buy stock in a harness factory.

The question of the influence of regulation can never be answered by an enumeration of regulatory policies. A thousand statutes now forbid us to do things that we would not dream of doing even if the statutes were repealed: we would not slay our neighbor, or starve our children, or burn our house for the insurance, or erect an abattoir in the back yard. Whether the statutes really have an appreciable effect on actual behavior can only be determined by examining the behavior of people not subject to the statutes.

An order to a trucker not to haul goods between cities A and B is even more difficult to assess. He may not wish to have this route, in analogy to the laws governing our personal behavior. But let him wish with all his heart to have it, and be denied;

there still will be no economic effect of the regulation if others are allowed, in adequate number, to have the desired route.

The point at issue may be restated in the language of economics. An industry's output and price are normally governed primarily by the basic economic and technological determinants of supply and demand: by whether the demand curve is D_2 or D_1, and the supply curve S_1 or S_2 (see Fig. 1). Regulation will affect price and output only if it shifts the curves or the point on a curve where the industry operates. Does regulation introduce shifts in curves of the magnitude of S_1 to S_2 or S_1 to S'_2? Then its effect will be negligible. Does regulation shift the effective operating point from p_1 to p_2? Then its effect will again be negligible.

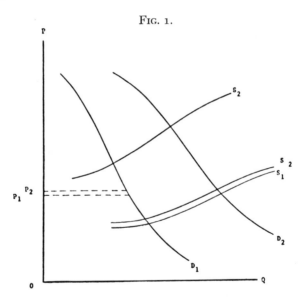

FIG. 1.

The test of the economic effect of regulation is essentially independent of the content of the formal regulations. No degree of care in analyzing the regulations, or even their administration, will tell us whether they rubber-stamp or slightly heckle the state of affairs or substantially alter it.

What does one mean in saying that regulation has had large or small effects? He means that of the observed economic behavior in a certain industrial sector, a large or small part can be explained only by recourse to regulation. Consider these examples:

1. Is the decline of railroading due in any important part to ICC regulations? If in other economies with rising incomes and extensive adoption of automobiles and trucks the railroad traffic shows a pattern similar to ours, then regulation has not been the primary influence.

2. Do utility commissions reduce the differential in prices of utility services to large and small buyers? If in a group of unregulated markets we observe a mean ratio of rates of large to small buyers of m_{nr}, and in regulated markets a ratio of m_r, do m_{nr}, and m_r differ significantly? If of the total variance among markets in the ratio of rates of large to small buyers only 2 per cent can be explained by regulation, the regulations have negligible impact.

3. Do regulatory bodies succeed in preventing monopoly profits? We take it that they will usually prevent such profits from appearing explicitly in accounting statements. Whether they go beyond this may be judged, for example, by the fortunes of investors in stocks of regulated companies over periods extending from preregulation on, compared with those of investors in similar but unregulated enterprises.

These summary remarks will deceive no informed person as to the analytical and empirical complexity of the task of isolating the effects of regulation. They are intended only to suggest why one does not read the regulations to reach the answer.

We propose now to make an investigation of one regulated industry to explore techniques and hopefully reach tentative results. This is the electric utility industry. Here we face three major problems: (1) What firms are regulated? (2) What effects of regulation shall we study and how shall we measure them? (3) How do we explain our findings?

WHEN IS A FIRM REGULATED?

Every enterprise producing and distributing electricity has been regulated since its founding by way of charter limitations and franchises; its use of public thoroughfares was enough to insure this. It would therefore be possible to say that there is no unregulated sector to provide a base for judging the effects of regulation. This statement would not be acceptable to the professional writers on public utilities: they hail the beginnings of effective regulation with the establishment of the public service commissions in New York and Wisconsin in 1907.[1] Yet these specialists have assuredly not faced the problem of measuring the effects of regulation, so their judgments are suspect. Indeed, if we accepted their judgments our problem would be solved, for they never question the importance of (effective!) regulation.

There is no substitute for an objective measure of regulation, and the one we choose is the creation of a special state commission endowed with the power to regulate rates of electric utilities.[2] It may be complained that some of these commissions were long ineffective, or that municipal regulation was effective earlier in some states. Such assertions can only be tested by a study invoking another criterion of the existence of regulation: the year the commission issued its first rate order upheld by the courts, the year the commission first spent $100,000 or published 100 pages of orders, etc. But it is intrinsic to the problem that there be an independent criterion of regulation, and that findings on effectiveness be conditional on acceptance of that criterion. There is a strict analogy with the problem of estimating the influence of monopoly, where the result is conditioned by the criterion of monopoly (concentration ratio, number of firms, etc.).

The classification of states by the existence of regulatory commissions with jurisdiction over electric utilities . . . varied as shown in the accompanying tabulation. Two-thirds of the states had commissions by 1915, three-quarters by 1922.

	States
Before 1910	6
1910–20	29
1920–30	1
1930–40	3
1940–50	2
1950–60	2

1. L. S. Lyon and V. Abramson, Government and Economic Life 636 (1940); Twentieth Cent. Fund, Electric Power and Government Policy 65, 235 (1948).

2. In our statistical work we measure regulation from three years after the creation of the commission, on impressionistic evidence of the lag involved in organizing the commission, hence all statements regarding, for example, states regulating in 1917 should be interpreted to refer to states initiating regulation no later than 1914.

THE EFFECTS OF REGULATION ON RATES AND RETURNS

There are two basic purposes of the public regulation of prices: the curtailment of the exercise of monopoly power and the elimination of certain forms of price discrimination. There will no doubt be other effects on prices, including unintended effects such as the short term rigidity of price commonly associated with regulation, but we shall concentrate upon these basic purposes. Our analysis of effects will be limited to the period up to 1937, simply because by that time thirty-nine states had regulating commissions. By that date every unregulated state had at least two adjoining states with regulatory commissions, and even a showing of no difference in rates thereafter would be ambiguous; it could be argued that the threat of regulation was always latent in the unregulated states. This position does not seem wholly convincing to us—in a sense the threat of regulation was operative as soon as the Interstate Commerce Commission was created—but the small number of unregulated states after 1937 offers statistical support for this terminus.

The Level of Rates · We shall make little use of the direct comparison of the average level of rates in regulated and unregulated states, of which a sample summary is given in Table 1.[3] The ambiguity of simple differences may be illustrated by the data for 1917. In this year the average revenue per KWH was 1.88 cents in regulated states and 3.20 cents in unregulated states, which might suggest that regulation lowered rates by almost 40 percent. But we can classify the rates of these states in several years (see Table 2). This classification makes clear the

3. The complete average rates are reported in the Appendix in Table A2 [Ed. note: Shown only in the original publication of this article]. These average revenues per kilowatt hour involve the following adjustments of census data: for 1907 to 1922 revenues include sales by private electric companies to ultimate consumers, domestic and industrial, plus net sales to out-of-state electric companies, municipal electric companies, and electric railroads, but exclude intercompany sales within states. KWH figures are for KWHs generated by private electric companies plus net purchases of KWHs from electric railroads or out-of-state electric companies. For 1927 to 1937 revenue and KWH data are for current sold to ultimate consumers, including gross sales to electric railroads but excluding all sales to other electric companies.

fact that rates were lower on average in the regulating states, not only *after* but also *before* regulation.

TABLE 1. *Average Revenue per KWH, States with and without Regulation, 1912–1937* *

	Regulated		Unregulated	
Year	States	Revenue (cents)	States	Revenue (cents)
1912	6	2.30	41	2.99
1917	31	1.88	16	3.20
1922	33	2.44	12	3.87
1927	35	2.85	10	4.21
1932	34	2.91	8	3.69
1937	34	2.32	6	3.04

*A state is considered regulated in a given year if commission regulation was established three years previously.

TABLE 2.

	Number of States	Average rate		
		1917	1912	1907
States instituting regulation before 1912	6	1.88	2.30	2.76
States instituting regulation from 1912 to 1917	25	1.88	2.30	2.93
States not regulating before 1917	16	3.20	4.07	4.34

The basic fact is, of course, that regulation is associated with economic characteristics which also exert direct, independent influences on rates—the size and urbanization of the population, the extent of industrialization, etc. To isolate the effects of regulation we must take direct account of these economic factors. We do so by the following procedure.

The main determinants of the level of rates for an unregulated monopolist would be the size of the market and its density (which affect both production and distribution costs), the price of fuel, and the incomes of consumers. We approximate the market size and density by the population in cities with 25,000 or more population; the fuel costs by an equivalent BTU cost and by the proportion of power derived from hydroelectric sources; and consumer incomes by per capita state income. We fit the equation, $\log p = a + b \log U + c \log p_F + dH + e \log Y + fR$, where

p = average revenue per KWH (in cents);
U = population in cities over 25,000 (in thousands);
p_F = price of fuel (in dollars per BTU equivalent ton of bituminous coal);
H = proportion of power from hydroelectric sources;
Y = per capita state income, in dollars;
R = dummy variable, o if an unregulated state, 1 if a regulated state.

The results of fitting this equation to 1922 data are presented in Table 3. The regression of millions of KWs of output, in logarithms, on these variables is also added.

TABLE 3. *Regression Equations of Average Revenue per KWH and Output on Urban Population, Cost of Fuel, per Capita Income, Proportion of HP from Hydroelectric, and Regulation, 47 States, 1922*

Regression coefficients and their standard errors

Dependent variable	Constant term	Urban population	Cost of fuel	Per capita income*	Proportion of HP from hydro-electric	Regu-lation	R^2 Includ-ing regu-lation	Exclud-ing regu-lation
Average revenue per KWH	.0918	− .0592 (.0248)	.0604 (.1665)	.230 (.204)	− .498 (.083)	− .0109 (.0068)	.567	.540
Output	.166	.395 (.052)	− .577 (.349)	.718 (.428)	.491 (.174)	.0172 (.0143)	.694	.684

*Linear interpolations between averages for the following years: 1919–21.
SOURCES: Maurice Leven, *Income in the Various States* (1925); 1929–31. U.S. Office of Business Economics, *Personal Income by States since 1929*, Supplement to the Survey of Current Business, 1956.

The effects of regulation may be expressed in two ways: by the regression coefficient of the dummy variable representing regulation or by the difference in the coefficient of multiple determination including and excluding regulation. By either standard, regulation had no effect upon the level of rates in 1922.

For the other census years we use the abbreviated regression equations summarized in Table 4. No effect of regulation is ob-

TABLE 4. *Regression Equation of Average Revenue per KWH on Urban Population, per Capita Income, Proportion of Hydroelectric Power and Regulation, 1912–1937*

Year	Number of states	Constant term	Urban population	Per capita income[*]	Proportion hydro- electric[†]	Regulation	Includ- ing regu- lation	Exclud- ing regu- lation
					Regression coefficients 4 *and their standard errors*		R^2	
			I. ALL SALES					
1912	47	.663	— .0291 (.0134)		— .552 (.062)	.0028 (.0590)	.654	.654
1922	47	.730	— .0533 (.0240)		— .508 (.081)	— .0708 (.0596)	.546	.531
1932	42	.380	— .0478 (.0144)	.141 (.090)	— .336 (.058)	— .0630 (.0409)	.580	.554
1937	39	.323	— .0486 (.0157)	.123 (.121)	— .257 (.059)	— .102 (.043)	.496	.413
			II. SALES TO DOMESTIC CUSTOMERS					
1932	42	1.036	— .0044 (.0125)	— .0804 (.0781)	— .132 (.050)	— .0371 (.0358)	.286	.266
1937	39	.726	— .0223 (.0130)	.0187 (.1002)	— .146 (.409)	— .0337 (.0358)	.271	.251
			III. SALES TO COMMERCIAL AND INDUSTRIAL CUSTOMERS					
1932	42	.622	— .0496 (.0149)		— .349 (.059)	— .0306 (.0391)	.546	.539
1937	39	.572	— .0520 (.0159)		— .262 (.061)	— .0925 (.0417)	.493	.422

[*] Per capita income variable introduced only in years in which annual data are available.

[†] In 1912 and 1922, ratio of HP capacity of water wheels and turbines to HP capacity of all prime movers; in 1932 and 1937, ratio of KW capacity of hydroelectric to KW capacity of all generators.

servable through 1932. The 1937 equation does display a regulation effect, but it is localized in the sales to commercial and industrial consumers—the class of consumers that regulation was *not* designed to protect. We believe even this modest 1937 effect would be eliminated by a fuller statistical analysis.

4. The regression coefficient of regulation becomes nonsignificant if we shift from measuring urban population by the logarithm of population in cities over 25,000. A set of alternative regressions, reported in Tables A4 and A5 [of the original article] are also relevant; these equations employ total output and output per customer as independent variables, and thus raise identification questions which led to their replacement by those in the text, but seem worth reporting.

We conclude that no effect of regulation can be found in the average level of rates.

The Rate Structure · We have examined two aspects of the rate structure for possible influences of regulation. The first is the ratio of monthly bills of domestic consumers for larger amounts of

TABLE 5. *Differentials by Size of Monthly Consumption 1924 and 1936*

Year	Class of states	Number of states	Average ratio of larger to smaller monthly bills
A. 100 AND 25 KWH PER MONTH			
1924	{ Regulated	29	3.02
	{ Unregulated	10	3.25
1936	{ Regulated	30	2.79
	{ Unregulated	9	2.86
B. 250 AND 100 KWH PER MONTH			
1924	{ Regulated	29	1.90
	{ Unregulated	10	2.15
1936	{ Regulated	30	1.83
	{ Unregulated	9	1.82

SOURCE: U.S. Federal Power Commission, *Trends in Residential Rates from 1924 to 1936* (Washington, D.C.: 1937), Table 11. The observations are unweighted average rates for cities of over 50,000 population in each state.

electricity relative to smaller amounts. Here our expectation was that the regulatory bodies would recognize the greater potential political popularity of low rates for the numerous consumers who buy small quantities. The evidence is essentially negative (Table 5); in only one of four comparisons was the ratio of monthly bills significantly different in regulated states from unregulated states.[5] The quantity rate structure for domestic consumers seems independent of the existence of regulation.

A second aspect of the rate structure where regulation might be expected to be influential is in the comparative charges to domestic and industrial buyers. The regulatory bodies would reduce domestic rates relative in industrial rates if they sought to

5. In 1924 the ratio of bills for 250 and 100 KWH is barely significant at the 5 percent level; the difference is opposite to that predicted as resulting from regulation.

reduce discrimination; the industrial users presumably have better alternative power sources and therefore more elastic demands. Or, again as a political matter, the numerous domestic users might be favored relative to the industrial users. To test this expectation, the average ratio of charges per KWH to domestic users to charges to industrial users was calculated for two years (see Table 6). The ratios are therefore directly opposite to those which were expected.[6] But a scatter diagram

TABLE 6. *Average Ratio of Domestic to Industrial Price per KWH*

	1917	*1937*
Regulated states	1.616 (29 states)	2.459 (32 states)
Unregulated states	1.445 (16 states)	2.047 (7 states)

analysis reveals that the ratio of domestic to industrial rates depends primarily upon the average number of KWH sold to domestic customers divided by the average number of KWH sold to industrial customers, and the relationship does not differ between regulated and unregulated states.[7] Again no effect of regulation is detectable.

Stockholder Experience · The final area to which we look for effects of regulation is investors' experience. Our basic test is this: Did investors in companies which were not regulated, or were regulated for only a few years, do better than investors in companies which were regulated from an early date?

To answer this question, we invest $1,000 in each electrical utility in 1907, reinvest all dividends and cash value of rights, and calculate the accumulated investment in 1920.[8] The year 1907 was chosen as the first date to reduce the possible impact of expectations of regulation, and even this date—which is later than we should like—reduced the number of companies we could trace to twenty. The basic data are given in Table 7.

The pattern of increases in market values appears erratic. A

6. The 1917 difference is significantly different from zero at the 5 percent level; the 1937 difference at the 10 percent level.

7. In 1937, six of seven unregulated states had KWH per domestic buyer divided by KWH per industrial buyer above the mean of all states, but only seven of twenty-nine regulated states had ratios above the mean.

8. A separate termination in 1918 yields the same results.

TABLE 7. *Market Value in 1920 of Investment of $1,000 in 1907*
(20 Electric Companies)

Year of regulation	Company	Market value in 1920	Relative change in sales, 1907–20 (percent)
1887	MASSACHUSETTS:		
	Edison Electric Illuminating Co. of Boston	$1,689	246
	Lowell Electric Light Corporation	1,485	295
	New Bedford Gas & Edison Light Co.	1,528	164
	Edison Electric Illuminating Co. of Brockton	2,310	558
1907	NEW YORK:		
	Buffalo General Electric Co.	2,632	718
	Kings County Electric Light & Power Co.	2,356	279
	N.Y. and Queens Electric Light & Power Co.	1,059	225
1909	MICHIGAN:		
	Detroit Edison Co.	4,273	1,412
	Houghton County Electric Light Co.	1,959	130
1910	MARYLAND:		
	Consolidated Gas, Electric Light & Power Co. (Baltimore)	6,547	286
	NEW JERSEY:		
	Public Service Corp. of New Jersey	1,546	206
1911	OHIO:		
	Columbia Gas and Electric Co.	3,952	999
	CONNECTICUT:		
	Hartford Electric Light Co.	2,028	728
	CALIFORNIA:		
	Pacific Gas and Electric Co.	2,051	212
1913	ILLINOIS:		
	Commonwealth Edison Co.	2,179	299
1914	PENNSYLVANIA:		
	Philadelphia Electric Co.	4,254	296
Not regulated in 1920			
	Galveston-Houston Electric Co.	1,001	262
	Northern Texas Electric Co.	4,861	272
	El Paso Electric Co.	4,046	281
	Tampa Electric Co.	2,830	183

TABLE 8. *Regression Equations of Market Value in
1918 and 1920 of $1,000 Investment in 1907,
on Growth in Sales and Regulation* *
(20 Electric Companies)

Terminal year (t)	Constant term	Growth in sales	Regulation	R^2
1918	3.28	.332 (.227)	− .015 (.010)	.16
1920	3.27	.395 (.232)	− .017 (.010)	.21

* Market values in logarithms; growing in sales = log $(sales_t/sales_{1907})$.

simple regression of market value as a function of the increase in dollar sales of the utility system and the number of years of regulation is presented in Table 8. There is thus a slight, statistically insignificant effect of regulation on market values.[9]

CONCLUSION

Our study was undertaken primarily to investigate the feasibility of measuring the effects of regulation, but our inability to find any significant effects of the regulation of electrical utilities calls for some explanation. This finding is contingent upon our criteria of regulation and of the areas in which we sought effects, but both of these criteria are accepted by much of the literature of public utility economics.

The ineffectiveness of regulation lies in two circumstances. The first circumstance is that the individual utility system is not possessed of any large amount of long run monopoly power. It faces the competition of other energy sources in a large proportion of its product's uses, and it faces the competition of other utility systems, to which in the long run its industrial (and hence many of its domestic) users may move. Let the long run demand elasticity of one utility system be on the order of —8; then the system faces demand and marginal revenue curves such as those displayed in Figure 2. Given the cost curves we sketch, price will be MP.[10]

The second circumstance is that the regulatory body is incapable of forcing the utility to operate at a specified combination of output, price, and cost. As we have drawn the curves, there is no market price that represents the announced goal of competitive profits; let us assume that the commission would set a price equal to average cost at some output moderately in excess of output OM, say at R. Since accounting costs are hardly unique, there is a real question whether the regulatory body can even distinguish between costs of MS and MP. Let the commission be given this knowledge; then the utility can reduce

9. An analysis of variance was also made of Table 7, grouping states into four classes, by year of regulation: 1887, 1907–1910, 1911–1914, not regulated in 1920. No significant effect of regulation was found.

10. An elasticity of —8 implies that a utility will set prices 14 percent above marginal cost. In the constant cost case, given a capital/sales ratio of 4, rates of return will exceed the competitive level by 3½ percent.

costs below *MS* by reducing one or more dimensions of the services which are really part of its output: peak load capacity, constancy of current, promptness of repairs, speed of installation of service. It can also manipulate its average price by suitable changes in the complex rate structure (also with effects on costs). Finally, recognize that the cost curve falls through time, and recognize also the inevitable time lags of a regulatory process, and the possibility becomes large that the commission will proudly win each battlefield that its protagonist has abandoned except for a squad of lawyers. Since a regulatory body cannot effectively control the daily detail of business operations, it cannot deal with variables whose effect is of the same order of

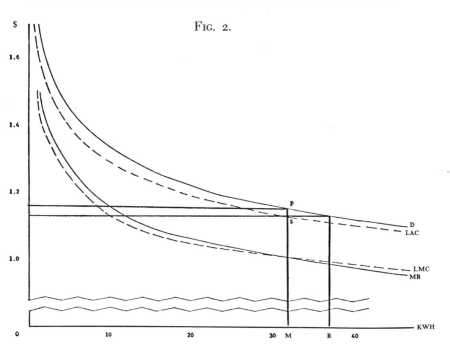

Fig. 2.

magnitude in their effects on profits as the variables upon which it does have some influence.

The theory of price regulation must, in fact, be based upon the tacit assumption that in its absence a monopoly has exorbitant power. If it were true that pure monopoly profits in the absence of regulation would be 10 or 20 percent above the competitive rate of return, so prices would be on the order of 40 or 80 percent above long run marginal cost, there might indeed be some possibility of effective regulation. The electrical utilities do not provide such a possibility.

Comment

RONALD H. COASE

*Ronald Coase, professor at the University of Chicago Law School,
published these remarks in criticism of two papers delivered before the American Economic Association in 1963. They have been
revised here by deleting specific comments on the papers because
it appeared that the remarks were appropriate to the general state
of research on regulation.*

WHAT THE REGULATORY COMMISSIONS are trying to do is difficult
to discover; what effect these commissions actually have is, to a
large extent, unknown; when it can be discovered, it is often
absurd. This grim report gave me a good deal of satisfaction, and
for the only reason which really weighs with a scholar: it would
appear to be true.

When we discuss the effects of regulation we are, of course,
interested in much more than in what ways the subsequent
course of events would have been different if this particular
commission had not been set up or that statute passed, and the
pre-existing conditions had been allowed to continue. We are
also interested in evaluating these differences in order to come
to a conclusion as to whether the original decision was wise.
But if we are interested in economic policy, it would clearly be
a mistake to confine ourselves to this question alone. We should
also be interested in other possible modifications in the system,
with, for example, what would happen if the powers of a commission were enlarged or narrowed or changed since this might
well produce a state of affairs better than either now exists or
would have existed if the commission with its present powers
had not been established. It is in this broad sense of an enquiry
into the effects of a whole range of regulatory arrangements that
I conceive our task when we talk about discovering the effects
of regulation.

The main concern is with the method to be used in ascertain-
ing these effects. . . . There are two possible approaches. With
the first we compare the performance of the regulated industry

with "an ideal norm derived from the familiar optimum conditions of economic theory," an approach commonly used by economists when dealing with questions of economic policy. It is, in most cases, a thoroughly bad approach. It is obvious that if you are comparing the performance of an industry under regulation with what it would be without regulation, there is no reason to assume (indeed there is good reason not to assume) that either of these situations will correspond to anything an economist would call optimal. The same is true if one is thinking of modifications in the system. None is likely to be optimal since it is quite certain that, whatever may be the characteristics of the ideal world, we have not yet discovered how to get to it from where we are. Contemplation of an optimal system may suggest ways of improving the system, it may provide techniques of analysis that would otherwise have been missed, and, in certain special cases, it may go far to providing a solution. But in general its influence has been pernicious. It has directed economists' attention away from the main question, which is how alternative arrangements will actually work in practice. It has led economists to derive conclusions for economic policy from a study of an abstract model of a market situation. Until we realize that we are choosing between social arrangements which are all more or less failures, we are not likely to make much headway. . . . The kind of question which usually has to be decided is, for example, whether the administrative structure of an agency should be changed or a certain provision in a statute amended. That is to say, what we are normally concerned with are social arrangements and what is economically relevant is how the allocation and use of factors of production will change with a change in social arrangements. There is little that we can learn about this from a study of theoretical optimal systems.

Given these views, it will not surprise you to learn that I found a second approach—the comparison of a regulated industry with an industry not subject to regulation—more congenial. It does focus attention on the actual working of alternative arrangements. The only drawback to reliance on this approach is that we will very rarely have an opportunity to use it. It is hard to find industries which are otherwise comparable apart from the kind of regulation.

Is there an alternative? I think there is, although what I have to say here cannot go beyond assertion. I believe that by a detailed study of an industry or organization it is possible to obtain sufficient understanding of how it operates to be able to say how its performance would be affected by changes in circumstances —for example, the introduction of a particular form of regulation. I think that to study other industries or organizations which have been subject to similar regulation would enlarge our understanding and would assist in forming such a judgment. But a mechanical comparison of A (with the regulation) and B (without) is not likely to be helpful since the effect of the regulation in A need not be the same as it would produce in B. What is needed is an act of imaginative reconstruction. This must, however, be based on detailed knowledge and such knowledge can only come slowly as the result of the work of many scholars over many years. But this should not cause us to despair. Ours is not an enterprise in which everything has to be sacrificed for speed. After all, we are not trying to get to the moon. . . .

The legal framework is perhaps the most important institutional factor which economists interested in securing the kind of regulatory agency and the kind of regulation which would promote economic efficiency should take into account. Professor Cramton [of the University of Michigan] quoted a statement in which it was said that lawyers "focus on the fact that public officials and tribunals are going to be fallible at best and incompetent or abusive at worst." This is not the way in which economists habitually think about governmental bodies. We tend to think of them as benevolent associations waiting to take over when the Invisible Hand points in the wrong direction. As I remarked earlier, in economic analysis we have "market failure" but no "government failure." A lawyer's experience may perhaps lead him to take too jaundiced a view of human nature; but his experience affords a welcome corrective to what is implicitly assumed in much economic discussion. . . .

I have one final point. Professor Cramton ascribes some of the ineffectiveness of the commissions to the difficulty of the economic problems which they face. This is no doubt true. But these problems are difficult because economists have not yet learned how to solve them. Part of the poor performance of the regulatory commissions must be attributed to "economists' failure." I trust that we will all be as anxious to remove this failure, which it is perhaps within our power to do, as those other failures, which we should recognize in our work but which, in general, it is not within our power to remedy.

PART THREE The Gains from Deregulation in Transportation

The Effect of Rate Regulation on
Resource Allocation in Transportation

GEORGE WILSON

*George Wilson is professor of economics at Indiana University.
He has published widely in transportation economics, including
the important* Essays on Some Unsettled Questions in the Economics of Transportation *(1962). This essay was first published in
the* American Economic Review *in May, 1964.*

THE CONSEQUENCES OF RATE REGULATION depend upon the type
of such regulation, its effectiveness, and extent. Since we are
worried about misallocation within transportation, which implies
a concern with the distribution of traffic among the various competing modes, I shall concentrate on one regulatory body,
namely, the ICC, since it has jurisdiction over those modes of
transport deemed to be most closely competitive—in particular,
rail, truck, and, in some instances, water. Furthermore, the most
important and analytically interesting questions are those involved with rate policy as it affects specific commodities between particular points. I will therefore resist the temptation to
make caustic comments about the regulation of what is loosely
referred to as the general rate level.[1]

1. Few persons are concerned any more over railroads making "excessive
returns." There is more interest in truck profitability, but the commission
artfully covers this up by using the operating ratio as an index of profitability.
Comparison with railroads is further confused by using return on investment
as the index of rail profitability. If, however, we take the ICC's conception of
normal profits in trucking to be an operating ratio of .93 and normal rail
profits to be 6.5 percent return on investment, the interesting result emerges,
on certain normative assumptions regarding capital turnover, that equilibrium

It is not easy to determine what ICC rate policy in fact is. Although exceptions can be found, the following appear to be the most frequently used criteria. I will examine each to ascertain the extent to which regulation, even if complete, creates differences from what might be expected in the absence of regulation and then assess the allocative implications.

EACH CASE SUI GENERIS

Although from time to time the commission may enunciate certain general rules, these are normally put in a *ceteris paribus* context. Since transportation markets, properly construed in terms of city-pairs, are characterized by substantial diversity, there are in fact few general principles that are directly relevant to particular circumstances. But in this sense, the situation is precisely what it would be in the absence of regulation. If firms are rational, they will adjust rates to meet the exigencies of particular times and places. Each rate change, even when based upon profit-maximization principles, will differ because the marginal costs and revenues relevant to a particular transportation firm depend upon the demand for and nature of the commodity to be shipped, the rates and service of competing forms of transport, particular shipper and carrier circumstances, and so on. Even under regulation all of these considerations enter into any pricing decision, although they are frequently accorded difference weights by the commission than would be the case without regulation.

RATE FLOOR AT OUT-OF-POCKET COSTS

One of the major purposes of minimum rate regulation is to prevent rates from falling below something referred to as out-of-pocket costs on the assumption that rates below this level constitute an unfair or predatory method of competition. Out-of-pocket costs may appropriately be taken to refer to marginal

---

ensues when rails earn 6.5 percent and trucks earn over 30 percent, a conclusion fraught with intriguing implications which cannot be pursued further here. It seems to me, however, that this issue is of some practical as well as theoretical importance. Indeed, the origin of the problem is to be found in Adam Smith where profits are construed in both senses.

costs;[2] hence, rate regulation seeks to prevent any rate lower than marginal cost.

The commission likewise makes a distinction between short-run (i.e., immediately escapable) and long-run marginal costs. Although there are serious analytical, interpretive, and statistical complications regarding this distinction, it is clear that the Commission construes the rate floor in terms of at least a proxy for the economist's concept of long-run marginal cost and that it frowns upon any cost analysis that includes only those costs that are immediately escapable. Without rate regulation would there be a tendency for rates to fall below long-run marginal costs? The answer to this depends upon two main factors: (1) knowledge of specific costs, including cost behavior, and (2) the long-run profitability of predatory pricing.

Our knowledge of specific costs and cost behavior in transport is most inadequate. Despite important advances in recent years, none of the techniques of cost finding hitherto employed yields results that have any necessary connection whatsoever with what the economist means by long-run marginal cost. Not only do all the empirical studies use accounting cost data which may deviate substantially from economic costs, but for rail, barge, and pipeline transport in particular the significant gap between the sales and output unit creates problems of cost indivisibility over and above those other cost categories traditionally deemed nonassignable to specific output (and especially sales) units on a cost-occasioned basis, namely, fixed and joint costs. It is frequently forgotten that all variable output costs are divisible or traceable to specific sales units only if the output and sales units coincide. Where they do not, many variable output costs become

2. There have been, from time to time, doubts raised concerning the equation between out-of-pocket costs in the commission's sense and marginal costs in the economic sense. (G. L. Wilson and J. R. Rose, "Out-of-Pocket Cost in Railroad Freight Rates," *Q.J.E.*, Aug., 1946, pp. 546–60. More recently, M. J. Roberts, "The Regulation of Transport Price Competition," in *Law and Contemporary Problems, Transportation: Part I*, Autumn, 1959, p. 568, f.n. 39, has restated the argument of Wilson and Rose.) However, the commission's definition is essentially the same as the appropriate economic conception, namely, the increment in costs associated with the increment in output. The basic difficulty, like so much else in transportation economics, resides in defining a unit of output as distinguished from a unit of sales. These and other points are elaborated more fully in my *Essays on Some Unsettled Questions in the Economics of Transportation* (Foundation for Economic and Business Studies, Indiana University, 1962).

indivisible. Unlike the problem of cost fixity, the magnitude of both the indivisible and joint costs is independent of time. Although the appropriate conception of what actual, calendar time span constitutes "long run" remains a serious difficulty, especially in empirical cost studies, it is clear that the relevance of time from the point of view of cost assignability is in deciding what amount of output costs are variable. If there exists a constant gap between pricing (or sales) units and output units, the variability of the number of output units does not affect the relative magnitude of joint and indivisible costs. In short, the long-run marginal cost of an extra sales unit (LRMCs) will regularly be below the long-run marginal cost of an extra output unit.

But even finding LRMCs requires a host of assumptions and choices prior to any statistical analysis. From an empirical point of view, one must select the sample carriers in any cross-section analysis, the years for which the accounting data are to be used, the appropriate form of the regression function, the variables to use in determining coefficients, the degree of cost refinement, and so on. When all of these choices have been made, even if each is perfectly reasonable, the result gives a "sort of central tendency" when in fact what is required for pricing purposes is a set of estimates that encompasses the wide variety and variability of carrier and shipper circumstances for particular shipments between specified points. If there were less variety and change in this regard than in fact appears to exist, central tendency results would be good enough; but contemporary transport markets appear to contain substantial variety on both the cost and demand side and it is this variety as well as variability that ought not to be averaged away and that needs to be exploited.

For these and many other reasons it is not surprising to find many transportation economists as well as company officials lamenting the lack of good cost data that would provide appropriate guidance to pricing policy. But the point here is that costs in transport, as elsewhere, are not the objective, tangible things so frequently presumed. The avoidable economic costs in any particular circumstance depend upon a host of subjective factors, as well as technical and pecuniary facts. Cost, then, is a pretty elusive and ambiguous concept. This implies that any management can demonstrate statistically that whatever rate it sets, or proposes to set, is above its own subjectively estimated long-run marginal costs. Thus, whether through ignorance or intent, rates in specific instances can easily fall below long-run marginal costs in the economic sense. Even under regulation, however, this situation would exist. The only difference is that the probability of below-cost rates would be reduced since regulatory authorities generally employ cost data that probably overstate costs for a particular, efficient carrier and for particular kinds of traffic.

However, the regulatory process, as distinct from its use of broad cost averages, would discourage below-cost rates even if cost is not adequately known. Respondents will generally determine the costs to be higher than the carriers initiating a rate decrease and in the ensuing compromise of statistical techniques and estimates a rate higher than originally proposed will often be ordered. Generally, the need to defend cost estimates tends to make these or the proposed rates higher than would be the case if a carrier merely sought additional traffic. At the same time, however, there is a strong incentive for the initiating carrier deliberately to employ techniques of cost finding and assumptions which yield low cost estimates relative to the rates and vice versa for protesting carriers. On balance, it is difficult to assess the net regulatory impact upon rates, for, like cost itself, much depends upon particular circumstances, such as the care with which the parties to the dispute prepare cost estimates, the projections of traffic volume anticipated at the proposed rate, and so on.[3] Nevertheless, it seems reasonable to conclude that rate regulation would deter below-cost pricing, even in the absence of good cost estimates, and would eliminate

3. It must be stressed that costs (variable as well as fixed) and rates are intimately interconnected so long as long-run cost linearity is not assumed; that is, since marginal cost depends upon volume and volume is some function of the rate, then marginal cost is likewise a function of the rate. This suggests that there may be some equivocation regarding "cost-based rate making" if this is meant to imply that the level of any rate is made dependent upon a prior calculation of cost. This also suggests that if the ICC is to retain minimum powers, it must make independent estimates of the effects of the rate on volume of traffic. It is, therefore, inconsistent to argue, as some have done, that the ICC retain the minimum rate power but give up any attempt to substitute its own estimates of demand elasticity.

obviously predatory pricing. On the other hand, in the absence of rate regulation, past history suggests that many carriers have found predatory pricing sufficiently profitable to warrant its use from time to time either to eliminate or discipline a competitor. The net effect of this aspect of rate regulation is therefore to reduce the frequency and extent of below-cost rates that would result either from ignorance or intent.

RATES TO CONTRIBUTE A "FAIR SHARE" ABOVE LRMC'S

The commission is normally reluctant to permit rates as low as LRMCs and, indeed, some amount must be added to LRMCs if any profit on output units is to be achieved. However, the amount to be added is interpreted rather loosely in terms of no lower than "necessary" or not so low as to "unduly burden" other traffic. The precise meaning of these phrases is ambiguous, but there are two main implications. The notion that each rate must be sufficiently compensatory so as not to burden other traffic unduly leads to an emphasis upon fully allocated costs in the belief that if a particular rate is below fully allocated or average total costs (ATC) other rates must be sufficiently above ATC so that total revenues equal total costs including normal profit. The frequent allusions by the commission to the fact that fixed costs are no less real than variable costs becomes a rationalization of ATC as a more appropriate rate minimum in the sense that such a rate on particular traffic requires no "excess" revenue contribution from other traffic which may be hard to get.

Now this addition of a predetermined prorata share of the fixed costs to computed marginal cost is what has drawn the scathing critique of professional economists who rightly repeat Jevons' famous "bygones" dictum. But the commission is perfectly aware that this is arbitrary and contrary to sound economic principles. As Commissioner Webb recently put it: "The allocation of constant costs to specific traffic . . . is essentially arbitrary. . . . There is no doubt in my mind that such fully distributed cost constructions are bottomed on economic fallacy. . . . [But] this form of economic nonsense . . . may be entirely sound from a regulatory point of view . . . [because] regulation is designed to achieve a number of important objectives, the value of which cannot be determined on purely economic grounds."[4] Ignoring for the moment the noneconomic criteria, it appears that in a very crude way the commission is groping for some potentially tangible or measurable standard to determine how much should be added to computed LRMCs. However rough or uneconomic the ATC standard may be does not deny the fact that something has to be added to LRMCs even on strictly economic grounds. Furthermore, the commission, as the occasion warrants, prevents rates as low as ATC and under some circumstances permits rates below ATC but above LRMCs. This implies that the commission may be attempting to seek for the regulated carriers a rate on each commodity that maximizes the net within the constraints of equity among shippers and regions, normal overall profits to carriers, and the other noneconomic objectives of regulation.[5]

If this is the case, then the situation under regulation is not basically different from what the carriers would seek if let alone, except that personal and place discrimination would logically receive no consideration, nor would the other features of national transportation policy such as the "needs" of the post office and national defense. There is, however, an important exception, even ignoring noneconomic criteria. If two or more regulated carriers are competing for the same traffic, the commission will prevent the unraveling of the rate structure and will generally establish rates higher than would be the case without regulation. It will force a kind of compulsory cartel and for commodities that have a low elasticity of transport demand will generally maintain

4. "Costs for Rate Making Purposes," remarks of Charles A. Webb, Member, Interstate Commerce Commission, before the Annual Meeting of the National Accounting and Finance Council of American Trucking Associations, Washington, D.C., May 13, 1963, mimeographed, pp. 7–8.

5. For example, Commissioner Webb in a recent case argued that "inflated out-of-pocket cost computations will prevent carriers in some cases from making rates which enhance net revenues to the maximum extent possible. Rates which barely exceed out-of-pocket costs may be condemned in some cases because they do not maximize net revenue and are apparently motivated by a desire to destroy competition, but on the other hand, rates at such a level may be the only means to obtain a modest contribution to fixed costs on the traffic involved." (Lumber—California and Oregon to California and Arizona, I & S Docket No. 6933, decided Aug. 10, 1959, p. 57.) Again, the commission in another case approving proposed rate reductions stated that "the reduction in the level of rates in a competitive situation such as here has as its purpose the maximizing of net revenues through increased volume of traffic." (Paint and Related Articles—Official Territory, I & S Docket No. 7027, decided Aug. 27, 1959, mimeographed, p. 9.)

rate levels well above any measure of ATC. Of course, it is possible that without regulation the oligopoly solution might prevail, but it is doubtful whether it can be as successful in maintaining as high a rate as a commission-supported compulsory cartel arrangement jointly exploiting aggregate demand inelasticity.

The impact of completely effective rate regulation, insofar as the present criterion is concerned, is therefore to maintain rather higher rates where the aggregative elasticity of transport demand is low than would be the case without regulation, since demand elasticity will appear higher to the individual carriers. This is probably true even where the rational oligopoly solution would exist.

However, an important misapplication of such discriminatory pricing is that form of pricing which links the rate to the value of the commodity. All too frequently the commission as well as the carriers appear to believe that the value of the transportation service, even when all modes are considered together, is closely related to the value of the commodity. In fact, of course, the value of the commodity is only one determinant of value of the service and in many cases not the most important one. The value of the transport service depends on the level and elasticity of the demand for the product and the ratio of the freight rate to the delivered price of the commodity. More precisely, the total elasticity of transport demand is simply the product of the elasticity of demand for the commodity and the ratio of the present freight rate to the delivered price of the commodity. From the point of view of an individual mode of transport or single carrier, the rates and service quality of actual and potential competitors as well as their expected reactions are also significant determinants of value of the service. The value of the commodity is then but one among several factors essential to a pricing policy aimed at absorbing as much shipper surplus as possible for a particular carrier or carrier group. The important determinant of the value of the service—a term most appropriately defined from the economic point of view as the maximum profit rate on any commodity between a given city-pair—involves, in short, the demand function facing an individual carrier or group of carriers if they act in concert, as well as marginal cost. There is no point whatsoever in attempting to set rates on the basis of the level and elasticity of total transport demand if in fact the demand function facing the group or firm is lower and more elastic due to actual or potential competition. Yet, in many cases, this is precisely what has been done even where the possibility of nonregulated carriage exists. I suspect that it is this type of thing for which not only the commission gets its lumps but also value of service as a pricing principle gets disparaged. Yet, in fact, this represents misapplication of the principle. There is a vital distinction between the principle itself and misuse thereof, and the fact of the latter should not be used as evidence of the inappropriateness of the former. Nevertheless, the commission is prone to argue that high-value products in some sense "should" pay differentially higher freight rates and there is no question that this ethical judgment makes no economic sense in many cases.

THE SHARE-THE-TRAFFIC CRITERION

Where the aggregate elasticity of transport demand is low and where the feasibility of unregulated carriage is also low, the commission is reluctant to permit either the elimination of one form of common carriage or such a reduction in rates that the amount of shipper surplus jointly absorbed by the common carriers is seriously depleted. In seeking to enhance or maintain the profitability of common carriage, the commission will often prevent rate competition and establish a set of rate relationships such that the various modes each get some share of the total business available at rates that may well yield greater total profits to each mode than if one got all the business at a lower rate.

There is little doubt that this policy, which may in fact be on the wane and which involves very tricky estimates of shipper preferences and costs of private carriage, constitutes an important difference under regulation. In effect, the commission is seeking to find the limit price for the common carriers involved above which private carriage would be invited and below which aggregate profits would be reduced. The share-the-traffic criterion thus implies an extramarket restraint whose motivation is uniquely bound up with the preservation of common carrier profitability by joint common carrier exploitation of demand inelasticities up to the limit price.

RATE STABILITY

The entire regulatory process, including the foregoing policies as well as the thirty days' notice requirement and investigation and suspension procedures, inevitably leads to less frequent rate changes than would otherwise occur. Although designed for purposes other than prevention of "instability" per se, the necessary effect is a high degree of rate stability or rigidity, depending upon one's valuation.

ATTITUDE TOWARD VARIOUS FORMS OF DISCRIMINATION AND OTHER NONECONOMIC FACTORS

According to the law of ICC interpretation thereof, commodity discrimination is eulogized, place discrimination tolerated under special circumstances, and personal discrimination outlawed. But in economics, discrimination is discrimination, and there is thus no valid economic reason for these diverse attitudes towards differential pricing. In fact, the apparent moral repugnance manifest in the views regarding personal discrimination frequently leads to a kind of reverse discrimination by limiting, for example, quantity discounts to carload lots although this, too, seems to be changing. If large and regular shipments assist the economical operation of a carrier, they should be encouraged and not restricted by a set of noneconomic considerations which in the final analysis cause not only additional economic waste but do not have the desired effect, since private carriage is a feasible option where substantial traffic on a regular basis is involved.

Without regulation these divergent attitudes toward various forms of discrimination would not occur. Furthermore, the many other noneconomic considerations and externalities would also be irrelevant so long as carrier managements rationally pursued their profit objectives. In reality, of course, the existence of noneconomic objectives makes any decision of the commission "reasonable" on some grounds. It may well be of some value to the nation that these noneconomic objectives be pursued. But the carriers should not be judged on strictly economic grounds if required to perform noneconomic functions, and as economists we are rightly concerned that whatever the objectives, they be achieved by methods that occasion least cost.

THE NATURE OF RATE REGULATION: A GRAND BENTHAMITE DESIGN

The foregoing sections may be summarized as follows. Rate regulation as practiced by the ICC, if completely effective, would maintain higher rates on specific traffic than would otherwise occur, would involve greater rigidity, tend to preserve a demand-oriented rate structure, reinforce misapplication of value of service pricing but emphasize commodity discrimination as the most effective way of covering the nonassignable costs, frequently allow more than one mode to participate in a given piece of business regardless of relative costs, consider a wide variety of noneconomic objectives and externalities, treat each case as *sui generis*, more effectively prevent rates from falling below marginal cost, and would force a kind of public accountability and greater cost consciousness upon the common carriers. Insofar as one can impute rationality to contemporary regulation, the overall impression is that the commission seeks a rate structure such that all nontraceable costs including those additional costs arising from pursuit of noneconomic objectives and the added duties of common carriage are recouped from shippers on the basis of willingness and ability to pay; that is to say, the markup over computed out-of-pocket costs would be determined by the relative level and elasticity on the demand for transport of particular commodities. Individual rates would be adjusted from the maximum profit level by consideration of external economies and diseconomies as far as regulated carriers are concerned and overall profit limitation is implied. Rate regulation, if completely effective, thus attempts, albeit in a crude and implicit way, to assess the benefits to the regulated carriers as a group and weigh these against whatever externalities appear to emerge in particular instances. It is true, of course, that, unlike Bentham, the ICC does not explicitly add up the net benefits to each shipper, carrier, and community involved or affected and then strike the balance, approving those rate changes for which the sum of the net benefits exceeds zero and disapproving all others. But the frequent references to injury or noninjury to some shippers, regions, defense interests, or other carriers due to proposed rate changes, suggests that an interpretation of rate policy in terms of Bentham's felicific calculus may not be so farfetched as it seems on the surface.

In fact, however, the commission cannot follow this grand Benthamite design, even if such were clearly envisioned. As is well known, the extent of effective rate regulation differs widely among modes, and less than 3 percent of the proposed rate changes by regulated common carriers are generally investigated. This does not mean that rate regulation is ineffective because many of the cases have wide ranging effects. But it does suggest that modifications need to be made in the conclusions regarding stability, rigidity, and inertia fostered by the regulatory process. Likewise, the large unregulated segments, especially in truck and water transport, put serious constraints on commission policy. Where unregulated costs or rates are below those of common carriage, the commission is forced to permit lower rates (close to computed marginal costs) than it would normally sanction. This also reduces the ability to maintain a pricing structure oriented toward the total transport demand for particular traffic and prevents sharing the traffic among common carriers where rates fall below sustainable levels for all modes save one. It also jeopardizes the fulfillment of noneconomic goals through rate regulation and reduces the ability to accommodate the revenue needs of the regulated carriers to external diseconomies as well. Since competition from unregulated carriage differs widely from market to market, this explains the shifting weight given to the several criteria from case to case. Where unregulated competition is intense, the commission is forced to consider costs more fully, give them more weight, and abandon the share-the-traffic criterion, defense needs, and so on. On the other hand, where unregulated competition is less vigorous or feasible, rate levels will be oriented more toward what the traffic will bear and externalities will receive greater weight.

In short, because of incomplete regulation the grand design cannot be fulfilled. It is this fact that lies at the heart of the commission's attempts constantly to narrow the scope of exemptions and oppose their extension. But the commission persists in

attempts to realize the grand design, even with limited jurisdiction. As a result each case is *sui generis* not only in terms of
costs and revenues but also in terms of the influence accorded
the noneconomic considerations and externalities.

HOW DOES RATE REGULATION AFFECT ALLOCATION?

It is impossible to assess the amount of misallocation involved
in the forgoing. Economic cost estimates are not sufficiently accurate to enable us to specify with any degree of precision the
wastes of regulation. Furthermore, many things contribute significantly to misallocation in transportation. There is, for example, no way of determining whether truckers pay their fair
share of the publicly-provided right of way. Various forms of
transportation are differentially taxed and restricted by the several states. Union rules and regulations affect carriers in a wide
variety of ways. Massive public investments of different sorts
result in discriminations among modes. Many other factors condition resource allocation in transport, and to separate that portion of waste attributable to rate control is clearly beyond the
scope of present knowledge. Indeed, it may even be the case
that, for example, if some motor carriers are paying more than
their fair share of highway costs, the prevention of rail rate
reductions, in rail-motor competitive situations, might even induce a degree of relative use more closely related to the real
economic costs of providing the service even though relative
accounting costs suggest the reverse. Apparent misallocations
occasioned by rate regulation might partially offset misallocation due to other reasons.

Moreover, in the absence of rate regulation there is no assurance that particular rates would exceed real economic cost
and, in fact, it seems probable that many rates would fall to
below-cost levels given the subjective nature of costs. This
would provide as much uneconomic incentive as far as relative
use of the varying forms of transport, industrial location, and so
on are concerned as the artificially higher rates upheld by regulation, although for other reasons it is preferable to err on the low
than the high side since the division of labor is still limited by
the extent of the market. Rate changes would be more frequent
without regulation and since these would not necessarily be

based upon costs, the uncertainty engendered may inhibit investment in locations where on strict economic grounds it would be warranted. While I believe there has been an overemphasis upon the virtues of rate stability, nonetheless many shippers are less concerned about particular rate levels than in knowing that their rivals are paying comparable rates. If we could be sure that the rate differentials reflected even roughly real economic cost differences, there would be no legitimate cause for complaint. But this is precisely what we cannot be certain of. Indeed, the absence of all rate regulation is liable to result in the kind of rate secrecy, rebates, and so forth that was partly responsible for regulation in the first place. And this has important consequences for allocation among all transport-using industries.

Let us not forget that there are certain advantages to society of regulation as well as competition, even though both may be highly imperfect. We are, of course, a long way from an optimal mix of the two, but competitive pressures are clearly not absent under contemporary circumstances. However, the real case against economic regulation of transport today is the administrative impossibility of complete and effective regulation, the disincentive to change once a regulatory pattern has been established, and the existing collection of numbers gratuitously referred to as the "rate structure." The incomplete regulation imposes an artificial restraint and higher costs upon those carriers subject to ICC jurisdiction, and this occasions a relative over-expansion of unregulated carriage, leaving regulated carriers in the role of residual participants in many cases. Even though it cannot be demonstrated that competition in transport is such that far better economic performance would ensue should rate controls be eliminated, it is still the case that incomplete regulation may be worse than none unless it adopts a much higher degree of flexibility in adapting to particular changing situations than hitherto shown. But delay is probably inherent in the regulatory process, and complete regulation of all forms of transport is unfeasible. Nor can it be doubted that the present rate structure is unduly cumbersome, complicated, and extremely wasteful independently of its failure to relate correctly to either cost or demand factors. When firms can exist by taking a share of the gains to a shipper from a third audit of rate bills, when many shippers must maintain large staffs merely to assess the accuracy and legality of the rates actually charged, there is, to put it mildly, great need for tariff simplification which is unlikely to come from present regulatory practice. Although the economic consequences of substantial reductions in regulatory restraint cannot be adequately nor unambiguously deduced in advance in the present state of knowledge, we would learn much from the experiment. But we should also be prepared to abandon the public utility aspects of transportation and the noneconomic features as well. This would be less serious if the experiment could be expected to result in improved efficiency and, indeed, the satisfaction of the noneconomic goals of regulation might better be attempted by other techniques, such as direct subsidy in the case of unprofitable services deemed desirable. . . .

Whatever the extent of decontrol, I have few illusions that the results will approximate those postulated by the competitive or workably competitive models. If our hunches regarding the level and shape of the cost functions of the various modes have much validity, and if the ubiquity of de facto competition in transportation is less than recent assertions would have us believe, the results will be far removed from any reasonable vision of optimality. In short, I am not convinced that the effects of abandonment of rate regulation would result in any significant reduction in economic waste but welcome the chance to be proved wrong. As Ricardo might have put it, "the opinion entertained by those who believe that deregulation may not resolve the transportation problem is not founded on prejudice and error, but is conformable to the correct principles of political economy."

Competitive Policy for Transportation?

MERTON J. PECK

While the Wilson paper indicates the effects of present trans-
portation regulation, this essay shows the results from fundamental
changes in regulatory policies. Merton J. Peck, professor of eco-
nomics at Yale University, has published a number of books and
articles on the economics of government and business—studies of
the weapons acquisition process, Federal research and develop-
ment policies, as well as transportation regulation. He has re-
cently served as a member of the President's Council of Economic
Advisors.

THE QUESTION MARK added to the title reflects the fact that the
central question in transportation is the extent to which competition should be substituted for the existing forms of direct regulation. Elsewhere in the economy, apart from the special case of
public utilities, it is a settled question that competition should be
the dominant public policy, although such agreement on the first
principle leaves economists and lawyers a delightful margin of
dispute over the meaning of competition and how to achieve it.

In transportation, public policy took the quite different form of
extensive direct regulation. The Interstate Commerce Commission now controls rates, entry, and service of interstate rail, water,
and motor carriers.[1] These controls represent the culmination of a
seventy-five-year history in which each major piece of transportation legislation since the Interstate Commerce Commission Act
of 1887 has increased the regulatory authority of the ICC.

The transportation message of April 5, 1962, by the late President Kennedy, was widely hailed as a reversal of this historical
trend of increasing regulation. It called for "greater reliance on
the forces of competition and less reliance on the restraints of
regulation." More specifically the message proposes the elimina-

1. The Civil Aeronautics Board exercises similar controls over aviation. In
addition, state commissions exercise controls over intrastate traffic. Since
truck, rail, and water transportation are often close substitutes in freight
carriage, I have concentrated upon these sectors of the transportation industries.

eliming-

tion of all minimum rate regulation for bulk commodities where substantial nonregulated transportation now exists. The Congressional Commerce Committees held hearings in the summer of 1962 on the specific legislation implementing the message, but adjourned before filing their reports. These hearings clearly identified the warring parties: the proponents being the railroads and the executive branch, the opponents being the water carriers, the truckers, and the majority of the Interstate Commerce Commission.

This paper examines, first, the economic costs of the present regulatory policy, second, the specific presidential proposals for deregulation, and third, some further solutions to the organization of transportation.[2]

THE FAILURES OF REGULATION

The general tone of the presidential message was a vote of no confidence in the regulatory process—delivered with perhaps undue cruelty on the seventy-fifth birthday of the ICC. Since the message also proposed that "practices by carriers freed of minimum rate regulations would be covered by existing laws against monopoly and predatory trade practices," the implied long-run objective is to reduce the uniqueness of transportation policy and to bring public policy here in line with that for the rest of the economy.

Such a direction of change is not, I think, prompted by an abstract desire for policy uniformity or consistency. The Kennedy administrative style exhibited a New England pragmatism and Irish concreteness rather than a search for intellectual tidiness. I read the message as reflecting two assumptions: first, that the transportation sector today represents a singularly inefficient allocation of resources—capital and labor; and, second, that compe-

2. The transportation message is a comprehensive statement of transportation policy, including sections on taxation, passenger traffic, urban mass transportation, and international transportation. Since these topics are not central to competitive policy, I cheerfully leave their discussion to others. The presidential message has a fairly substantial discussion of railroad and airline mergers—matters of obvious central importance to competitive policy. But the discussion really says no more than that there are good and bad mergers and it is difficult to tell one from another. I shall follow this precedent on this topic and forgo a substantive discussion of the current enthusiasm for transportation mergers.

tition rather than regulation is the best way of improving the allocation of transportation resources.

Inefficient allocation of transportation resources is defined here as an allocation that falls substantially short of meeting the transportation needs of the economy with a minimum total expenditure of resources. More concretely, rails carry a great deal of short haul and small lot traffic that could more cheaply move by truck, and trucks carry long haul and bulk traffic that could more cheaply move by rail. The overall extent of such a misallocation cannot be completely quantified with present data. Using only partial information, a study of relative costs of transportation in which I collaborated indicated a substantial degree of misallocation.[3] With more complete data, my guess would be that the "price" of the present misallocation would turn out to be several billion dollars per year.

A major source of the misallocation is, I would argue, the high degree of economic price discrimination in transportation rates. Economists generally define price discrimination as price differences that do not reflect cost differences. Price discrimination so defined is a long-standing characteristic of railroad rates, though it is better known as value-of-service rate-making. In 1956 railroad rates ranged from a low of 15 percent to a high of 566 percent of fully distributed costs.[4] The elaborate detail of railroad price discrimination explains the existence of 75,000 tariffs, including a distinction between horses for slaughter and draft horses, sand for glass manufacture and sand for cement, and lime for industrial use and lime for agriculture.[5] Table 1 indicates the general direction of the price discrimination. Manufactures and miscellaneous traffic bear a substantially higher mark-up over out-of-pocket rail costs than commodities of lower value such as minerals or agricultural products. Although such discrimination

3. John R. Meyer, Merton J. Peck, John Stenason, and Charles Zwick, *The Economics of Competition in the Transportation Industries* (Cambridge, Mass., 1959). Much of this paper draws from ideas in that work, although I must take sole responsibility for the interpretation. Some ideas are also borrowed from my "Transportation in the American Economy" in *American Economic History,* Seymour Harris, ed. (New York, 1961), pp. 340–365.

4. U.S. Interstate Commerce Commission, Bureau of Accounts, "Cost Finding and Valuation, Distribution of the Rail Revenues by Commodity Groups, 1956."

5. D. Phillip Lockin, *Economics of Transportation* (Homewood, 1954), p. 455.

is of long standing, it has narrowed since 1939.

Through the 1920s the railroads, at least collectively, had the monopoly that extensive price discrimination requires.[6] Not only could railroads practice price discrimination, but most distinguished economists of that day argued that they should. The argument for price discrimination or value-of-service rate-making was that low rates on commodities that would not have otherwise (high elasticity of demand) and that covered the additional costs of their carriage would make some contribution to railroad

TABLE 1. *Ratio of Rail Carload Revenues to Out-of-Pocket Costs*

	1939	1949	1959
Agricultural products	135%	142%	122%
Animal and animal products	125	128	109
Products of mines	178	129	113
Products of forests	153	135	122
Manufactures and misc.	203	192	159
ALL TRAFFIC	172	157	135

SOURCE: 1939 and 1949: ICC Bureau of Accounts and Cost Finding, *Distribution of the Rail Revenue Contribution by Commodity Groups—1952*, (1955), pp. 8–9; 1959: *Distribution . . . by Commodity Groups—1960* (1962), p. 11.

fixed costs. Thus, such traffic would ease the burden on the higher price traffic and make fuller use of society's heavy investment in railroad roadbeds. Value-of-service rate-making would also add to railroad profits. Consequently, it was argued that with differential rates everyone would be gainers and no one would be a loser—the welfare economists' ideal.

The appearance of competitive alternatives to the railroads, beginning in the 1930s with large-scale trucking, the revival of the waterways, and the construction of pipelines eliminated the monopoly required by this kind of pricing. This fact—the relative decline of the railroads and rise of their competitors—is clear from the changing distribution of traffic shown in Table 2. The major factor in the shift of traffic was the technological changes that made it possible for these newer forms of transportation to de-

6. This discussion ignores the problem of competition between railroads and water carriers, important for some locations and commodities even in the 1920s. In addition there was intrarail competition which was moderated by the introduction of the ICC.

velop. Yet the value-of-service railroad rates played a contributing role, particularly in connection with the growth of trucking. The truckers, naturally enough, concentrated their traffic-gathering activities on the high-profit traffic of the railroads, that is, as Table 1 indicates, on the manufactures and miscellaneous traffic. Here the motor carriers could successfully compete even though both their average and marginal costs were higher than the railroads, for it was on such traffic that the railroads recouped a major portion of their overhead. The consequences were obvious; traffic was shifted from the low-cost to the high-cost carrier, and the resulting loss for the railroads of their overhead-contributing traffic had a major impact on their financial fortunes.[7]

We should be careful, however, not to overrate resource misallocation associated with the rise of trucking. For a considerable volume of traffic, trucks were, in fact, the low-cost carrier when allowance was made for the inventory and warehouse savings of the shipper made possible by the quicker and small shipment characteristics of truck transportation. But there were enough shifts from the low-cost to the high-cost mode of transportation, as measured in the sum of shipper and carrier costs, to produce the misallocation of transportation resources that now confronts us.[8]

In response to the growth of intercity trucking, ICC regulation was extended to the motor carriers, thus permitting regulatory policy to maintain value-of-service rate-making. In administering rail and truck rates, the ICC held to the general view that rail rate reductions to meet truck competition should be limited

7. These consequences were clearly seen at the time. The ICC Annual Report for 1938 states that since value-of-service rate-making had "resulted in rates disproportionately high from a cost standpoint, it has provided opportunities for competitors that might not have otherwise existed. Where rail freight rates have been considerably higher than the cost of service would justify . . . trucks and waterlines have not been slow in availing themselves of the opportunity to compete." Quoted in Henry J. Friendly, *The Federal Administrative Agencies* (Cambridge, Mass., 1962), Chapter VI, p. 111. But this foresight was not matched with effective action.

8. Business logistics, the newest wrinkle in traffic research, places great premium on formally analyzing the overall costs of distribution, although shippers have obviously always done so on a more informal basis. For a discussion of business logistics, see E. Grosvenor Plowman, "For Good or Ill, Users Influence Transportation," *The Annals of the American Academy of Political and Social Science* (January, 1963), pp. 6–13.

TABLE 2. *Percent Distribution of*
Intercity Ton-Miles by Form of Transportation

	1930	1935	1940	1945	1950	1955	1960
Railroads	74%	68%	61%	67%	57%	49%	44%
Truck, private, and for-hire	4	6	10	7	16	18	22
Pipelines	5	10	10	12	12	16	17
Waterways	17	16	19	14	15	17	17
rivers and canals	n.a.	n.a.	(4)	(3)	(5)	(8)	(9)
Great Lakes	n.a.	n.a.	(15)	(11)	(10)	(9)	(8)
	100%	100%	100%	100%	100%	100%	100%

SOURCE: *ICC Seventy-Sixth Annual Report* (1962), p. 16, and James C. Nelson, *Railroad Transportation and Public Policy* (Washington, 1959).

to those necessary "to regain or to retain a fair share of the traffic."[9] In practice this meant parity between truck and rail rates, so that the division of traffic turned largely on service competition in which the trucks had an inherent advantage.[10] Thus, the ICC's rate policy (1) denied the shipper the advantages of the lower-cost transportation by rail, (2) diverted resources toward the high cost carrier, (3) added capacity to the nonrailroad sectors of transportation at a time when the railroads had substantial excess capacity, and (4) encouraged the growth of private truckers as a way for a shipper of higher rate commodities to escape the consequences of value-of-service rate-making. Surely this is almost a *prima facie* case of resource misallocation.

It would, however, be an obvious oversimplification to make value-of-service rate-making the sole culprit in the misallocation of transportation resources. A balanced view would recognize the effects of the maintenance of uneconomical rail service, the public provision of transportation facilities without adequate user's

9. For a lucid discussion of the founderings of the ICC in minimum rate regulation, see Henry J. Friendly, *op. cit.*

10. On occasion the ICC did allow the railroads to charge lower than truck rates to offset their service disadvantages. One of the difficulties in generalizing in this field is that ICC decisions are like the Bible; textual support can be found for any position. I rely on Professor Williams' summary of his study of nine hundred truck-rail decisions as follows: "The attitude of the Commission has not been fixed and certain. In some cases it has ignored service differences and insisted upon rate parity, or at least disapproved rail reductions below the motor carrier basis. In other instances it has permitted differentials. And in a number of cases, it has permitted rates below motor rates by the amount of the proved added costs to the shipper of using rail reserves." Ernest W. Williams, Jr., *The Regulation of Rail-Motor Rate Competition* (New York, 1958), p. 44.

charges, the resistance of unions to cost-reducing technical changes, the possible failings of carrier management, and the unwise specifics of regulatory administration. But since the focus here is on prices and competition, there is no need to examine all of these factors. Indeed, since prices and competition are the crux of the present transportation difficulties, this parochialism may well be an asset.

THE PROSPECTS FOR COMPETITION

The preceding harsh words about economic consequences of regulation do not prove the case for deregulation, unless one emulates Professor Stigler's king, who in judging between two singers, heard only the first before awarding the prize to the second. Relying on competition also has problems which can best be examined in the context of the specific proposals for deregulation.

The Proposals for Deregulation · The president's proposals for deregulation were limited to removing minimum rate regulation for traffic in bulk and agricultural commodities. The ICC would retain its other regulatory powers on such traffic, including control of maximum rates and the right to disallow rates granting undue preference. No changes were proposed for the regulation of other traffic.

Yet the two commodity classes proposed for deregulation account for 44 percent of rail revenue and 70 percent of rail tonnage, 47 percent of ICC regulated water carrier revenue and 84 percent of the tonnage, and 22 percent of ICC regulated truck revenue and 55 percent of truck tonnage.[11] The discrepancy between revenue and tonnage is explained by the fact that bulk and agricultural commodities both have shorter hauls and carry lower rates than other traffic.[12] And as discussed subsequently,

11. *Transportation Act Amendments—1962*, Hearings before the House Committee on Interstate and Foreign Commerce, 87th Cong., 2d Sess. (1962), p. 161. Henceforth cited as *House Hearings*.
12. These data omit the unregulated carriers. On the waterways about 90 percent of the traffic is now exempt from regulation. Data are not available on the bulk and agricultural commodity traffic of exempt and private motor carriers.

minimum rate regulation may be the most economically significant form of regulatory control.

Bulk and agricultural commodities were selected for deregulation in part because unregulated carriers now compete for such traffic. Water transport of bulk commodities was exempted from regulation by the 1940 Transportation Act, which otherwise extended regulation to water traffic, because such traffic was not considered competitive with the regulated rail and motor carriers. During and immediately after the war, however, technological advances in tug design and in handling of large tows widened the range of bulk commodities that could be competitively carried on the Mississippi River system. (As indicated in Table 2, the share of river traffic in all traffic rose from 4 percent in 1940 to 9 percent in 1960.) Motor transport of agricultural commodities was exempted from regulation by the 1935 Motor Carrier Act, which otherwise extended regulation to motor carriers, on the grounds that farmers and small carriers serving the farm-to-market trade were not competitive with regulated transportation. Once more technological change, this time in the form of the large trailer truck, made the exemption economically significant, with exempt carriers hauling agricultural commodities hundreds of miles.[13]

The opponents of the provisions of the message rest their case largely on four predictions as to effects of removing minimum rate regulations: (1) geographic price discrimination will become pervasive; (2) the railroads will engage in rate wars that will drive the truckers and water carriers out of business; (3) the competition among railroads will be ruinous; and (4) the final outcome will not improve the financial position of the railroads.

---

13. While comprehensive data on the growth of exempt traffic are lacking, the following truck receipts at Chicago as a percentage of total receipts illustrate the trend.

	1939	1949	1955
Two dairy products	52%	73%	89%
Seven fruits and vegetables	15	26	28
Four livestock groups	37	70	90
Four poultry and egg groups	66	86	98

SOURCE: Department of Agriculture, Agricultural Marketing Service, *The Marketing and Transportation Situation* (1956) p. 17, as quoted in James C. Nelson, *Railroad Transportation and Public Policy* (Washington, 1959), p. 61.

The opponents of deregulation offer an alternative proposal—to place the regulated and unregulated carriers on a parity by extending regulation to the presently unregulated bulk water carriers and agricultural motor carriers.

The Brief Economics of Competition in the Transportation Industries [14] · To consider these objections to deregulation requires a brief economic profile of the rail, water, and motor carrier industries, including the staples of competitive analysis—concentration of sellers, economies of scale, and the relative costs of the different modes of transportation.

The railroads are, of course, the highly concentrated sector of transportation. Although there are over one hundred Class I railroads, the major cities are connected by one to five railroads, with the smaller communities served by more than one. Most of the longer-haul traffic passes over major routes which have more than one but never more than six railroads.

Common carrier trucking represents the other extreme—one of the most atomistic industries in the economy. The hundred largest firms realize about half the common carrier revenues, the next 2,000 firms a quarter, and the 14,000 smallest firms account for the rest. Of course, the numbers are considerably fewer on individual routes, but the higher volume routes have as many as sixty carriers. Inland water carriers are likewise a highly unconcentrated industry of about 1,000 firms in total, with numerous carriers operating on the high volume routes.

These differences in market structure are easily explainable by obvious differences in technology. The trailer-truck and the tug-barge are highly divisible units of capital and so available equally to large and small firms. The railroad is a relatively indivisible and capital-intensive collection of roadbed, switching yards, and terminals, all of which preclude small firms. The differing technologies not only create differences in economies of scale, they also create differences in the relative importance of fixed and variable costs. With capital highly divisible and easily transferred from one route to another, costs in trucking and waterways are variable with changes in traffic, whereas the indivisibilities and immobility of capital in railroads create a sub-

14. See Meyer, *et al.,* for a fuller discussion, *op. cit.,* particularly Chapter VII.

stantial proportion of fixed costs, at least in the short run. Exactly what proportion of rail costs are fixed depends on the time period selected, but for the purposes of this discussion it may suffice to regard about a third of rail costs at today's traffic volume as fixed, allowing about a decade for adjustment to changed traffic volumes.

Costs vary not only by type of carrier but also by type of shipment and other characteristics of the haul. The "cost" of each type of carrier is a nonsense number, for relative cost rankings vary with type of traffic, volume, terminal facilities at the origin and destination points, length of haul, availability of return traffic, and the time period for adjustment of capacity to traffic. Yet this analysis requires some notion of relative long-run cost standing of the different modes of transport (where "long-run" means a sufficient time period, say a decade, to adjust capacity to volume). For traffic ideally suited to river barges (large volumes, little value placed on early delivery, both origin and destination on the water so trans-shipment is not required, and so forth), the water carriers have at least a 50 percent long-run cost advantage over the railroads. Similarly for traffic clearly suited to railroads (private siding at both ends, long hauls, and so forth), the railroads have at least a 50 percent advantage over the trucks.[15] Trucks, on the other hand, have a cost advantage for shorter hauls, for small shipments, and along routes with low traffic volumes. But a good deal of traffic does not fall into these "ideal" cases, so that there is a volume of traffic where the identity of the low-cost carrier is not clearly apparent.

Thus, the various types of carriers in direct competition with one another are strikingly dissimilar in firm size, market structure, and cost characteristics. Such differences account for the difficulties of forecasting the outcome of competition in transportation and, indeed, of devising a workable public policy.

Geographic Price Discrimination • Geographic price discrimination, involving the first of the four objections to deregulation, means geographic rate differences unrelated to cost differences. Existing rail rates are characterized by a considerable degree of geographic price discrimination—the most extreme and obvious

15. Under other assumptions the difference is four to one. See Meyer, *et al., ibid.*, Chapter VI.

examples being the "long and short haul" cases where traffic carried the greater distance is charged a rate less than traffic carried a shorter distance over the same route.[16] The marked instances of geographic price discrimination are associated with the prevalence of water competition, where historically the railroads cut rates to meet water competition while leaving inland rates unchanged. While the ICC largely accepted the geographically discriminatory rate structure it inherited, the effect of its regulation has been to moderate the railroad efforts to reduce rates to meet water competition. The opponents of deregulation predict that with the removal of minimum rate regulation, the railroads will reduce rates even further to meet water competition, thus adding to the degree of geographic discrimination.[17]

The objections to a greater degree of geographic price discrimination center, first, on the possibility that railroads would raise their rates on inland traffic to offset the rate reductions on water-competitive traffic. The difficulty with this argument is that if the railroads can raise rates on inland points, why have they not already done so? Railroad management is certainly under considerable pressure to increase prices, in view of a 1960 return on railroad stockholders' equity of 2.21 percent.[18] Nor is regulation a limiting factor. The ICC has repeatedly voiced its concern over low rail earnings and has not to any major extent prevented rate increases. From the 173,248 rail, motor, and water tariffs filed with the ICC in 1962, the Suspension Board of the ICC considered only 5,170, the others becoming effective without formal regulatory review. Of these 5,170 rates, about 95 percent were rate decreases so that, as noted previously, the intervention of the ICC in rate-making is directed largely at preventing rate reductions rather than rate increases.[19] I would submit the reason inland rates are not now increased is that intracarrier competition, the railroads' concern with the competitive stand-

16. Specific ICC approval, however, is now and would be required for this particular kind of geographic discrimination, although not for less obvious cases.

17. Railroad witnesses argue that the reduced rates to meet water competition tend to spread to inland points. While evidence indicates there is this diffusion effect, the present existence of substantial geographic price discrimination would indicate it is by no means an automatic result.

18. ICC, *Seventy-Sixth Annual Report* (1962), p. 214.

19. Of the 5,170 rates, 4,712 were decreases, 212 increases, and 173 both increases and decreases, *ibid.*, p. 42.

ing of its shippers, intercarrier competition, and political prudence hold inland rail rates down. Lower rail rates on water-competitive traffic would not remove these restraints on inland rail rates. A second argument against more geographic discrimination is more compelling. The water-located towns, of course, have an inherent advantage over inland towns, which only the most rigid kind of regulation could alter. The removal of rate regulation would intensify their advantage, for the railroads could cut rates and the barge lines could meet the competition, thus further adding to the inherent advantage of river and lake towns over inland cities. But surely the question that ought to be asked is how large such an additional advantage would be.

The revitalization of inland waterways has been the significant factor in the river location of such transportation-intensive operations as large coal-fired electric power plants serving aluminum reduction plants on the Ohio River. Yet deregulation will have little effect on such operations, for here the advantages of water transportation are so decisive that the railroads cannot compete. Rather, deregulation would affect traffic on the margin between rail and water. I estimate such marginal traffic to be about 10 percent of the current revenue of the inland waterways or $140 million.[20] Rate reductions that affect traffic volume of this magnitude, even if the reductions spread to other traffic, will hardly induce a large-scale relocation of industry. Yet the uncertainties, particularly in a system where political representation is on a geographic basis, dampens Congressional interest in deregulation. The problem, however, can be kept within manageable bounds because the ICC will retain the power to prevent undue preference on specific rail rates, and thus the commission can limit the extent of geographic discrimination. Nonetheless, some increase in the extent of geographic discrimination may be reckoned as a cost of deregulation.

Intramodal Competition · The hypothetical computations of the preceding paragraph raise the second objection to deregulation —that the railroads will cut rates and eliminate their truck and

20. I base the percentage estimate upon the type of tonnage carried by water carriers. The sources of the estimate of revenue are given in Table 3. The distressing feature of the extensive Congressional testimony is the lack of quantitative estimates of the effect of deregulation. This omission is rightly bothering Congressmen. See *House Hearings, op. cit.,* p. 419.

water competitors, and then raise rates to monopoly levels.

The costs of the water carriers are a quarter to a half that of the railroads for much of their traffic. Indeed, for this traffic the bulk water rates, now unregulated, are largely determined by competition among water carriers and the latent opportunity for private water carriage by big shippers.[21] Thus, even though 85 percent of water traffic is bulk commodities for which rail minimum rate regulation would be removed, the cost advantages of water, as noted above, would protect this traffic from rail competition. Traffic on the margin between water and rail is estimated in the preceding section as about 10 percent of current water traffic. The transfer of such volumes of traffic would leave a viable water carrier industry.

The rail-motor cost comparison favors the railroads by about the same two-to-four factor that exists between rail and water. About 24 percent of the regulated motor carrier revenue is realized in bulk and agricultural commodities. I would hazard a guess that no more than half this traffic can be regained by the rails, which would reduce truck industry revenues again by 10 percent. Again, a traffic shift of this magnitude would leave a viable trucking industry.

Thus, I would argue that the kind of competition involved would shift no more than 10 percent or so of their present revenues from the trucks and water carriers. Both of these are variable cost industries and could economically adjust in a relatively short time to a lower volume, though they can hardly be happy at such a reduction in their sales. Indeed, extrapolating the postwar growth trends of trucking and river water traffic shows that a 10 percent shift of traffic would be more than recovered by the trucking industry in two years and by the inland waterways in three years.[22]

21. The importance of competition between water carriers would explain the long-standing sentiment in favor of regulation for themselves by executives of the common carrier barge lines.

22. From 1939 to 1959, excluding four war years, the annual growth in ton-miles for all common carriers averaged 4 percent, with the following distribution between transportation sectors: 9 percent for unregulated motor carriers, 8.6 percent for regulated carriers, 38 percent for pipelines, 3.5 percent for inland waterways, and 2 percent for railroads. Data from Arthur P. Hurter, "A Summary of a Theory of Private Carriage and Its Empirical Testing" (paper presented at the Conference on Private and Unregulated Transportation, Northwestern University, October 29–30, 1962).

Intrarailroad Competition · Another argument against removing minimum rate regulation is that, without such controls, rate wars between railroads will jeopardize their financial stability. This argument assumes that railroads differ from other small numbers markets like steel or automobiles where, if I read the records of the late Senator Kefauver's hearings on administered prices correctly, violent price-cutting has not been a major problem. To be sure, the railroads prior to their regulation had a history of rate wars, but it is often forgotten that the rate wars were the exception and rate stability the rule.[23]

We should note, however, that the likelihood of rate wars is increased by the fact that the bill providing for deregulation also removes the antitrust exemption of railroad rate conferences for other than joint or through rates. Railroad men will no longer be able legally to discuss rates with one another. While it is true that railroad rates are more complex than other prices, the public filing of rates combined with a thirty-day notice and the illegality of off-list pricing should strengthen the oligopolistic discipline of a small numbers market. Thus, the elimination of rate bureaus would probably have little effect. There may be somewhat more rate innovation, since the practice of full discussion of rates with competitors and near unanimity for rate bureau decisions may dampen experimentation.[24] The railroads, of course, have always had the option of filing rates independently of the rate bureaus.[25]

The Effects on the Railroads · A final contention is that deregulation would not improve the financial position of the rail-

23. Professor Troxel states: "References to rate wars are common in historical writings on transportation. Perhaps this follows from the business mind that sees even an occasional extremity in price competition as a terrifying event. Or perhaps it follows from habitual concern for person-to-person struggles. In any event, for every rate war we can count many more, possibly thousands or tens of thousands of days, of no rate wars. There were some spectacular rate pricing conflicts in the earlier days of railroad; e.g., a few battles for Chicago to New York traffic were notable. Yet order was soon restored in each instance and most buyers throughout the country had infrequent experience with competitive bargains in railroad rates." Emery Troxel, *Economics of Transport* (New York, 1955), p. 428.

24. The rate bureaus have also provided a forum for shippers to state their views on rate changes, which is considered by some to be beneficial. A railroad could still discuss rate changes with its customers.

25. There seems to be more independent pricing by railroads in recent years. See the testimony of Jervis Langdon, president of the Baltimore and Ohio, *House Hearings*, p. 297.

roads. While the presidential proposals ought not to be viewed as a rescue operation for one industry, the persistent low profits of the railroad industry surely acted as a catalyst for a change in transportation policy. Therefore, a crude estimate of how deregulation might affect the profits of the railroad industry is in order.

I emphasize the adjective "crude," for such a calculation requires arbitrary assumptions and the use of considerably less than ideal data. In Table 3 it is estimated that deregulation might double rail profits. Suppose these estimates are correct. Railroad profits before taxes would then be at about their 1956 levels, a year in which the railroads were hardly considered financially prosperous. Only if these estimates understate the effect on railroad profits by a factor of two would railroad profits be above the postwar peak of 1952. If on the other hand, as I think likely, the estimate in Table 3 is 50 percent too high, the effect would be to restore rail profits to about their 1957 level. The preceding remarks about 1956 apply with more emphasis to 1957.[26]

The calculations show, then, that deregulation is likely to turn the clock back to recent years of better, although absolutely not very good, railroad profits. Thus, I would argue that deregulation falls considerably short of a cure for the ills of the railroads. I find unpersuasive, however, the view that deregulation would make the railroads worse off, which is based on either a proposition that rate reductions will not shift traffic from one carrier to another (which is unsupported by the evidence in numerous rate hearings),[27] or that the railroads will conduct ruinous rate wars, a point discussed above. My conclusion that deregulation will make the railroads better off is confirmed by the vigor with which railroad executives argue for deregulation.[28]

Extending Regulation to the Nonregulated Carriers · The opponents of deregulation offer an alternative—extend regulation to

26. Profit data from Department of Commerce, *Survey of Current Business* (July, 1962), and *U.S. Income and Output* (Washington, 1958), Table VI–17.

27. Nelson, *op. cit.*, Chapters 3, 10.

28. Their belief in deregulation may also reflect the fervor of a convert. Until recently, the dominant view of railroad management was that regulation should be extended to the nonregulated carriers rather than removing regulation from the presently regulated.

TABLE 3. *Estimated Effect of Deregulation on Railroad Profits (millions of dollars) (three-year average—1957, 1958, and 1959)*

I. Assumed Existing Revenue Diversions to the Railroads by Deregulation		
1. 10% of for-hire truck revenue other than agriculture		$670
2. 25% of agricultural commodity carriers revenues		475
3. 5% of the private trucking traffic		390
4. 10% of the bulk water carrier revenues		140
TOTAL		1675
II. Allowance for Change in Rail Rates to Divert Traffic		−460
Net railroad		1215
III. Rail Out-of-Pocket Cost to Serve the Additional Traffic (⅔ the gain in revenue)		−805
IV. Addition to Profits Before Tax		410
V. 1957–1959 Rail Profits Before Tax		+483
VI. Recomputed Profits		$893

NOTES: The methods underlying Table 3 are extremely straightforward. Item I provides an estimate of the percentage of existing revenues that might be diverted to railroads; II adjusts these revenues downward to reflect the reduction in rail rates to shift the traffic from other modes of transportation; III deducts the rail out-of-pocket costs to serve the additional traffic; IV provides the addition to gross profits before income taxes; V simply indicates 1959 profits; and VI provides the resulting gross profits. Data are a three-year average for 1957, 1958, and 1959, the last three years for which data were available. The three-year averages minimize the unique economic circumstances of any one year.

the presently nonregulated water carriers of bulk commodities and restrict the scope of the agricultural commodity exemption. These two unregulated sectors of transportation are doing extraordinarily well; they show a marked growth in traffic, both have a good record of cost-reducing technological change, and both the majority of shippers and the carriers (apart from the common carrier barge lines) appear content with their unregulated status. Thus, regulation would be extended largely to protect other sectors of the transportation industry.

Would such a change improve the allocation of transportation resources? Presumably its purpose and effect would be to raise rates in these unregulated sectors. Yet both are relatively susceptible to competition from private carriage so that higher rates here would add further to the overcapacity in the transportation industry and to the cost of transportation.

The Public Gains from Deregulation · The preceding examination of deregulation has been in economic terms. The administration witnesses at the hearings tended to refute the possibility of predatory competition, price discrimination, and ruinous interrailroad competition by arguing that such behavior would be checked by the antitrust laws which would now apply to transportation. This leads to the conclusion, as Senator Monroney pointed out to Mr. Loevinger, then Assistant Attorney General in charge of the Antitrust Division, that "It would appear to me from your testimony that all we are asking for is transference of regulation which we now have from the ICC to the Courts." [29] But if our economic analysis is correct, competition can be largely self-maintaining, with the proviso that antitrust laws may be needed here, as in other industries, to treat pathological extremes.

Yet if deregulation will not result in major increases in geographic price-discriminating, destructive rail competition against water and motor carriers, or ruinous competition among railroads, and is of some aid to the hard-pressed railroads, there remains the question of what are the public benefits from this change in policy. They are, I would submit, lower transportation rates,[30] associated with some reduction in excess capacity in transportation by higher utilization of the railroad plant, matched by some withdrawal of capital in water carriage and trucking (or more likely a slower rate of growth in these sectors), and the transfer of some traffic by higher-cost trucking to lower-cost railroads. By the definition and analysis in the first part of this paper, these are changes in the direction toward a better allocation of transport resources.

Yet we ought not to expect too much. The adjustment will be via relatively small changes at the margins of the various sectors of transportation. Still, such marginal changes are the substance of economic analysis and even limited Washington experience

29. *Proposed Amendments to Federal Transportation Laws,* Hearings before the Senate Committee on Commerce, 87th Cong., 2d sess. (1962), p. 84. Henceforth cited as *Senate Hearings.*

30. By the analysis in Table 3, the rate reductions would reduce the transportation cost by $460 million (item II), a not too impressive amount compared to the $20 billion expended in 1961 for purchased freight transportation. On the other hand, the difference between an efficient and inefficient economy is such differences in each industry which amount in aggregate to considerable.

creates an appreciation for small shifts in public policy in what one considers the right direction. There is, of course, the possibility that deregulation will alter the entrepreneurial climate in the transportation industry sufficiently to trigger both marketing and technical innovations. In this way, the gains from deregulation would be much greater than estimated here. Even so, the specific presidential proposals leave many questions of transportation policy untouched.

LONGER-RUN SOLUTIONS TO THE ORGANIZATION OF TRANSPORTATION

In an academic environment, there is the duty to go beyond the present policy proposals and to consider more broadly and boldly what should be the overall direction of American transportation policy. Past experience suggests that the transportation problem will still be here, whatever the outcome of the specific proposals now being considered by Congress. After all, Mr. Childe, a transportation expert of fifty years' standing, began his Congressional testimony by noting, "During my lifetime there has always been a railroad problem serious enough to command the attention of Congress." [31]

Specifically I would suggest that the further changes in transportation policy ought to include fairly complete removal of direct commission regulation of transportation, combined with the massive simplification of railroad rate structures. The final result would be a public policy for transportation that differs little from that for the rest of the economy. [32]

31. *Senate Hearings, op. cit.,* p. 339.
32. These two measures are most directly related to competitive policy. I would rank as of equal importance in an overall transportation policy (1) considerable railroad disinvestment in branch lines, private sidings, and low density routes that can be more cheaply served by trucks, combined with investment in railroad modernization; (2) increased reliance on intermodal transportation such as truck-trailers or flat cars; and (3) freer entry into trucking. The rationale for these measures is discussed in Meyer, *et al., op. cit.,* Chapter IX. I attach much less importance than most to a proper system of user taxes on water carriers and trucking, for I find the advantages of government-furnished public ways not too significant in the allocation of traffic between carriers. Water carriers now pay nothing, but these carriers have such significant cost advantage over the railroads for much of their traffic that user taxes would make little difference. Trucks now pay substantial user taxes and they ought to pay more, but again, even doubling

The Further Reduction of Regulation • If the proposals of the late President Kennedy become law, the ICC will retain (1) minimum rate regulation over all traffic other than bulk and agricultural commodities, (2) maximum rate regulation for all traffic, and (3) the control of undue preference or discrimination between rates on all traffic.[33] In each case, however, ICC jurisdiction excludes the water carriage bulk commodities and private carriage, traffic now and always exempt from regulation. All the arguments for deregulation for bulk and agricultural commodities apply also to manufactured miscellaneous traffic, and for the latter there are additional arguments that reinforce the case for the removal of minimum rate regulation. Such traffic has traditionally been the high-profit traffic of the railroads, so that, as Table 1 indicates, rates depart the most from rail costs. Thus, with the development of trucking, this kind of traffic has been the most subject to shifts from the low- to the high-cost carriers and hence a sector with considerable resource misallocation. Second, competition between truck and rail does not raise the problem of geographic price discrimination, since for-hire truck competition is widespread and private carriage is available to shippers. Third, rates are a much smaller proportion of the delivered price of the individual commodities in this group, so that shipper adjustments to rate changes introduced by competition is of lesser significance.

The political wisdom of excluding this traffic from the first step in deregulation is also clear. This traffic is not now subject to direct competition from for-hire unregulated carriers, so that the competitive equality argument does not apply. An even more potent political reality is that this traffic is the life-blood of the trucking industry. Therefore, prudence suggests that deregulation be applied first to the bulk and agricultural commodities. But there seems no reason on economic grounds to distinguish between this traffic and that for which the removal of minimum rate regulation has already been proposed, except that the ad-

user taxes would change truck costs by little. Thus, the case for user taxes is a matter of good government housekeeping, and it is on these grounds I support them. I exclude labor relations on the grounds of ignorance.

33. The ICC will also continue to control entry into all sectors of interstate surface for-hire transportation except, again, motor carriage of agricultural commodities and water carriage of bulk commodities.

justment problem will be more severe for the trucking industry. Even here the service advantage of trucking would ensure the survival of a substantial long-haul for-hire trucking industry.

Maximum rate regulation was initially devised as a protection against excessive railroad profits. With the inadequate earnings problem, this function has disappeared along with the steam locomotive. Maximum rate regulation can still provide useful consumer protection against excessive rates on specific traffic that is not subject to intercarrier competition. As so applied, this control becomes indistinguishable from the third kind of control —the prevention of undue preference or discrimination between rates.

This regulatory control, I think, must remain. Competition in all parts of the economy is notoriously uneven, but outside of transportation it is difficult, as a practical matter, to separate out the various buyers, so that competition-induced, selective price reductions are eventually extended to most buyers. In transportation the fact that the purchase is consumed on the seller's property permits a high degree of discrimination, as the first section of this paper indicates. Furthermore, tradition by now allows considerable price discrimination in transportation rates. It is not only that high value commodities are generally charged more, but about 85 percent of rail traffic moves on "commodity" rates—that is, separate prices devised for individual commodities for specific origins and destinations. Such tailor-made pricing offers possibilities for the bargaining power of large shippers, management arbitrariness, and sheer inertia to create inequities between consumers of transportation.

Rate Simplification · One way out of this problem may be a massive simplification of the transportation rate structure to replace the present complex rate structure. A new rate structure could be based on such simple and objective phenomena as distance, special cost of handling a particular commodity, and so forth. The ICC might well take the lead in the simplification of the rate structure. A rate structure composed of a limited number of commodity classes would automatically reduce the unevenness of competition by forcing transportation companies, like manufacturing companies, to make price reductions on broad classes of products rather than to devise more special rates to meet specific competitive situations.[34] But such a rate simplification carries with it a danger that it might impose a new orthodoxy and rigidity upon the transportation system.

A CONCLUDING COMMENT

I have indicated my view that a competitive policy is not only possible but desirable in transportation. To be sure, there will be problems, but they will be no more vexatious in transportation than in steel or the automobile industries. What is more decisive, the results of competition in transportation should be superior to what regulation is now achieving in terms of economic efficiency. Indeed, the failings of regulation provide an interesting insight into achievements of competition. As my collaborators and I wrote in 1958:

Thus in a very real sense, the American experience with transportation regulation stands as an eloquent, though negative, testimonial to the great strength of free enterprise: an ability to adapt quickly and efficiently to change in the economic environment.[35]

34. The president's transportation message states that Congress should "Direct the regulatory agencies to sanction experimental freight rates, modifications, and variations in systems of classification documentation, and new kinds or combinations of service." The context of the message does not indicate whether the objective would be the kind of rate simplification I have discussed.

35. Meyer, et al., op. cit., p. 272.

PART FOUR   The FCC in the
Television Wasteland

The Economics of Broadcasting
and Public Policy

RONALD H. COASE

*Professor Coase here follows the prescriptions for research laid
down in his "Comment" earlier in this book. By "detailed study
of an industry . . . it is possible to obtain sufficient understanding of how it operates to be able to say how its performance
would be affected by changes in [regulation]." The author has
carried out such studies of the communications industries over a
number of years, and wrote this essay for the* American Economic Review *in 1966 as partial summary of this extended research.*

THE BROADCASTING INDUSTRY, with its various methods of finance,
its intricate organization and its close, and peculiar, relations
with the government offers a rich field for study by the economist. But I will not dwell on those aspects of the industry which
would mainly be of interest to students of industrial organization. I wish to consider a more general question. I want to
examine the part the economics of broadcasting has played in
the formulation of government policy and to consider what
conclusions we should draw from this in making our own policy
recommendations and in the conduct of our researches.

We must first note that economic factors are taken into account in a world in which ignorance, prejudice, and mental confusion, encouraged rather than dispelled by the political organization, exert a strong influence on policy making. I will illustrate
this by a quotation from the Canadian Royal Commission on
Broadcasting of 1957 (the Fowler Commission). The Commis-

sion was discussing the proposal to finance the broadcasting service by means of an annual license fee for set owners. This is what they said:

This certainly seems a logical way for a group of people to make a joint purchase of a service they want. It is not strictly equitable as presumably a flat fee would be charged and all licencees would not make the same use of the service; but it seems much more equitable than the ear-marking of a particular tax paid both by those with radio and television sets and by those who hope never to have one in the house. The yield from the licence fee is reasonably predictable and the support required or desired to be given can easily be adjusted upwards or downwards, by changing the amount of the individual licence fee.

But the Commission concluded:

The flaw in this approach to the problem is that virtually nobody favors it, and many people feel quite strongly in their opposition. The arguments against it range from the inefficiency and excessive cost of collection, through the likelihood of evasion and difficulty of enforcement, to the simple claim that a license fee is a nuisance tax and generally unpopular.

Thus we see that a method of finance which was considered "logical," "more equitable" than the alternatives, which could be "easily adjusted" to meet the changing requirements of the service was politically impossible because it would be "generally unpopular."[1] The main reason for this unpopularity, heightened in Canada, as always, by describing the hardship a license fee would impose on the old-age pensioner, is an objection to paying for anything. This is, of course, bad economics. It is our duty to point this out, but at the same time we can hardly ignore, in deciding whether or not to advocate particular government policies, the extent to which political considerations will prevent the execution of those policies in a manner which is economically efficient. In Britain the BBC is financed by the proceeds of a license fee, but the BBC has not usually been allowed by the Treasury to receive the total proceeds, while the level of the fee has not always been as high as officials of the BBC desired. If the withholding of part of the license fee and the

1. See the *Report of the Royal Commission on Broadcasting* (1957), pp. 274–75.

reluctance to raise it were due to political considerations unconnected with the needs of the service and if most licensees would have been willing to pay a higher fee to secure the additional service that this could have made possible, a reason for the introduction of commercial television is provided which would have been absent if one assumed that the license fee was fixed at an "optimum" level, however that may be defined.

Of course we may hope that, over time, the influence of the economics profession will be such as to make it more difficult to gain political advantage by the propagation of bad economics. But there are other features of the system which I think we must regard as permanent. The first is that the businessmen in the broadcasting industry will try to make as much money as possible. I know that there are some economists who would argue that businessmen merely seek a reasonable return on their capital. But consider the facts. We know from recent figures that the profits of television stations in the first fifty TV markets represented, on an average, 36 percent of gross revenue and that the rate of return on capital for some stations was 200 or 300 percent per annum (after taxes). One wonders what an unreasonable rate of return would be. I personally believe that the only reason the rate is not 500 percent per annum (after taxes) is that the businessmen have not yet discovered how to achieve this. If one reads the trade press about changes in programming, it is apparent that the aim is almost invariably to gain audience (which facilitates the sale of time) and that the adjustments in rates which occur are designed to increase the receipts of the stations. I do not wish to moralize. As has been said, a man is seldom more innocently employed than when he is making money.

So much for the first permanent feature. The second is that we cannot expect a regulatory commission to act in the public interest, particularly if we have regard to its actions over the long period. I am not primarily thinking of the fact that commissions in the United States tend to be responsive to the wishes of Congress or committees of Congress or that, appointed and reappointed by the executive, their views are liable to be in tune with those who have political power. What I have in mind is a feature which, with the best will in the world, it seems to me very difficult to eliminate. However fluid an organization may be in its beginning, it must inevitably adopt certain policies and organizational forms which condition its thinking and limit the range of its policies. Within limits, the regulatory commission may search for what is in the public interest, but it is not likely to find acceptable any solutions which imply fundamental changes in its settled policies. The observation that a regulatory commission tends to be captured by the industry it regulates is, I think, a reflection of this, rather than, in general, the result of sinister influences. It is difficult to operate closely with an industry without coming to look at its problems in industry terms. The result is that the commission, although thinking of itself as apart from and with different aims from the industry, will nonetheless be incapable of conceiving of or bringing about any radical changes in industry practices or structure. In fact, the regulation of the broadcasting industry by the Federal Communications Commission resembles a professional wrestling match. The grunts and groans resound through the land, but no permanent injury seems to result.

It is of course wholly proper that public discussion of broadcasting policy should have centered on programming, since public policy must be appraised by considering its effects on the programs. But the discussion, particularly in Britain but also in the United States, has taken on a somewhat peculiar character and has tended to confuse rather than clarify the basic issues. Perhaps the best example is to be found in the Pilkington Report of 1962.

The report examines the question of whether it is desirable "to give the public what it wants." It states that at first sight this aim seems to be "unexceptionable," but adds that "when applied to broadcasting it is difficult to analyse." The reason is that not everyone wants the same things. It is somewhat surprising that the Committee should have thought this peculiar to broadcasting. Had they realized that this was a general problem that every economic system has to solve in dealing with every product or service, and that, in most Western countries, it is solved with the aid of a pricing system, I think the committee would have been led to a more useful discussion of the question. I would not wish to imply that we fully understand the logic of a pricing system or that special institutional arrangements are not necessary for its tolerable performance. But an understanding of the pricing system does lay bare the nature of the problem. As it is, what follows in the report is a discussion of an economic problem without benefit of economics.

I can give you the flavor of the argument by quoting some passages, the character of which will not be altogether unfamiliar to those of you who know only the American literature:

No one can say he is giving the public what it wants, unless the public knows the whole range of possibilities which television can offer and, from this range, chooses what it wants to see. For a choice is only free if the field of choice is not unnecessarily restricted. The subject matter of television is to be found in the whole scope and variety of human awareness and experience. If viewers—the public— are thought of as "the mass audience," or "the majority," they will be offered only the average of common experience and awareness; the "ordinary"; the commonplace—for what all know and do is, by definition, commonplace. They will be kept unaware of what lies beyond the average of experience; their field of choice will be limited. In time they may come to like only what they know. But it will always be true that, had they been offered a wider range from which to choose, they might and often would have chosen otherwise, and with greater enjoyment. . . . "[T]o give the public what it wants" is a misleading phrase: misleading because as commonly used it has the appearance of an appeal to democratic principle, but the appearance is deceptive. It is in fact patronising and arrogant, in that it claims to know what the public is, but defines it as no more than the mass audience; and in that it claims to know what it wants, but limits its choice to the average of experience. In this sense we reject it utterly. If there is a sense in which it should be used, it is this: what the public wants and what it has the right to get is the freedom from the widest possible range of programme matter. Anything less than that is deprivation. . . .

It is I think apparent that these passages, full of sound and fury, do not give us any criteria by which to decide whether any particular program should be transmitted. It is easy to talk about "the widest possible range of programme matter" but there is surely some point at which, as more and more resources are devoted to increasing the supply of programs, the gain from additional broadcast programs is of less value than the loss in output elsewhere. And if the resources devoted to broadcasting are limited in this way, it follows that the provision of programs which are liked by one group will have deprived some other group of programs that they would have liked. According to what principles is it to be decided which demands are to be satisfied? The committee never tells us this. But later they tell us how this problem should be solved. I will quote another passage:

The broadcasting authorities have certainly a duty to keep sensitively aware of the public's tastes and attitudes as they now are and in all their variety; and to care about them. But if they do more than that, this is not to give the public "what someone thinks is good for it." It is to respect the public's right to choose from the widest possible range of subject matter and so to enlarge worthwhile experience.

Up to now we have heard of respect for the public's right to choose and of need for the widest possible choice. It is at this point that the trap closes. They continue:

Because, in principle, the possible range of subject matter is inexhaustible, all of it can never be presented, nor can the public know what the range is. So, the broadcaster must explore it, and choose from it first. This might be called "giving a lead": but it is not the lead of the autocratic or arrogant. It is the proper exercise of responsibility by public authorities duly constituted as trustees for the public interest.

Thus the committee avoids the question of how it should be decided which programs to transmit and for the phrase "what the public wants," they substitute another and better, "what the public authority wants." What the public authority should want, how it would get the information which would enable it to do what it should, and how in practice it would be likely to act are questions which all disappear in a cloud of pious platitudes.[2]

In the United States it is improbable that many would seriously suggest that a public authority such as the Federal Communications Commission should be given the power to determine in detail what programs should be broadcast, and while sentiments similar to those found in the Pilkington Report will no doubt continue to be expressed in the United States, there is no likelihood that they will lead to the establishment of a broadcasting system operated by some organ of the government (leaving aside the question of whether this would be held constitutional by the Supreme Court). The broadcasting system in the United States is likely to continue as a decentralized

2. These quotations will be found in the *Report of the Committee on Broadcasting*, 1960 (Cmnd. 1753, June, 1962), pp. 16–18.

system, operated in the main by private enterprise. What programs will be broadcast will therefore be determined by the economics of the industry. Put shortly, the programs that will be broadcast will be those that it is most profitable to broadcast. I would not wish to argue that all the businessmen consider is money. A television station operator earning 200 percent per annum (after taxes), if he had been grasping and less aware of the finer things, might no doubt have earned 210 percent per annum. I do not doubt that some programs will be broadcast which reduce the profits of the station, but I am quite certain that the broad pattern of programming will be determined by profitability. My view is that we should not bewail the fact that businessmen maximize profits. We should accept it and use it. The task which faces us (and the task of good government policy) is to devise institutional arrangements which will lead the businessman, as it were by an invisible hand, to do what is desirable (by making it profitable for him to do so).

I would emphasize that belief in the invisible hand does not imply that the government has no part to play in the economic system. Quite the contrary. If it is in general true that men, following their own self-interest, act in a way that is of benefit to society, it is, to quote Edwin Cannan, "because human institutions are arranged so as to compel self-interest to work in directions in which it will be beneficient."[3] Our task as economists is to help in the devising and improving of those institutions. In doing this, we should not ignore the noble side of human nature when this can be brought into play. But we should never forget the words of Alfred Marshall to which Robertson has drawn our attention: "progress chiefly depends on the extent to which the *strongest* and not merely the *highest* forces of human nature can be utilized for the increase of social good."[4]

I think we should ponder these words of Cannan and Marshall when we contemplate the institutional framework within which the broadcasting industry operates in the United States. It is obviously incredibly bad. But how should it be improved? The allocation of the major resource used in the industry, the radio frequency spectrum, is carried out by a method which is inefficient, inequitable, and inflexible. I have explained my grounds

3. See the *Econ. Rev.*, July, 1913, p. 333.
4. See A. C. Pigou, ed., *Memorials of Alfred Marshall*, p. 310.

for holding this view on other occasions and there is no need for me to spend much time going over them now, particularly as there is really no dispute about the correctness of my position. If I may quote Dr. Goldin when he was with the FCC, but giving, I need hardly say, his personal views, the present procedure for choosing among competing applicants for the radio frequency spectrum is "ritualistic, formalistic, wasteful, and inefficient." [5] I have proposed that radio frequencies should be disposed of to the highest bidder because it would avoid the costs of the present procedure, would tend to allocate these frequencies to those who could use them most efficiently, would prevent the unjustifiable enrichment of those (commonly wealthy) private individuals who obtain these grants from the FCC, and would facilitate changes in the use of radio frequencies when this seemed to be called for.

I would not argue that there should be no government regulation of the broadcasting industry. But such regulation is not inconsistent with use of the pricing system. There is no industry which is not in some way regulated. What is extraordinary if we contemplate the allocation of the radio frequency spectrum is that it makes no use at all of the pricing system. Of course there would be difficulties in introducing a pricing scheme. Dr. Goldin has said that "after the initial shock of rationally considering the use of the pricing mechanism in frequency allocations, the virtually unanimous view of communications specialists" would be that these practical difficulties were too great and he adds that until I, or a friendly ally, make a study of how such a system would actually operate, my suggestion will not get into "the mainstream." [6] I think that this is right. The FCC is rather like a whale stranded on the seashore, waiting while the local inhabitants, ignorant of whale anatomy, try to show it the direction in which it should swim. If we are to get sensible government policy in this area, it will, I am afraid, have to come from the work of economists outside the government service (and, for that matter, outside the industry).

The position is the same if we think of another fundamental question: the finance of the industry. With commercial broadcasting, the person who pays for the broadcast of a program is

5. *Land Econ.*, May, 1965, p. 168.
6. *Ibid.*

the advertiser. It follows that the programs broadcast are those which maximize the profits to be derived from advertising. The market for broadcast programs is one from which the consumer is barred: what he would pay plays no part in the determination of programs. The result is that some sectors of the public feel that they are not being catered to. The FCC is uneasily aware that all is not well. And so it has exhorted the businessmen to act in the public interest and, incidentally, against their own. It seems clear that in this case the highest motive was not the strongest.

The obvious way of dealing with this problem is to introduce some form of pay-television. If this were done, consumers who were willing to pay more for resources used in the broadcasting industry than were the advertisers could secure the kind of programs they wanted. This proposal has been strongly opposed by the broadcasting industry. This opposition comes, as Dr. Frank Stanton of CBS has told us, not because the industry has any "economic axe to grind," but because it would not be in the best interests of the public.[7] It is, I think, a universal rule that businessmen never act from higher motives than when they are engaged in restricting potential competition. Of course, the opposition has been successful. Proposals for pay-television were first made in the late 1940s, but in spite of determined attempts to secure the approval of the Federal Communications Commission, all that has been granted is authorization for experimental pay-television services operating under restrictive conditions which make it impossible for pay-television to realize its potentialities. So far only one such service has been started, that in Hartford, Connecticut. I do not know what the future will be. But there are no signs that the Federal Communications Commission intends to change its policy of support for the commercial broadcasting system.

What should be done? The task of charting a sensible future for the broadcasting industry is not one which can be left to the industry, which has its own interests to protect. It cannot be left to the Federal Communications Commission, which cannot conceive of any future which is not essentially a repetition of the past. Who, therefore, is to perform this task? I suggest that it

7. CBS Statement on Pay-Television by Dr. Frank Stanton, president of Columbia Broadcasting System, May 19, 1955.

has to be assumed by academic economists. You may recall what Adam Smith said about university education: "The parts of education which are commonly taught in universities, it may, perhaps, be said are not very well taught. But had it not been for those institutions, they would not have been commonly taught at all; and both the individual and the public would have suffered a good deal from the want of those important parts of education." [8] The position seems to be similar in the present case. I would not argue that academic economists are technically the best qualified to investigate what government policy should be toward the broadcasting industry. But unless they do it, no one else will.

8. Adam Smith, *Wealth of Nations* (Modern Library edition), p. 721.

Monopoly and Competition in Television: Some Policy Issues

Peter Steiner wrote this appraisal of policy alternatives in television channel allocation while a visiting professor at the London School of Economics during the time the government of the United Kingdom was preparing to allot a third channel to either public or commercial use. The issues encountered then exist today with respect to frequency bandwidth allocation in the United States. Professor Steiner is a member of the Law School and economics department faculties at the University of Michigan.

THE NEW DEBATE upon public policy toward television has centered on the award of broadcasting rights for a third channel. Should it go to the BBC, to a new public corporation, to a new or existing commercial organization, or to toll television? More is at stake than the nature of the new channel since the additional service may fundamentally alter the behavior and performance of the existing services and thus affect the pattern of development of the whole broadcasting system. This is one of those rare moments when the public has a real opportunity to choose among alternatives; the purpose of this paper is to explore them.

The procedure used is (1) to define the standards of judgment employed, (2) to relate performance with respect to these criteria to the form of organization by considering two prototypes of organization, (3) to sketch the possibilities of an ideal mixed system, and (4) to compare such a mixed system with the existing British mixed system. In this context the uses of a third channel are then discussed.

Among the many standards of judgment that have been suggested the following will be used in this paper.[1]

1. The omission from this list of the criterion "provision of a technically adequate national service" is justified because of the ample international evidence that it is consistent with such a wide range of alternative forms of market organization as to be irrelevant to the subsequent discussion. The striking common characteristic of the very different broadcasting systems of Britain, the United States, Canada, Australia, and others is their success in overcoming the technical problems of distance and interference.

1. *Provision of an ample and unbiased source of news and an open forum for commentary and public discussion.*

2. *Existence of a sufficient number of independent sources of employment* for specialized personnel to prevent capricious or discriminatory treatment, and to provide a fair market for valuation of their services.

3. *A commitment to public service.* This phrase is intended to embrace attention to social objectives, such as public information and education, stimulation and encouragement of creative activity, preservation of the distinctive national and regional cultural patterns, and observation of canons of good taste in entertainment and argument. For brevity it will subsequently be called *public service responsibility.*

4. *Provision of a rich and varied choice of programs with due regard to the preferences of the population.* A wide choice of programs at any time, and over time, is important for two reasons. The first is that tastes vary widely. The product of the industry—the program—is one for which there is no inherent, unambiguous index of quality. Rational and informed consumers choose differently and there is neither need for nor likelihood of a consensus of judgment. Second, choice is essential for the formation of tastes since it permits the experimental sampling of the unfamiliar. Given only two or three channels, choice is necessarily limited; the problem is to avoid further, unnecessary restrictions.

Each of these objectives is critically influenced by the structure of the industry and the motives of its members. Each is thus influenced by the question of public or private ownership, by the method of financing and by the extent and form of competition. Since there are several standards of judgment employed there is a real possibility of a conflict of criteria; a form of organization that performs well when judged by one standard may do poorly by another. Indeed, this sort of conflict is the crux of the debate detween the advocates of public monopoly and private competition in broadcasting. This debate is worth exploring, not to resolve it,[2] but to find if there exists a mixed system that achieves the benefits of both. For this purpose it is helpful to

2. It is impossible scientifically to resolve it without an agreement on the ordering (or weighting) of the objectives. Since I believe this agreement to be impossible, I believe it is unwise to force an election (by majority vote, or in any other way) if it is unnecessary.

use as prototypes (a) a monopoly under a public corporation as in British sound broadcasting, and (b) a private, commercial, competitive system under overall public surveillance as in American television.

THE CHARACTER OF AMERICAN TELEVISION[3]

Three national network organizations (NBC, CBS, ABC) dominate American television. Each offers its affiliated stations about twice as many hours of programs per week as BBC television. Some of these programs are sponsored, some not; of the former some are network produced, some produced by advertising agencies or independent producers. While the networks own a few key stations, most stations are independent, private, commercial organizations that have voluntarily affiliated with the networks, yielding to the networks options on a significant portion of their time, the major share of the revenue from the sale of their time, the major share of the revenue from the sale of their time to network advertisers, and much of their jurisdiction over programming. In return they are provided with the cable interconnection that makes simultaneous national broadcasting possible, with a stream of programs of all types, and with the minor share of the revenue from the sale of their time as part of the network. The two biggest networks are enormously profitable by any standard; ABC is less profitable, but is above the average of American corporations of its size. Stations typically enjoy moderate profits and are clearly better off with network affiliation than without it.

Stations, rather than networks, are licensed by the Federal Communications Commission and renewal, while subject to standards of overall performance, is virtually automatic. Stations receive additional revenue from spot commercial announcements and from sale of their time for local or non-network "national spot" broadcasting.[4] Non-network sources account for perhaps

3. For more detail, see F.C.C. *Report on Chain Broadcasting* (1941); *Network Broadcasting* (1958) House Report 1297, 85th Congress, 2nd Session; P. O. Steiner, *Workable Competition in Radio Broadcasting* (1949) Harvard University Library.

4. "National Spot" is the phrase used to describe the practice of purchasing a film series and telecasting it in a series of selected cities at varying times. Sponsorship may be by one national advertiser or by local or regional advertisers who cooperate in the venture.

a quarter of the total time of stations and more than half of their revenue. These fractions should not lead one to underestimate the importance of network programming for two reasons: firstly, virtually all of the high budget programs, entertainment and public service alike, are network and their drawing power creates the audience at which both spot commercial announcements and the adjacent programs aim; [5] secondly, with only two or three stations in the typical market area, virtually all stations are affiliated to one of the networks and rely heavily on their network programs for the "quality" programming with which they justify themselves to the FCC.

The networks' dominance, influence and affluence reflect a substantial degree of monopoly power *vis-à-vis* all other elements in the industry. They are insulated (mainly by past allocations decisions) from new networks or from other challenges to their dominant position. This position permits them to pursue a multiplicity of goals and gives them wide scope for decision. They do, however, compete actively with each other for the related (but not identical) goals of audience, revenue, and public prestige. This is the competition of rivalry—of the "big few" —rather than the impersonal competition of classical economics. External influences, such as the residual responsibility of stations, preferences of listeners and advertisers, and public opinion limit but do not wholly determine network practices. Since the limits are wide it is more of a mistake to be preoccupied with them than to ignore them. In the main, networks can do what they want. When they choose, for example, not to resist advertiser pressure it reflects lack of courage or desire rather than lack of power.

COMPETITION, MONOPOLY, AND THE PUBLIC INTEREST: PROTOTYPES COMPARED

1. *An Ample, Unbiased Source of News and an Open Forum for Commentary and Public Discussion* · The arguments against monopoly power in these areas need no rehearsing here. Nor is it the fear of outrageous abuse of freedom of thought or expression that motivates opposition to a benevolent and public spirited

5. The value of "adjacencies" (as they are called) to a station from a particular popular network program may exceed its direct revenue from it.

monopoly like that of the BBC in sound broadcasting. It is, rather, that the centralization of authority over the selection and presentation of public issues imposes an awesome responsibility for a benevolent monopoly; it must be prudent and it must be studiously impartial. This responsibility leads, apparently inevitably, to paternalism. At best, and the BBC frequently achieves this best, it produces the broadcasting equivalent of a superbly balanced book. But this is not the equivalent of a balanced library. The brilliance of individual items may obscure the fact that there is no appeal from the decision *not to cover* a particular story, or to give it merely routine coverage. This can, of course, occur under any system, but is less likely if there are several independent decision units than if there is one.[6] This is a major objection to monopoly in broadcasting.

How does American experience compare? With respect to news reporting it is by usage free from advertisers preview or editing. Both unsponsored and sponsored broadcasts are common, at both the station and network level; selection and production decisions reside with the broadcasters in all cases. The frequency of such news broadcasts is great, and because of the diversity of the selection, the number of stories reported in a given day is substantially larger than on the BBC. News commentary is also frequent and exhibits substantial range of opinion—from the extreme right to the middle left.[7] While punditry far outweighs polemic, both are present. In the field of public discussion, panel interviews and documentary coverage in depth are frequent—once in a while in bad taste, typically informative, and occasionally superb.

It is necessary to note that while pluralism of decision making

6. A recent American experience is instructive. During Khrushchev's attendance in New York during the fall of 1960, a major boycott on interviewing him was agreed to by the networks on a suggestion from Washington. This boycott was broken by an independent station in New York and the resulting broadcast attracted international attention. At stake is not the wisdom of the particular decision but the character of an open society. Compare the decision of the BBC not to broadcast the results of the American presidential election throughout election night with its decision to broadcast the heavyweight fight between Patterson and Johansson at 3:15 A.M. for an example of the capriciousness of a monopoly.

7. Most broadcasters and commentators are regular staff members of the station or network news departments. A few commentators are chosen by the sponsors which include trade unions as well as more traditionally conservative organizations.

inheres in competition, they are not the same thing, and it is the former that is more important here. Limited competition appears to be more satisfactory than automistic competition; the two largest networks are the clear leaders in quality news and discussion programming. This is partly due to their intense competition between themselves for public prestige and partly to their secure (monopoloid) financial position which permits maintenance of an expensive public service establishment. ABC, the weakest of the networks, falls well short of NBC and CBS, and the multitude of individual stations lag behind the networks. High quality coverage probably owes more to affluence than to competition, but they are not wholly incompatible. And even limited competition avoids the major objections to monopoly in this area.

2. *Existence of a Sufficient Number of Independent Sources of Employment* · The market for television performers, directors, producers, and technical personnel is necessarily discontinuous and imperfect. The advantages of having even two or three potential employers rather than one are obvious. They are particularly compelling where artistic judgments are involved. Blacklisting, favoritism, and discrimination may occur, but they may also be imagined if there is no real alternative source of employment. Pluralism of decision making provides an essential element of protection.

Because skills are specialized and markets are imperfect, appropriate levels of compensation are difficult to determine. It is clear that introduction of independent television in Britain has led to a significant increase in the pay scales of the BBC as a response to the loss of personnel to its competitor. This suggests that monopoly, public or private, exercises significant monopsony power as well.

If one accepts the view that these considerations are important, it is clear that competition—even competition limited to a few competitors—has a major advantage over monopoly.

3. *Public Service Responsibility* · A semipublic monopoly has one enormous asset: it is free to undertake a wholehearted commitment to public service. Freed from any crass scratching for revenue, freed from competition for listeners, and insulated

from pressure groups, it may consciously and conscientiously pursue its image of the public interest. The BBC's worldwide reputation and its many programming triumphs attest to the public benefits that can be achieved. These benefits are not without costs. The image served is that of the monopoly. That it may be paternalistic, that it may identify too closely with the Establishment, that it may resist changes in itself and become impervious to changes in the public climate, are real rather than phantom dangers. They are the hazards of power wherever it is found. Complete lack of power, the characteristic of atomistic competition, while avoiding the dangers, negates the benefits as well in cases where public service is not identical with private interest. The challenge is to find the mixture of monopoly and competition that gives the best balance.

The American mixture does not. Not that the conscious pursuit of public service is absent; the networks do have such an image and it is reflected in news and documentary programs, and elsewhere as well. But even networks can afford to be "uneconomic" in some areas only if they attend to the business of collecting revenue most of the time. If one makes a rough distinction between entertainment and other programming it is only slightly unfair to say that networks abdicate public service responsibility in the former and embrace it in the latter. As to entertainment, the creed is to "give them (the listeners and/or the advertisers) what they want." (How well they do this is discussed below.) For the other they can be magnificent. As examples consider their decisive role in the destruction of Mc-Carthy by the simple expedient of relentless coverage of his investigation of the Army; the coverage of political campaigns and elections; the CBS documentary on Polaris; the NBC documentary on the U-2, with its restrained if devastating exposure of the ineptness of the government then in power. These are the equals of the best of the BBC.

But these activities are inversely related to competition. ABC has gained both listeners and profits by leaving prestige programming to its rivals and developing "adult" Westerns. National spot programming eschews it entirely, and individual stations frequently reject unsponsored network prestige programs in favor of national spot or locally sponsored film series if they have an option. Subjecting the networks to fiercer and more compelling competition, a goal frequently advocated and fruit-lessly pursued by the FCC, would work against, rather than for, public service responsibility.

The successes of the networks should not detract from the question of whether enough of the networks' time is devoted to programs of this sort. This is the problem of the program mix.

4. *The Provision of a Rich and Varied Program* · Here the dis-advantages of limited competition are most pronounced. This fact, and the reasons for it, are very important but only dimly appreciated. It is convenient to consider the problem in stages.

Consider first a situation in which there are three channels operating concurrently for a single period (say thirty minutes) broadcasting to a population of potential listeners whose tastes vary in the following very simple way; out of every one hun-dred potential listeners, eighty want a program of type A (e.g., Western), eighteen want a program of type B (e.g., dramatic show), and the remaining two want a program of type C (e.g., discussion of current events). Further assume to start with that a listener will turn on his set only if a program of the type he wants is broadcast.

A monopoly interested in maximizing the number of listeners (which in this case is the same as satisfying the largest number of people) will clearly produce one program of each type, one on each channel, and both capture and satisfy the whole audience. Three competing firms, each trying to get as many listeners *for itself* as it can, will probably *all* produce a program of type A for the simple reason that each one's share of the mass audience will be larger than the whole of the potential audience for programs of types B or C. If we assumed that two or more stations produc-ing the same program type will share the audience equally, it is easily seen that a fourth channel will also produce type A (20 percent of the audience) rather than type B (18 percent). Indeed, one would need five stations before one could expect type B to be produced, and at least forty-eight channels before type C would appear attractive. Duplication is a consequence of competition for listeners, and if choices are varied and the num-ber of channels limited, duplication will leave some listeners unnecessarily dissatisfied. While each of the duplicating pro-gram producers can claim that "we give people what they want," this is not so in the aggregate.

If viewers will accept (if grudgingly) less-preferred programs rather than none at all, the tendencies for duplication under competition are increased. To see this quickly, suppose 70 percent of the audience prefer type A and 30 percent type B, but will listen to either. If there are only two channels, both will produce type A and each will get 50 percent of the audience. A third channel has a choice of producing type B and getting 30 percent of the listeners, or duplicating type A and getting one-third of the total. If it aims strictly at maximizing its audience it will choose type A. (If viewers had not been shiftable, it would have chosen type B.)

When attention is directed to variation over time rather than to a single period, there are clearly substantial opportunities for increased variety. But there are major forces tending toward duplication as well, and a clear over-representation of the most popular program types. This can be shown theoretically, but the argument is somewhat complex, even tedious, and it will be omitted.[8] Empirically, duplication of program types by channels at the same time, and also over time, are perhaps the most clearly visible features of the American system. The near-saturation of prime evening hours on all networks with Westerns, "private eye" shows, and situation comedies has been noted by many critics. The cost is less coverage of minority tastes than their place in the reference pattern of the population warrants.[9]

So far, then, as satisfying as many listeners as is possible is a sensible objective, and so far as choice is only between program types, it is clear that complete monopoly is, in principle, a more effective instrument than maximum competition when there are binding limits on the number of competitors possible. Monopoly, even private monopoly, is motivated to avoid duplication; competitors are not.

8. For extended theoretical treatment of this and other complications, see P. O. Steiner, "Programme Patterns and Preferences and the Workability of Competition in Radio Broadcasting," *Quarterly Journal of Economics*, Vol. LXVI (May, 1952), pp. 194–223.

9. Nor does this observed behavior fully reflect the working of the simple assumptions of the above examples. Networks do temper their uninhibited search for listeners because of their sense of public service and their desire for critical esteem, which their partial monopoly allows them to indulge. Comparison of network programming with syndicated and local programming provides ample support for the networks' repeated assertion that they devote more time and money to providing both variety and quality than mere profit-seeking would dictate.

Some will quarrel with the objective. Broadcasting, they will argue, should strive virtually exclusively to edify and to educate rather than to cater to the wants of its audience. Whether or not one shares this view (I do not), it is clear that monopoly is again much the most effective way to achieve it, although a monopoly need not act this way. To carry this view to an extreme, the case can be made for only a *single* channel. While there are times (such as a major address by the head of state) when a case can be made for silencing distractions, this practice will find little general support in the basic tenets of an open society.

Viewers select specific programs as well as program types. A choice between two Western (or two religious programs, or two variety shows) is, after all, better than no choice. Not only do tastes vary within program types but competition between programs imposes standards of competence on program producers. But such choice is expensive if it precludes the wider alternatives. Further, the same forces that tend toward duplication of program type lead to imitative programming where competition for listeners is the spur.

The performance of our prototypes with respect to the quality of individual programs is not easy to assess because of the presence of differences in the form and adequacy of financing available. The American prototype taps additional sources of revenue and is much more generously financed. The results of this show, not only in the higher budgets available for popular entertainment but elsewhere as well. For example, the extensive (and in my view splendid) coverage on a regular basis of top sporting events, professional and amateur, occurs because the system generates revenues sufficient to compensate the promoters for the declines in attendance. The price paid for the affluence is the foothold given advertisers in choice and character of programming. The results are some of the best and worst programs in the world. It is not necessary to ask British viewers to accept this assertion on faith; they see a generous sampling of American television on their sets, somewhat biased in favor of the mediocre.

In summary, the comparison between the prototypes—public monopoly and private, commercial, limited competition—shows:

(1) The advantages of pluralism in providing an open forum for news and discussion and in providing alternative sources of

employment give competition a decisive edge.

(2) Public service responsibility flows from two sources: power and motivation. The public monopoly has both, and has the advantage. But the form of limited competition considered leaves substantial monopolistic power in the hands of the competitors who can (and do) choose to compete for public esteem as well as for audience. In either case the existence of a protected position provides the opportunity for conscious public service.

(3) Monopoly is inherently motivated to provide the complementary programming that leads to maximum variety; competitors are not so motivated and a significant restriction on choice owing to both duplication and imitation is to be expected.

(4) Competition, if it generates substantial additional resources for programming, can do some things better than a (relatively) underfinanced public monopoly, and (while it should not be overstressed) the need to compete for audiences may have a beneficial effect on the particular programs of the kinds most heavily demanded.

If choice is limited to one or the other of these prototypes, judgment as to a "balance of advantage" is required. The challenge is to find a mixture that can tap the advantages of both.

AN "IDEAL" TWO-CHANNEL SYSTEM

Suppose that one channel is given to an adequately financed public corporation, called the Public Broadcasting Company (PBC) and that the other is licensed or leased to the Commercial Television Corporation (CTV), a private company, organized for profit, that sells advertising as its chief source of revenue.

Subject to such overall terms as the appropriate authorities may designate, the CTV is encouraged to pursue its own interest, which we may crudely designate as seeking to maximize its audience. It will, in the main, cater to the dominant preferences of its audience, although if care is taken in granting of the license there is no reason to suppose that the drives for prestige and status will be entirely absent. The form of commercial activity permitted (sponsored programs or commercial announcements) is left to the licensing authority; if adequate financing is possible without sponsorship, it seems preferable.

The PBC is instructed to conduct itself so that the *total* broadcasting service (CTV *and* PBC) is as rich and varied as possible. During hours in which both channels are operating this will mean that the PBC will complement rather than compete with CTV and provide the best possible *choice* for those not attracted to the CTV. If the private channel produces or imports splendid Westerns or variety shows, the PBC will provide opposite them a real choice, hour by hour. Of course, where the PBC feels the CTV is doing a poor job it is free to compete—to discipline, if you like, the commercial channel and force the absolute standard of its programming up to a higher level. What the PBC will *not* do is to schedule a Sunday night drama series opposite a similar series on CTV (although it may do so at another time, opposite a variety show, if it thinks wise). Nor will it cover horse racing at one track while CTV is covering racing at another. During hours when CTV is not broadcasting—PBC is licensed to broadcast from early morning to midnight—it will act as the public monopoly that it is, with due regard for the nature, needs, and desires of its potential audience.

While the PBC will thus be imbued with its role as a complementary service it will not always aim for the second largest audience—it will vary its programming to appeal, at least sometimes, to all minority preferences and will not always present the same choices. Further, it will be quite free to over-represent minority tastes if is believes that public information, education, or welfare requires it. In short, it will do very much the same thing as if it were the second service of a *public monopoly* in which the program of the first service were previously settled by higher authority. Coordination does not require mutual agreement; it merely requires that one participant be adaptable and properly motivated.

Two consequences, at first glance unfortunate, will emerge almost by definition if the PBC plays its role properly. First, it will surely lose the battle for audience ratings most of the time (there may be occasional surprises) since it is inviting CTV to cater to the largest audience. This should neither discourage nor deter it. Its job (as a crude first approximation) is to maximize the total audience, not its *share* of the audience. The danger here is that the financing authorities will take this as a measure of failure and withhold funds. Perhaps ideally, the PBC could have its revenue geared to the *total* satisfied audience, not the potential audience, and thus be motivated to play the desired role. The second consequence is that neither the CTV nor the PBC will provide a fully balanced diet. The former will be biased toward popular entertainment, the latter away from it. Some may object to this lack of balance in the offerings of each channel authority, but, surely, this would miss the point. Viewers are not required to choose a *channel* for the duration, but to choose programs. Comparative shipping is easy and cheap (it would be easier and cheaper if the PBC's publication *Broadcasting Times* provided information about programs on *both* channels). Choice between channels, instead of between programs, greatly reduces options, and it should be discouraged rather than fostered by the public-serving PBC. In this connection the PBC will take pains to avoid unnecessary impediments to choice owing to scheduling times; if the CTV schedules programs to begin on the hours and half hours, PBC does the same, rather than on the odd quarters.

In what senses is this "ideal"? First of all, it provides for the complementarity of programming that is a major advantage of monopoly over competition without forfeiting competitive prodding when deemed necessary. Second, it retains the unique organization dedicated to public service that is possible only if financing is at least at one remove from the pressures of commercialism. Third, it provides the pluralism that is absent in monopoly. And finally, it provides an ample source of non-public financing and uses it where it can do the job well, reserving the public funds for those things that private enterprise can not do, is not motivated to do, or does indifferently. In short, it achieves the advantages of complementarity and public service responsibility without loss of the advantages of competition and of private financing. . . .

THE EFFECTS OF A THIRD CHANNEL

A third channel will, according to the way it is allocated, affect the motives and behavior of the existing channels as well. In net effect it may create a system which, alternatively (1) consists of three channels actively competing for share of audience, not unlike the American prototype, whatever the forms of financing;

(2) has one truly complementary service, and achieves the basic benefits of the "ideal" two-channel system; (3) while not introducing a thoroughly complementary service, adds a new form of programming that does widen choice; (4) both creates a complementary service *and* adds a new *third* alternative type of choice.

While any one of these changes represents some improvement, in terms of public objectives, the first seems least attractive and the fourth most promising. Between the second and third, opinions may differ since the benefits and costs are distributed differently. . . .

If one use of the third channel is to try and approximate the results of an "ideal" two-channel system, an alternative is to introduce a thoroughly new form of television. The most frequently discussed is toll television. The promise of toll television lies in (1) its ability to tap new sources of programming, previously beyond reach because of extraordinarily high costs of production or because of the need to compensate other industries for loss of revenues caused by the grant of broadcasting rights; (2) its ability to finance itself from the willingness of consumers to pay; and (3) the impetus to quality provided by competition for the consumers support with other uses of consumers income.

A toll service will not by itself provide the incentives for the existing channels to act in a complementary way, nor is it without problems of its own. The principal danger is that it will skim the cream from existing programs and program producers rather than enrich the mixture. One suspects that viewers would be willing to pay something for much of what they now see free, and this willingness could easily be exploited by toll television.[10] This danger exists if toll television is an independent service, through its ability to offer premium fees to particularly popular actors, playwrights, and others; it exists equally if toll television is part of an existing service through diversion of the most productive effort into the profitable pay-off field. Thus the form of organization of a toll service is of real importance if the promise is to be achieved and the dangers avoided.

10. The expectation of such exploitation has been the major deterrent to the introduction of toll television in America. The fear seems to me justified on a reading of the testimony before the FCC.

Carnegie, Ford, and Public Television

STEPHEN WHITE

This review of recent policy toward improved noncommercial television, written for The Public Interest *issue of fall, 1967, provides two recent answers to the questions raised by the Coase and Steiner articles. As the author shows, the answers of the two foundations are not at all similar. Mr. White, former assistant to the chairman of the Carnegie Commission on Educational Television, is now consultant to the Sloan Foundation.*

BEFORE THE END OF 1968, the 90th Congress brought into being a noncommercial television service intended for the general public. The legislation provided the structure of a Corporation for Public Broadcasting. The United States will thus be in a position to enjoy, after nearly half a century of broadcasting, what most countries have had since the very beginning: a broadly conceived television service not financed by the sale of advertising.

The consequences are not yet calculable. However carefully the structure of the new service, and however lavishly it may be supported, in the end it is nothing but a device to produce pictures and sounds in the living room. It is the kinds of pictures and kinds of sounds that will be consequential. The new system will be the direct descendant of the educational television system that now exists; and if it has no more impact than that system, it will leave matters substantially unchanged. On the other hand, if it becomes a highly professional, well-directed medium of news and cultural programming geared toward some kind of an elite, it will no doubt perform a major service—but it will leave commercial television still dominant and pretty much unchanged (or changed for the worse, as commercial television gives up once and for all upon this segment of its public). If, finally, Public Television enters into any kind of competition with commercial television, and begins to attract any measurable share of the general audience, we may well find ourselves entering a new era in mass communications. Any one of these three outcomes is possible; the legislation can serve any of them.

What can be said without equivocation is that with the new legislation, the potential for change will have been provided. American television need no longer be monolithic. It will at least be possible that other voices will be heard, of their own right and not merely upon the sufferance of the soap, drug, and cigarette manufacturers.

THE CARNEGIE COMMISSION

Only an unusually bold prophet could have suggested, as recently as 1965, that Congress would be persuaded to take action so pregnant with the opportunity for drastic change. True, there had been grumblings about commercial television from the moment it supplanted radio as the primary mass medium. There had been public statements, too, such as Newton Minow's memorable castigation of the "vast wasteland." But these, in effect, amounted to appeals to the conscience of commercial television, and the assumption was that change could be effected only by acts of persuasion directed toward the networks. Commercial television, with a good thing in its possession, sailed its own course.

The road that led to Congressional action was pioneered without foresight or conscious intention. It was opened in late 1964 by Ralph Lowell, trustee of the Lowell Institute and prime mover at WGBH, the educational television station in Boston. Mr. Lowell, at a meeting in Washington called by the National Assocation of Educational Broadcasters, proposed that a Presidential Commission be established to study the financing of educational television. What he had in mind was straightforward enough: ETV was so thoroughly poverty-stricken that its very survival was in question. Mr. Lowell hoped to begin a process that would lead to direct infusions of federal aid.

The notion of a Presidential Commission did not long survive. The [former] president himself owns a most profitable television station in Austin, Texas, and was quite properly reluctant to assume responsibility for a study that bore upon television. Instead John Gardner, at the time president of the Carnegie Corporation of New York, accepted the role the White House could not play, and established the Carnegie Commission on Educational Television, wholly financed by Carnegie (the bill in the end was more than half a million dollars) and operated directly by the foundation, Dr. James R. Killian, Jr., chairman of the corporation at the Massachusetts Institute of Technology, consented to serve as chairman of the commission, and went on to devote to it more than eighteen months of intensive and skillful direction. The White House, having formally established its disassociation, went on to maintain a close and continuing interest in the work of the commission.

Even before the commission came into being, a significant modification had been made in Mr. Lowell's proposal. Educational stations are predominantly operated by educational institutions of one kind or another. In large cities, however, nonprofit corporations have come into being to run educational stations; and these community stations, although they number only about one-fourth the total, have been in general the strongest and the most nearly lively ("most lively" would be too much to say). They have the best channel allocations, the largest audiences, and, in the context of educational television, the widest ambitions. Carnegie decided to concentrate its efforts on the community stations and decided further to study the manner in which those stations operated, as well as their balance sheets. It thus directed its commission away from mere cost-accounting into matters which involved aims, values, and manner of performances of noncommercial television.

The commission itself took that decision a significant step forward at one of its early meetings. It decided to limit itself to that part of noncommercial television which was directed toward the prime-time home audience. It left to another time, another place, and above all another commission the task of dealing with instructional television and the use of television in the classroom. This move transformed the role of the commission. The Carnegie Commission moved into the big leagues. It was now preparing to deal with matters of great public interest and importance—much greater than anyone had anticipated at the outset.

ENTER FORD

During the period when both the Carnegie Corporation and Mr. Killian were defining the study, Carnegie was in close touch with the Ford Foundation. Ford, after all, was the patron saint of noncommercial television, which had come into being largely because of Ford, had been kept in existence simply because Ford repeatedly pumped money into the system, and owed all its ambitious programming—little as it was—to National Educational Television, a creation of the Ford Foundation. It seemed to Carnegie that the good will of Ford was essential. That good will was formally expressed by Henry Heald, president of the Ford Foundation, although his privately expressed views on Carnegie's initiative were by no means amiable. Still, the study could not appropriately be carried out by Ford, for there it would take on the shape of a self-examination and would inevitably be suspect. In any case, in a certain sense Ford's approval had been sought and granted and Carnegie had every reason to believe that it was free to proceed and that Ford would stand aside while its study was in process.

Mr. Heald's expression of benevolent disinterest, however, quickly became irrelevant. He was succeeded at Ford by McGeorge Bundy, who had no reason to feel bound by earlier conversations, who had a profound respect for the power of mass communication, and who felt strongly that television was an area in which Ford should continue to be a major factor. Mr. Bundy was not the kind of man who would willingly remain passive while the Carnegie Commission deliberated.

Coincidentally, a palace revolution at the Columbia Broadcasting System set free Fred Friendly, president of CBS News. Mr. Friendly is a skillful television journalist with a most enviable record in the production of news and documentaries; he is, moreover, a man of great charm and persuasiveness. For reasons peculiar to the television industry and Mr. Friendly's place in it, nothing in commercial television appeared particularly attractive to him. Ford was back in business. Nor was there to be any secret about it, for neither of the two men is shy and retiring.

Some months earlier, before the commission was formed, Mr. Friendly—then at CBS—had commented that the problems of noncommercial television could be summed up in a few words: "A dollar an hour a mile." These are, approximately, the charges made by A. T. & T. for use of coaxial cable—charges which had more than once inhibited or oppressed Mr. Friendly when a big news story was in the making. He felt those charges to be unreasonable and to be, moreover, the principal barrier to more flexible—and hence better—television, whether commercial or noncommercial. At the time, Mr. Friendly's preoccupation with line charges appeared to be merely a personal peculiarity; they quickly took on significance when he moved the focus of his attention and his own vast energy to the Ford Foundation.

With Mr. Bundy in command and Mr. Friendly at his side, it was apparent that Ford would decide, as had the Carnegie Commission only a few weeks earlier, to concentrate its efforts upon prime-time home television. Thus both foundations had now determined to move in a direction that was quite new to Carnegie and that had been at Ford usually subordinate to the uses of television in formal education (though Ford had in fact already been shifting its emphasis before Mr. Bundy appeared). For the time being, both foundations were abandoning television as an educational instrument in favor of television as a social instrument.

WHAT IS "PUBLIC TELEVISION"?

At a latter date, the Carnegie Commission adopted the name "Public Television" for the subject-matter of its considerations, and Ford immediately followed suit. The phrase has since become generally accepted. It might be well to specify more closely what it means. Public Television is noncommercial, nonprofit television, directed in principal to all set owners (although it is generally conceded that any individual program may be directed to some segment of that all-inclusive audience). To that extent, there is general agreement between Carnegie and Ford, and the phrase "Public Television" is also commonly so understood both by those who favor and those who oppose it. There is no such agreement, however, on how a Public Television system might be organized. Above all, there is no agreement concerning the kind of television programs such a system should provide. As we shall see, Carnegie and Ford have adopted diametrically opposed positions in respect to organization and programming.

From the outset, it should have been clear to anyone who thought steadily about the matter that the adoption of the name "Public Television," and the decision to concentrate attention upon Public Television, were inferentially sharply critical of commercial television. Both Ford and Carnegie were implying that there were services of which television was capable and to which the general public was entitled, but which were not being provided by commercial television. Among those who participated in the Carnegie and Ford endeavors there could be no substantial differences of opinion on this point. Differences did appear, however, in the conclusions that were deduced. It could be held, and is held by some, that this is a natural and even a praiseworthy state of affairs—that commercial television has its own tasks to perform, in most respects performs those tasks well, and is in no way obliged to render any but the services it chooses to render. This could be read as a powerful argument for establishing some kind of Public Television. But there are also those who believe that commercial television, whether it likes it or not, should be required to provide a full range of television services, and that to create a Public Television service would simply relieve commercial television of its own deepest obligations and impose a charge upon the public in doing so. There is also a kind of intermediate position, whose proponents hold that commercial television should indeed do a great deal more than it does, but is not going to do so, and that consequently a Public Television system should be erected under conditions that oblige commercial television to support it out of commercial television's own ill-gotten gains. Nor does this exhaust the possibilities, for there is also pay-television to be considered, or variants on the existing commercial system, or still others that fecund minds can provide for future contemplation.

None of those considerations is to be found in the Report of the Carnegie Commission, and they are treated only tangentially in the various Ford documents. Instead, practical men came to the practical conclusion that there was little point in seeking a direct confrontation with commercial television. This strongly entrenched industry, with no shortage of friends in high places, was not going to change radically of its own volition, and there has never been any reason to believe that either Congress or the Federal Communications Commission is disposed to direct it to reform itself radically. Under such circumstances, to inflame the commercial television interests and to array them in opposition would be the worst conceivable tactic for any group which intended to add to the utility of a television set. For the Carnegie

Commission there was the further complication that three commissioners representing commercial television would be called upon to sign the final report. Thus, in the end, both foundations produced documents which are inferentially highly critical of commercial television and yet at the same time resolutely bland.

AN IDEA IS ORBITED

While the Carnegie Commission, during the first six months of its existence, went about its business quietly and behind closed doors, Ford found itself confronted with an immediate opportunity. Mr. Friendly's preoccupation with line charges had engendered an ingenious notion. Ford was developing a scheme which would free television of A. T. & T. line charges by replacing coaxial cables with a communications satellite. That satellite would provide interconnection and other services to commercial television, for a fee, and the same services to Public Television for no charge at all. What is more, the profits of the satellite broadcasting corporation would be turned over to Public Television and used for its support. The notion was in many respects an attractive one. For those who believed that a major deficiency of noncommercial television was its poverty, it provided funds. For those who believed that the principal need of noncommercial television was the kind of electronic interconnection that would make of it a network after the pattern of NBC and CBS, it provided the means for such an interconnection. For those hostile to commercial television, it provided a means—indirect but non the less real—of forcing commercial television to pay the costs of Public Television. Finally, it fed the familiar American faith that the solution to most problems lies in gadgets.

In order to pursue this plan, it was necessary to straighten out the entanglements into which communications satellites had fallen. Congress had awarded to COMSAT exclusive operating rights to satellites operated for international communications, but the locus of such rights for domestic operations had not been determined. Such rights might be awarded to COMSAT, or to a new common carrier incorporated for the purpose, or to new or existing corporate entities which would not act as common carriers but would use specific satelites for specific purposes. The

Ford scheme was reliant upon a decision favoring the last of these three lines of action, and hence the Ford Foundation was an interested party to an inquiry into the matter being held by the FCC. Briefs were requested by the FCC on August 1, 1966, and Ford hastened to file.

The effects of the Ford filing were prodigious. The Ford proposal was radical, sensational, and different, and it caught both the public fancy and the public attention. This public response was not long in making itself heard and it revealed a widespread discontent with commercial television and a broad body of belief that something should be done to provide a kind of television which was lacking and for which a real general need was felt. Where earlier the Carnegie Commission may have wondered, in its quiet moments, whether there was any substantial demand for what it was seeking to build, and whether any forceful public support for its proposals could ever be generated, the Ford intervention made it clear once and for all that those concerns need no longer occupy its attention. The desirability and the propriety of Public Television were no longer an issue.

But at the same time Ford's new idea represented a kind of declaration of war between it and Carnegie. Undeclared war, for on both sides all parties strenuously denied that hostilities had been opened. Mr. Bundy and Dr. Killian tendered and accepted invitations to one another's deliberations at propitious moments and missed no public occasion to express warm respect for one another. Nonetheless, at Ford there was a general sense of elation that the initiative had been recaptured by it; among friends of the Carnegie Commission, a strong feeling that the commission had been "betrayed" by Ford, and that its own attempts to provide a thoughtful, reasoned study of Public Television had been nullified by Mr. Bundy and Mr. Friendly, shooting from the hip.

Both reactions were reasonable. Ford had indeed recaptured the initiative. But in doing so, it had defined Public Television in a fashion that prejudged many of the issues with which the Carnegie Commission was grappling. To buttress a brief that dealt fundamentally with technical issues, Ford was obliged to describe the brave new world of television which the receipts from a privately-managed satellite would sustain, and Ford's brave new world differed in many respects from the Public

Television that the Carnegie Commission was laboriously whipping into shape. The precise nature of those differences will be considered below; for the moment it is enough to say that they are real, and friends of the Carnegie Commission were painfully aware of them—painfully aware, too, that by the time a dissenting Carnegie report was laid before the public, the Ford Foundation might have fixed forever in the public mind the shape of Public Television.

In addition, the Ford filing had inextricably intermingled the notion of Public Television and the notion of a communication satellite. Their only link was the link forged by Ford when it proposed that the costs of one be sustained by the receipts from the other. That link was a tenuous one, for the first hard look at the Ford proposal made it clear that receipts from a satellite could never, under the best of circumstances, pay more than a small part of the full cost of a Public Television system. Nonetheless, an association had been established, and it remains, despite the fact that the arguments for a Public Television system, whether they are persuasive or not, are unaltered by the existence or nonexistence of a communications satellite and would be the same if no satellite had ever gone into orbit.

A NEW NETWORK OR LOCAL CONTROL?

During the months that elapsed until the Carnegie Commission filed its report, Ford continued to press, privately and publicly, for its own design. The Report of the Carnegie Commission was issued late in January, 1967. It was well received, by press and public, and almost invariably linked with the Ford proposal. Mr. Bundy hailed it as complementing and supplementing the work of his own organization—putting the fine finish, as it were, upon what Ford had already accomplished. Dr. Killian had equally kind words to say of Ford.

Yet in its two most important aspects, the Carnegie Report is so fundamentally opposed to the Ford proposal that there can be, in fact, no meeting between the two. Both Ford and Carnegie speak of a Public Television system, and consistently do so in terms that make it appear they are speaking of the same thing. Instead, the two plans have little in common but the name.

To begin with, the Carnegie design is persistently erected on the base of the local station. It anticipates complete local control of program scheduling, substantial local production, and a broad reliance on local talent. It explicitly opposes the concept of a fourth network. It enthusiastically supports electronic interconnection among the stations, but looks upon it as a distribution device which will give every station access to programs produced anywhere within the system, without prescribing for any station the manner in which those programs are to be used—the station is in fact freer not to use a program that to use it, since it will have access to far more programs than it can possibly air.

What underlies that design is the belief that a fourth network would fail to serve needs that are not now being met by commercial television. Any system structured as commercial television is structured will ultimately obey the same imperatives as commercial television: maximization of audience, centralization of decision, and the appeal to a least common denominator. It may be a higher least-common-denominator than that served by commercial television, but there is no guarantee that it would be high enough to serve any real public needs. Put somewhat more broadly, a fourth network would encourage the same kind of uniformity that commercial television demands—uniformity that would perhaps exist at a slightly higher level, but a uniformity none the less. The commission preferred to believe that against the constant and unremitting pressures that exist to make our society uniform, there should remain at least one area of diversity —that at least one station in Atlanta should have the opportunity to be something more than a faithful image of corresponding stations in Seattle, New York, Los Angeles, and Omaha.

The Ford design, in contrast, is firmly suspended from the satellite. It calls explicitly for a fourth network. Like CBS and NBC, the system would arrange for production of programs in a few locations, would then arrange nightly schedules, and would transmit those programs for use by affiliated stations. Again, like commercial affiliates, the local stations would plug into the network at some early hour of the evening, and pull the plug again a few hours later.

That design, too, has its rationale. It is, to begin with, the only way that television now works. It is economical; each program receives maximum use. It responds to the acknowledged fact that great talents are to be found congregated only in a few cities and that it is thus easier to create television of high gloss and finish in those cities. But there are hidden assumptions in the Ford design. The most important is the assumption that there is no room in television for programs intermediate between the purely local and the purely national. Television talent, in whatever field, becomes divided into two categories: those with national appeal and those with local appeal. This, of course, is the viewpoint of commercial television; the comedian who amuses a few million viewers must be denied access to the airwaves, which can utilize only the comedian who amuses tens of millions. It is true that the Ford proposal does take cognizance of local autonomy and local production; it fits them into the interstices of networking. The Carnegie proposal allows for high-gloss production and upon occasion for networking, but they are elements of the total system and are not the system itself. Basically, the two proposals are completely antithetical.

PUBLIC TV AND JOURNALISM

The second principal distinction is the Ford commitment to journalism and the Carnegie Report's antijournalistic bias. The Ford proposal represents Mr. Friendly's earnest and sincere belief that the single central purpose of television is the dissemination of news and commentary of national interest and significance, and that everything else is secondary. It was essentially on the basis of this belief that Mr. Friendly entered into guerrilla warfare at CBS and was forced to resign. He holds this belief as an article of faith and he can hardly be criticized if he does battle for it.

Thus, the network that Ford proposes is primarily a journalistic network; its proposal grows lyrical when it deals with the extent to which a well-supported, interconnected fourth network can provide news coverage of a depth, a breadth, and a substance that cannot now be found on television. For the rest, Ford speaks solemnly of great plays, great concerts, great art. But this, too, is a form of journalism as the Ford proposal deals with it. Essentially, Ford proposes to *reflect*, on the one hand, what happens in the world of politics, of social and military confrontation, and of catastrophe; on the other hand, it will also *reflect* what is happening in the theater, the opera house, the concert hall, the museum. In neither case does there enter any concept of creativeness. There is little notion that television, too, may be an art form and that it need not be at its best when it presents on a twenty-one inch screen *Carmen* or the New York Philharmonic or *Hamlet*.

The Carnegie report, on the other hand, implies that pure journalism, on the national scale, is more than adequately served over most of its range by commercial television and other news media, and that Public Television would be wasting its substance if it engaged in a hopeless attempt to enter into competition. There is, indeed, one member of the commission who has commented that the American public is too well served with news—much of it fabricated to fill the time that commercial television devotes to it—and that part of the current American malaise can be attributed to a constant exposure to commotion and catastrophe without the concurrent means of coming to grips with any of it.

The Carnegie Report identified the great journalistic need as a local need, for it is here that the commercial networks are least effective, the local newspaper less and less enterprising, and the national magazines by their nature inadequate. At this level, too, there is less temptation to sensationalize the news, for the local viewer is more likely to be in a position to check on the veracity of the newscaster. (Much national news is in fact local news sensationalized to the extent necessary to make it nationally titillating.) Thus the Carnegie Commission attempted to create means by which the local station would enjoy a greater capacity to produce local newscasts and local news commentary.

For the rest, the Carnegie proposal is epitomized in a few words with the epigraph by E. B. White which stands at the head of its report. Public television should be, Mr. White wrote, "our Minsky's, our Camelot." In short, the commission intended to rid Public Television once and for all of the sober pedanticism and the dull virtue that characterized educational television. Public Television should rather set out frankly to entertain and to satisfy, in its own terms and on any level where there is an audience to serve. It should have television presentations of quality and distinction for the person who at other times will go to the theater to see *Hamlet* or to the concert hall to hear *Carmen;* it should also have television presentations of quality and distinction for the person who at other times will go to the cinema to see the Marx Brothers or to the theater to see *My Fair Lady.*

The contrast between the two proposals is here cast in the starkest terms. The Ford proposal does speak of creativity, the Carnegie proposal of great Shakespearian productions. But the centers of gravity of the two proposals are as far apart as they can possibly be.

WHAT FLESH ON THE BONES?

These principal differences between the two proposals have not yet been resolved, nor is there any formal attempt to resolve them. The Corporation for Public Broadcasting, no doubt will in time be erected and put into operation, can move in either direction, or indeed in almost any direction at all. Congress is dealing only with the bare bones of Public Television; the flesh will be put on them by the men and women who become the corporation and who set about creating and directing the system.

The Ford Foundation has moved ahead with its own design. Mr. Bundy has established the Public Television Laboratory and staffed it with professionals of high skill and talent. They are now preparing to launch a two-hour television program each Sunday evening (or perhaps alternate Sundays) to consist primarily of pure journalism and secondarily of what might be called derivative journalism, to be fed to a network of noncommercial stations. This is the course of action indicated by the Ford proposal, and they are being consistent in pressing ahead with it.

The Carnegie Commission dissolved with the issuance of its report. A Citizens Committee for Public Television was created some five months later, but it has been inactive so far. In any case, there is no reason to believe that the Citizens Committee will adopt the viewpoint of the Carnegie Commission; indeed, it would be surprising if it should do so, for that committee itself has been bathed in the atmosphere of the Ford proposal, its executive secretary comes out of the Ford-Friendly shop, and it will find that its ground, too, has in part been pre-empted by the energetic Ford Foundation.

It would be salutary if broad public consideration could be given to the differences between the two proposals. That has not been done, in part because there has been no general recognition that they do indeed differ. It may be that my own bias—which I have taken no pains to disguise—is mistaken, and that the fourth network, dominated by journalism, is indeed the most desirable shape a Public Television system could assume. But there is surely some possibility that the position taken by the Carnegie Commission, once it is fully understood, is closer to American needs and American desires.

In the absence of further consideration, it is clear that the Ford position will prevail, if only because the Ford Foundation is pressing for it actively and with substantial resources. The likely outcome is that Ford's Public Television Laboratory will dominate program production, and that it will fall into a simple fourth network operation. Let it at least be clear that, if this happens, or if anything much like it happens, the intentions of the Carnegie Commission will have been largely ignored. What is more important, American television will have survived its crisis and will continue into the future essentially unaltered, if perhaps somewhat improved.

PART FIVE   Air Transport Regulation

Performance, Structure, and the Goals of Civil Aeronautics Board Regulation

RICHARD E. CAVES

This comprehensive review of air transport regulation centers attention on the regulatory commission and its interaction with the industry being regulated. The book by the title Air Transport and Its Regulators, *of which this essay is an abridgment of the last chapter, is a model of the new research by economists focusing on the commission in this manner. Richard E. Caves, professor of economics at Harvard University, is well known for his work in international economics, resource economics, and public utility economics.*

THE RECORD OF market performance in air transport is determined by structural factors, both the economic elements of market structure and the controls of the Civil Aeronautics Board. Consider these particular features of performance: approximately normal profits; some maldistribution of resources among city-pair markets (serious in the past, now substantially improved); firms of efficient size (also a recent achievement); a somewhat limited range of classes of service offered; costs that are affected by such undesirable factors as the survival of inefficient firms and "uneconomic" types of product rivalry; rigid prices that sometimes change perversely; reasonable selling costs; and reasonable rates of technological and marketing innovation. On the whole, the airlines' record is not bad if compared with unregulated industries of similar seller concentration in the American economy; and it is definitely good by comparison with many consumer-goods industries.

THE IMPACT OF STRUCTURE

Seller concentration, usually a key determinant of an industry's performance, here plays a lesser role because it is an effect of other environmental factors. Demand characteristics and the condition of entry (along with the cost characteristics that underlie it) seem more important. The traits of the demand for air transport rule out product differentiation, a fecund source of barriers to entry in other industries. They also have something to do with the minimum efficient scale of operation in a given city-pair market and thereby determine the maximum number of carriers likely to be found there. The efficiencies of marketing a variety of daily flight times, plus the economies of fully utilizing a carrier's planes and spreading overhead items, create moderate barriers to the entry of new firms into city-pair markets. On the other hand, cost conditions facilitate exit from a particular city-pair. This, plus the ease of entry by an established carrier, makes competition workable in these markets despite the necessarily high seller concentration. Now, contrary to first impressions, the Civil Aeronautics Board's absolute control of entry has not entirely upset the influence of these traits. Some city-pair markets have been exploited by monopoly carriers and by tight oligopolies now and then. But over the history of the Board, entrenched carriers have seldom been free from the fear that a route case would unleash new competition; the legal possibility of entry seems to have kept its economic ease effective. The national market for air transportation is really the sum of a great number of city-pair markets; so the implication of demand and entry conditions at the national level is much the same. Again, even with regulation that has been implacably hostile to direct forms of entry, the moderate ease of entry to the industry has been responsible in part for the existence at all times of potential entrants. In the past decade these have been the "nonskeds" or supplemental carriers. The local-service carriers are now taking somewhat the same role, and there is talk of a new layer of local airlines.

These features of demand and entry have some impact on the aggregate level of profit and, lately, a strong effect on the relocation of resources to even out the rates of return earned in different city-pair markets. These facts have also influenced the relatively moderate amount of interdependence recognized in many city-pair markets and have motivated various forms of seller rivalry and marketing innovation. Though many advantages of easy entry have been preserved, the Board's absolute ban on full-fledged entry has extracted a cost. The restricted choice of classes of service and cost-increasing phenomena, such as the general decline of load factors in the first years of the general passenger-fare investigation, probably must be explained this way. The same is true, in part, of the rigidity of fares and the slowness of such changes as the extension (or contraction) of coach service that has taken the place of fare adjustments.

Another group of important structural features is that which has tended to make smaller carriers less profitable than larger ones. This situation has partly rested on pecuniary advantages of size, partly on artificial disadvantages created for the small carriers by the "grandfather" route patterns of 1938. It seems to have had two major results. The direct one, indicated above, was to increase the market rivalry in the industry and multiply the kinds of product rivalry. Indirectly, this condition has been very important through its impact on the Board's policies. In a series of cases in the 1950s, a chance to allow new carriers into the industry was sacrificed, in a sense, to the goal of improving the position of the smaller carriers by putting them into profitable routes. Furthermore, the protection of weaker carriers must be one of the mainsprings of the Board's chronic fear that some types of competitive strategies may get out of hand.

Other economic traits of market structure deserve brief mention. All the facts suggest that the rapid growth of demand for air transport has influenced conduct and performance by raising the extent of market rivalry. The carriers' long-term schedules for penetrating new city-pair markets are but one feature of the many which point to their willingness to sacrifice today's profits to tomorrow's greater market share. Since air transport is not a readily differentiable good and is bought primarily by experienced customers, its nonfunctional advertising has been held at a minimum, and crippling barriers to entry have not arisen.

As an independent force, the Board's policies have had a number of effects on market performance. The certification provisions of the Civil Aeronautics Act have certainly increased the stability and quality of service to marginally profitable city-pairs. Taking a purely economic view of performance, this has both good and bad features. Subsidized service has no attraction in the absence of proof of external economies or other indirect social worth. On the other hand, fluctuations in marginal services resulting from the ebb and flow of oligopolistic rivalry in major markets have no particular virtue. The Board's restrictions on the forms of product competition and its methods of evaluating profits have given an enormous boost to the rate of development and adoption of new aircraft. These same restrictions on product and also on price rivalry have been largely responsible for the inflexibility of the price of air transportation and for the possibly inadequate variety of services offered. The control of entry and exit, both in the national market and in city-pair markets, has raised the cost of air transportation through protecting inefficient firms and through maintaining seasonally imbalanced route structures that require firms to own many types of aircraft. Paradoxically, the Board's policies, on the whole, have probably had little effect on the rate of profit earned by the industry; but, without the Civil Aeronautics Act and the Board, these profits would have resulted from quite a different sort of operation. Supporting this view is the lack of clear evidence that the Board's actions have either increased or decreased the recognition of mutual dependence and the achievement of collusion among the carriers. On the one hand, the regulatory setting tolerates a certain amount of common cause among the regulated firms; on the other, during the period of direct subsidy to the trunks of premium was taken off collusion and the highly rivalrous behavioral patterns which resulted are slow in dying out.

How would the traits of the air-transport industry change in the absence of direct public control? Seller concentration in the typical city-pair market would not differ much from what it is now, but seller concentration at the national level would probably be much lower. Giants like the present Big Four would still exist, but they could compete against different, smaller specialist carriers in particular markets. Both large and small carriers would have more homogeneous operations. Route structures of individual carriers would be stable in the short run but nonetheless adaptable to changes in the types of airplanes used and to shifts of demand. The total number of city-pairs served would be reduced, although the evolution of aircraft designs might have taken a different course and produced planes more suitable for thin markets, thereby partly offsetting the absence of subsidy. Without regulation, more flexibility and possibly more variety would exist in the range of product and price offered to the traveler.

These conclusions can be adapted to answer a variety of questions about the consequences of any partial change in the scope or substance of aeronautics regulation. For instance, a decade ago the proposal was often made that the trunk carriers merge into a few strong systems to improve their balance and self-sufficiency and to reduce the "costs of competition." [1] Assuming no other changes, this would result in an increase in profit rates earned by the carriers, in the near elimination of effective public control over the price and product policies of the surviving firms (because of an extensive recognition of mutual interdependence), and in unchanged costs to the industry. Assuming that the firms of the rationalized industry were similar in size and profitability, marketing innovations would be reduced to those deemed profitable for the industry as a whole. Sales-promotion expenditures and efforts at product differentiation generally would probably be higher to an undesirable degree. Price flexibility would be less, if possible, than today. The picture in general is quite unattractive.

The effort of lesser changes may also be predicted. For example, relaxing controls over price and product competition without changing the controls over entry would have a variety of effects. On the one hand, effective collusion among the trunks is probably such that the general fare pattern would tend to adjust to yield somewhat higher average fares than now. On the other hand, there would be more variety in the strategies of product rivalry used and more variability of price in particular city-pair markets. The emphasis on new aircraft as a product strategy would be reduced. On balance, the industry might possibly earn a higher aggregate rate of return and also furnish a more flexible and satisfactory variety and quality of product, perhaps at no higher an average fare; it is hard to tell whether any net gain in performance would be involved. To remove re-

<hr>

1. H. D. Koontz, "Domestic Air Line Self-Sufficiency: A Problem of Route Structure," *American Economic Review*, XLII (March 1952), 122–123.

strictions on entry without changing the existing policies on price and product changes (and assuming no subsidy to entrants) would tend to guarantee normal profits in individual city-pair markets and in the industry as a whole. It would insure the ending of unprofitable service by unsubsidized carriers in thin markets. The normal profits, however, would occur at whatever level of fares happened to prevail, with average costs being driven up through excess capacity and real or spurious product differentiation or improvement. If the Board still permitted fare adjustments to yield a normal profit over current levels of cost, both price and cost would rise in successive and possibly rapid stages, depending on the elasticity of supply of aircraft. The whole situation, again, would be highly undesirable.

Throwing open the major city-pair markets to unrestricted entry by *existing* trunks, however, would be much different. This change would improve the flexibility of the allocation of transport resources among major markets and keep the airlines' route structures in good balance with changes in the cost characteristics of new aircraft. Problems of seasonal imbalance would be substantially corrected. The rising recognition of mutual interdependence among the trunks would be set back sharply unless too many were eliminated from business in the process; this seems unlikely because, in spite of the operating disadvantages of some of the smaller carriers, all could surely survive on rationalized systems. The Board's problems with a rising cost level and the resultant price increases would be no worse than at present, and probably less troublesome for a while. Monopoly service to weak points would not be affected except in transition. The variety and flexibility of service offered in richer markets would improve, and the cost of producing it might well be reduced. Thus, a reform consisting of removing barriers to entry into major city-pair markets by existing certified trunks is the one partial loosening of the Civil Aeronautics Board's restrictions that has a number of points in its favor. To forestall an objection that the industry would immediately raise, there is no reason why it should induce cutthroat competition. At any one time, there are only so many aircraft in the hands of the trunks, and usually these are fully utilized. Such a reform would hardly reduce recognized mutual dependence enough to encourage great investment of capital in new equipment by the present trunks; without this it is difficult to envision the proliferation of any undesirable forms of competitive conduct.

GOALS OF THE CIVIL AERONAUTICS BOARD

The major standing policies of the Civil Aeronautics Board do not coincide with the economist's usual criteria of efficiency. The Board aims at more than a normal amount of resources in the air-transport industry, service in more city-pair markets than can sustain it commercially, and probably a faster rate of development of new aircraft than unrestricted market forces would produce. Any final conclusions about the best policies for air transport must depend on whether one concedes the worth of such objectives. The question is, can the loss of economic welfare so caused be repaid by what these policies achieve?

Let us recall those objectives, stated or implied, of the Board's regulation which lie outside of the usual norms of economic welfare. First, the airlines contribute to the military potential of the nation in a variety of ways. The Board has felt that some of them warrant subsidy and other actions to raise the output of the industry above what commercial considerations would indicate. A second objective is to maintain a regular network of air routes uniting the nation's cities and towns. On heavily traveled segments, private enterprise would do this without any public attention; if meaningful, the objective calls for service which commercial revenues would not support. A third major objective, one which this study has inferred from a great number of Board policies, is to speed the development of transport aircraft. A fourth objective, also implicit, has been to maximize the safety of air travel by maintaining economic stability in the industry. Finally, the Board has two minor aims relating to the sort of service offered by the industry. One is to keep air fares as stable as possible over time. The other, drawn directly from the Civil Aeronautics Act, is to restrict the use of certain types of price discrimination.

It is often said that the airlines' trained personnel constitute an important resource in the case of military emergency, and many of the large transport aircraft are subject to an agreement to cover their immediate transfer to military service. There is no evidence, however, that this defense potential requires more support than market forces would give. If so, this is no argument for departing from a market-determined situation. But the Board has felt at times that specific services require subsidy because of their contribution to defense. The military value of service experience accumulated by the helicopter airlines has been cited to justify their heavy subsidies,[2] and a local-service route was established in Montana and North Dakota at a subsidy cost substantially higher than usual because it served isolated military installations.[3] The Board has also said that air service desired by the military would justify *some* extra subsidy,[4] but there is no experience to tell how this worth for defense purposes is or ought to be evaluated. Thus, subsidy to particular air services has brought substantial returns in aid to the military, but these contributions come in specific cases and they do not seem to warrant the raising of the aggregate output of the industry above a market-determined level.

The annals of economic history contain example after example of public subsidy to forms of transportation. One justification for such policies is that the gain in national unity through making first-class transportation available to small cities is worth a certain amount of subsidy. A more technical argument would be that there are always a few persons in any small city who would pay much more than the nondiscriminatory market price for air travel; subsidy of minimum service is justified by the "surplus" which accrues to them but which cannot be collected directly. This argument cannot apply to large cities with good alternate means of transportation. Neither the economic argument nor the noneconomic one can be tested formally. One might doubt that such a case carries much weight in an advanced country like the United States, where there is no lack of national unity or no need to subsidize transportation in developing new regions. But there is no way of disposing of it entirely. Certainly, if public sentiment, expressed by Congress, supports it, there is not much ground for counterargument. The Civil Aeronautics Board has always favored the extension of air service to the largest possible

2. Chicago Area Service Case, Docket No. 6600 *et al.*, decided June 7, 1956, CCH Av. Law Rep. § 21,965.01.
3. Montana Local Service Case, Docket No. 6293 *et al.*, decided July 2, 1959, CCH Av. Law Rep. § 22,290.01.
4. The City of Portsmouth Service Investigation, Docket No. 7887 *et al.*, decided Nov. 9, 1956, CCH Av. Law Rep. § 21,997.02.

number of cities. When the trunks were receiving direct subsidy, this was done by trying to force the airlines to use the profits from lucrative routes to subsidize money-losing routes. With the withdrawal of subsidy it was no longer to the carriers' interest to do this. The Board gave tacit approval to their abandoning of this arrangement and started to spread air service by extending the local-service carriers. This step, which seemed responsive to the will of Congress, shunted the burden of subsidy from the "internal subsidy" reaped by overcharging passengers on dense routes to a straightforward subsidy from the government covering the losses of the local airlines. The newer arrangement is strongly preferable, if this sort of subsidy is desired at all. First, there is no reason why impoverished grandmothers flying from New York to Los Angeles should be the ones to subsidize well-off businessmen traveling between small towns. Second, enforcing internal subsidy required the Board to use many auxiliary restrictions, such as blockading entry to rich markets, that take a heavy toll in economic efficiency.

A third objective of the Board's policies that lies outside the normal criteria of economic welfare is to speed the development of new aircraft. This is not very explicit in the Civil Aeronautics Act or in the Board's policy pronouncements, but it is strongly implied by the general drift of the Board's decisions as well as by the results of its regulations curtailing the available means of price and product competition. Now, the rate of development of civil aircraft is no doubt a matter of concern to the American public. In the late 1940s the British embarked on a massive program of subsidization of turbine-powered aircraft. With the coming of the Comet I, it was clear that the United States was behind and numerous Congressional hearings were held to consider subsidization of a turbine prototype. There was much support for such a move, even though nothing substantial resulted because the aircraft industry was of several minds and the only legislation, the Prototype Testing Act of 1950, was never implemented.[5] Again, in the last few years there has been much alarm that the British or the Russians would be the first to produce a supersonic commercial transport, to the enduring injury of American dignity. Once again, no serious action has been taken, but

5. The President's Air Coordinating Committee, *Civil Air Policy* (Washington, 1954), pp. 62–63.

the existence of popular concern is undeniable. The public would prefer the rate of development of new aircraft to be, if anything, faster than at present, and the present rate is faster than an unregulated industry would generate. So the Board's policies cannot be rejected out of hand. As with service to unprofitable points, it is a case of hard-to-measure costs and intangible benefits.

It is hard to tell how much the influence of the Board's economic policies has to do with the promotion of safety in air commerce, the fourth major special objective. The only extensive discussion of this came during the debates over treatment of the irregular carriers in the 1940s. Whether or not these carriers cut corners on safety was widely argued, but the evidence is not conclusive. Furthermore, no evidence has turned up in the course of this study which shows that those policies which reduce the turnover of firms in the industry make a substantial contribution to safety. On the one hand, one can imagine a licensing system for air carriers that would require them to meet minimum safety standards independent of any economic regulation. Indeed, the division of labor between the Civil Aeronautics Board and the Federal Aviation Agency operates on that principle now. However, it is not possible to refute the assertion that regulating turnover is a safety measure.

There remain two minor objectives more directly economic in their significance. One is the Board's preference for stable air fares. This was officially adopted with the dismissal of the first general fare investigation and has been restated at various times. Whether or not fares should be stable in a regulated industry has often been debated but never settled. If we count on changes in relative prices to allocate resources properly throughout the economy, there is an *a priori* case against the rigidity of any price. On the other hand, regulation that aims at normal profits implies a movement of prices counter to the business cycle and counter to most other prices in the economy. Meaningless shifts of relative prices would occur—shifts that might draw too many resources into the regulated industry in time of prosperity only to force the regulatory authority to raise prices to guarantee a normal reward in time of recession.[6] This is not better than rigid prices, and probably is worse. If regulation is necessary on

6. For discussion, see Ben W. Lewis, "State Regulation in Depression and War," *American Economic Review*, XXXVI (May 1946), 384–404.

other grounds, the best the regulatory authority can do, when it is bent on setting *some* prices subject to normal constitutional guarantees, is to maintain rigid prices or, if possible, to encourage promotional discounts only in recession. But if the achieving of rigid prices is advanced as an argument against an unregulated status, then it has no economic standing. One regulatory goal of the Civil Aeronautics Act has been to restrict the amount of discrimination in the air-transport industry. However, most of the matters the Board has worried about are actually not forms of discrimination. Some price differences, such as special group fares, reflect cost differences. Only a few pricing practices of the airlines are discriminatory in the classical sense; one of these is the family fare, which the Board has regularly, if grudgingly, allowed. Would price or service discrimination be a major problem in an unregulated air industry? Certainly not in general, for discrimination is possible only when two conditions are satisfied: monopoly (or collusion achieving the same result) and the ability of the seller to distinguish among buyers and prevent resale of the product. Even in thin markets, where monopoly service would be normal, distinguishing among persons and preventing resale would not usually be possible. The opportunities for discrimination among persons that were exploited by rail freight services before the Interstate Commerce Act would not be open to the airlines in the absence of regulation.

Thus, none of the Board's special objectives seems very compelling. However, not all of them can be dismissed as worthless, and so we shall consider the workability of the present administrative arrangements—the efficiency of the Board's historic pursuit of its own goals, the current effectiveness of its policies, and the possibility of improvement through minor changes.

PERFORMANCE OF THE CIVIL AERONAUTICS BOARD

According to the terms of the Civil Aeronautics Act, how efficient has been the pattern of regulatory actions imposed by the Board? It has been reasonably faithful to the board goals set for it, and even in its detailed policies its performance compares very favorably with the other major regulatory commissions. It has largely avoided the trap of outright protectionism of the industry it regulates. It has handled well many of the problems of regulating a competitive industry, such as the need for manipulating the incentives rather than directly molding conduct and performance. Many other accomplishments have been mentioned above and should be recalled through the critique that follows. Still, a good deal has been wrong, and the situation is not clearly improving.

The difficulties of the past seem to come from three major sources. One is the restrictions of the political environment in which the Board works. Whether one sees in them the vices of government-by-pressure-group or the virtues of continuous voicing of the popular will, they are an ingrained feature of regulation by any independent commission. The political equilibrium surrounding the Board was analyzed in Chapter 12 (of *Air Transport and Its Regulators*) and will not be considered further here. A second general problem for the Board is appropriate timing for its policies. It has too often steered into the future while watching the rear-view mirror. A third problem, somewhat related to the second, is that the Board has not been able to foresee all the consequences of its decisions and has not secured the information necessary to clear its vision.

Taking the second of these problems, the Board has not only had to decide important questions of the future from a dated record of the past, it has also been particularly unlucky with accidents of timing. At about the time of the Korean War, the Board was holding back on authorizations of new point-to-point competition and declining to hold a general investigation of standards for setting fares. The prosperity of the early 1950s was an ideal time for extensions of competition. But it was only in the mid-1950s that these were actually granted, and the resulting shake-down losses from the new situation coincided with the severe 1957-58 recession and a period of heavy capital outlays for new equipment. Facing this rather accidental crisis of low profits and fast-rising capacity, the Board set out to find a general standard for fixing fares and profits. A worse time could hardly have been imagined, and the decision showed the scars of its environment.

Apart from the problem of forecasting the future, the Board has not been able to sense important changes in the conduct or structure of the industry and adjust its policies accordingly. In part this resulted from personnel conditions on the Board, which had a rapid turnover of members not fully trained to deal with the economic complexities of the industry. In part it resulted from the failure of the Board to secure from Congress appropriations that would give it a staff large enough to work beyond the press of current problems.

The best general illustration of these troubles is the Board's failure to anticipate the great changes in the industry's conduct that followed when the trunks went off direct subsidy. Under subsidy it was logical that the airlines would have little incentive to adjust fares upward with rising costs, that they would be willing to maintain good service over particular route segments on which revenues were not covering costs, and that cutthroat rivalry for shares of highly profitable markets might be a very real problem. It was also logical for the Board to be chary about admitting new firms to the industry. By the late 1940s, despite many short-run problems, the Board's policies had become rather well adjusted to this situation. With direct subsidy ended, and neither the Board nor the carriers anticipating its return, the incentives before the trunkline carriers changed completely. Unprofitable services were sloughed off or allowed to deteriorate. The carriers' interest in higher fares took a sharp upturn. The problem of excess competition, such as it was, threatened only where one carrier saw a good chance of driving a rival out of business; otherwise, there was enough, often more than enough, recognition of mutual interdependence to take care of the problem. A major rationale for restricted entry evaporated. The problem of weak and strong carriers, which could be ignored while subsidy existed, immediately became critical; of the several possible solutions to it, the Board picked the one (route extensions) most cumbersome administratively and most likely to fail in the short run. One might say that by the end of the 1950s the Board was adjusting to this new situation. From efforts in the early 1950s to keep the quality of air service down and the price up, it had gone some distance toward reversing the emphasis. Still, a lag of ten years is not very admirable.

There are many other examples of dim vision. The Board was handed an extremely inefficient network of airline routes by the "grandfather" certifications. Yet there has never been any comprehensive consideration of how these might either be rationalized or made sufficiently flexible to adapt to changing airplane technology or changing patterns of demand. There have been piecemeal efforts at correction through route extensions and mergers, but the former have been haphazard and the latter have often had undesirable side-effects. The weak record in the regulation of air fares and the doubtful general standard finally adopted have already been discussed. Lacking the confidence to force the industry to extend special services or to experiment with promotional fares, the Board has rendered important decisions in the industry's favor, announcing that it expected these reforms in return; yet it has not used any leverage to enforce its requests or obtained any impressive results. (One example is the *Transcontinental Coach-Type Service* case, which asked for prompt and extensive entry of the trunks into air-coach service; the 1958 fare-increase decision urged more experimentation with promotional fares, but few appeared before 1961.) The Board has understood some of the consequences of an increasing recognition of mutual interdependence among the carriers, such as the collusive increases of costs and reductions of load factors during the early phases of the second general fare investigation. Yet in the decision to that same case it accepted the carriers' arguments that there was *not enough* recognition of mutual dependence. The Board has not kept continuously in mind the sources of marketing innovation. Without the occasional entry of new firms, these come largely from small, aspiring, and "imbalanced" carriers. It has often seemed to accept the Air Coordinating Committee's 1954 suggestion that, with the industry reduced to a few giant carriers, "the greater strength resulting from merged operations would actually increase the keenness of competition within the industry." [7] This is refuted by all evidence of conduct within the air-transport industry, as well as by much evidence concerning unregulated industries in the American economy. And if this were not enough, the logic of the quotation implies that reducing the number of firms in an industry renders it more and more competitive until, with only two left, competition reaches its maximum effectiveness; no comment seems necessary. Thus, in the hope of securing more effective competition, the Board has attempted to equalize the size and profitability of the carriers, at the same time preventing the entry of new ones and allowing the normal attrition of existing operators—a combina-

7. *Civil Air Policy*, p. 12.

tion of policies almost sure to defeat the objective.

A similar critique could be leveled at the Board's detailed procedures, though this seems a task better left to a scholar versed in administrative law.[8] For better or worse, the efficiency of the Board's decision making is heavily impaired by the requirements of due process. The Board operates in the same way, and with the same attention to detail, as when it started operations.[9] It has spent enormous amounts of time on route cases, especially in mulling over great mountains of irrelevant evidence on which carrier ought to perform what service, without securing the information it really needs about the cost characteristics of various route structures. Procedures are generally aimed at giving a fair hearing to all carrier parties, and the Board has not faced the fact that this often makes impossible any firm or consistent pursuit of the public interest.

The results of these substantive and procedural inadequacies appear in the weaknesses of the industry's performance mentioned above—unnecessarily high costs and restrictions on the responsiveness of the industry to expressions of consumer choice. Is the situation getting better or worse? Unfortunately, the signs seem to point to continued deterioration. Consider some current trends. The number of trunklines threatens to shrink rapidly to eight or less, partly with the Board's encouragement. The probable consequences have already been seen. With entry to the industry blockaded by the Board's standing policy, but with carriers now and then leaving by merger, the chances for tacit collusion and the resulting payoff rise sharply. The outlook is for more collusive behavior by the carriers, though it may be enlivened at times by attempts to dispatch a vulnerable rival. With blockaded entry a carrier enjoys an enormous reward from seizing any opportunity to eliminate a competitor. It has

8. For some relevant discussion, see P. N. Pfeiffer, "Shortening the Record in C.A.B. Proceedings through Elimination of Unnecessary and Hazardous Cross-Examination," *Journal of Air Law and Commerce*, XXII (Summer 1955), 286–297; Louis J. Hector, "Problems of the C.A.B. and the Independent Regulatory Commissions," *Yale Law Journal*, LXIX (May 1960), 931–964; Earl W. Kintner, "The Current Ordeal of the Administrative Process," *Yale Law Journal*, LXIX (May 1960), 965–977; M. H. Bernstein, *Regulating Business by Independent Commission* (Princeton, 1955); E. S. Redford, *Administration of National Economic Controls* (New York, 1952).

9. United Research, *Federal Regulation of the Domestic Air Transport Industry*, p. 4.

antitrust immunity plus a guarantee that the rival will not be replaced at least until another existing carrier can win a route award.[10] The rising barriers to entry from economic sources reinforce this situation, as do the chronic disadvantages of the relatively small carrier with low historic profitability and a structure of weak routes. The Board made a brave effort at removing the weaknesses of the smaller carriers in the route cases, but its success has been incomplete. The Board wanted to preserve the same number of trunks but to equalize their profitability; earning power will probably be equalized, but for a significantly smaller number. Sources of marketing innovation and product rivalry may be drying up because of this trend, as well as because of the shift of the carriers' top managements from ambitious and combative operating men to "business" personnel of more conventional outlook.

Another worsening problem for the Board is reflected in the adequacy-of-service cases. Some of these (Baltimore, Fort Worth) seem to reflect tacit understandings by the airlines to force travelers at the smaller of two nearby cities to use the airport of the larger. Others (Toledo, Flint–Grand Rapids) reflect the decision of a weak carrier to concentrate its limited equipment in competitive markets. Similarly, the complaints of many small cities about their trunk service reflect either this same strategy of weak carriers or the unwillingness of stronger trunks to waste resources on unprofitable or marginally profitable services. All of the cases suggest that the Board is restricting competitition in strong markets without benefiting the traveling public at weaker points.

Finally, the Board still employs cumbersome proceedings to pass on particular strategies of price and product adjustment, although it has less and less control over the amount and substance of effective rivalry within the industry. This is the story of changes that have followed the ending of direct subsidy to the trunks. When subsidy was in force, the Board had powerful tools

10. Conversely, where entry is easy, predatory and exclusionary conduct is not likely to be either profitable for existing firms or a serious worry for public policy. Paradoxically, the most determined antitrust attack against alleged predatory conduct of recent years was mounted against the A & P grocery chain, which operates in markets of very easy entry. See M. A. Adelman, *A & P: A Study in Price-Cost Behavior and Public Policy* (Cambridge, Mass., 1959).

for shaping the quantity and quality of price and product to its own tastes. Its ability to enforce *any* set of tastes or preferences continues to decline, but no adjustment has been made.

IMPROVING THE REGULATION OF AIR TRANSPORT

How can the Board increase the efficiency of the pursuit of its present set of objectives? These include, beyond the usual criteria for good market performance, rapid development of new transport aircraft, subsidized service to weaker traffic-generating points, low turnover of carriers to promote safety, and price rigidity. One step is to recognize that the amount of internal subsidy in effect has been dropping sharply and that it always tends to disappear among carriers not receiving direct subsidy. Thus the best strategy, as the United Research report urged, is to continue shifting the trunks out of marginally profitable points, to continue direct subsidy to the local-service carriers, and to drop all policies toward the trunks that are used solely to protect internal subsidy. So far, this is a very helpful suggestion. The Board is already in the process of converting subsidy for the local-service carriers from payment to each of them according to need toward payment of the difference between average or normal costs and commercial revenues.[11] Of the policies affecting the trunks, restriction of entry to city-pair markets no longer protects profits significantly because the typical market has its full quota of authorized carriers. Also, the policy on fares designed to exploit the richer markets has been in large part frustrated by the extension of coach service and outright differences in the quality of first-class service from route to route. Thus it is pointless for the Board to spend much time in deciding whether four or five carriers should be authorized for a given market. Since the number of carriers that can efficiently operate in a given city-pair market is probably falling, this essentially means that there will be no more major route cases unless mergers should continue to eliminate a good deal of point-to-point competition.[12] There is no reason not to allow the carriers more freedom to experiment with changes in the fare structure, classes of service offered, and

11. Order Serial No. E–15696, Local Service Carriers Rate of Return Investigation, Docket No. 8404, Aug. 26, 1960.
12. For a similar position see the United Research report, p. 43.

the like; happily, the Board has been doing so in 1961 and 1962.

One definite implication for the Board's policy is that it should be very cautious about allowing mergers, let alone encouraging them as it periodically does. Mergers always have some attractions. They can eliminate a carrier whose route network has never been rationalized. They can bolster a carrier weakened through misjudgments of its management or predation by large competitors. Both of these gains will usually be accompanied by a short-term increase in the quality of service offered the traveling public. However, mergers also have their costs. The Board has recognized that they can reduce point-to-point competition and threaten the rivals of the merged carrier. It is high time that it recognized another effect of mergers: by reducing the total number of trunks and (usually) reducing the imbalance among them, they encourage the slow rise of parallel action by the carriers which is aimed at frustrating the Board's regulations. For this reason, even a merger between weak carriers that will strengthen both is a mixed blessing. As long as the Board blocks entry to the industry, it should be hesitant about allowing mergers. If mergers become inevitable, it should consider expanding the activities of the local-service carriers, giving continental routes to Pan American, or other devices that directly or indirectly involve entry.

It is often suggested that some change should be made to eliminate the Board's concern with the carriers' need for revenue. The usual argument is that the period of direct subsidy to all airlines infected the Board with the need for protecting the carriers' profits and that the provisions of the Civil Aeronautics Act relating to "need" should be amputated.[13] This would be a valuable change, but the Board would show concern with protecting individual firms, even if it had never authorized a cent of subsidy. The root of the problem is the notion of a certificate of public convenience and necessity. The certificate confers an obligation to serve upon its holder. Theoretically, public authority gives nothing in exchange except permission to operate and a promise not to revoke wantonly. In air transport there is no conveying of a monopoly privilege or a guarantee of profits. Nevertheless, for the regulatory authority, especially one charged

13. For example, see *ibid.*, pp. 111–112 and *passim.*

with promoting as well as regulating, there is a great difference between setting the conditions of service by all comers and setting the conditions of service by authorized firms. The public need for the services of a certified carrier is established by law. It becomes inconceivable for the Board to enforce some secondary policy that would drive a carrier out of business. From this, it is a short and easy step to granting any request that seems at all necessary to keep the holder of the certificate in good health.

Therefore, it seems that, as long as the Board keeps its present set of objectives and the certification machinery remains in effect, no major improvements are possible. It is hard to see how entry to the industry could be much less restricted than it is now. The problems of unnecessarily high costs of air service will remain. The variety of services offered to travelers can be improved somewhat if the Board allows the carriers more freedom to experiment, but the Board's ultimate fear of subnormal profits will remain. The number of carriers may continue to shrink, even if profits for the industry as a whole average better than normal, unless the Board sees the long-run danger in mergers. Maintaining a high quality of air service and steady competition for its improvement by means of point-to-point rivalry alone will probably no longer suffice. More direct controls may be necessary.

This is not a very attractive picture and not much of an improvement in the efficiency of regulation. Yet it seems to be the best that can be done if we allow the Board its traditional objectives—maximum safety, maximum incentive to develop new aircraft, continuous promotion, and extension of air service. Reasonable men, however, may surely doubt that these goals are worth the cost. If national prestige requires rapid development of transport aircraft, this could be done by subsidizing the development of prototypes directly, a practice widely used by other countries. There is no reason why adequate safety could not be assured in an otherwise unregulated industry by requiring letters of registration for all carriers from the Federal Aviation Agency, subject to stiff penalty or revocation for violation of safety requirements.[14] Internal subsidy to short-haul service in compe-

14. The mere fact that barriers to entry from economic sources are much higher now than after World War II means that the problem of enforcing standards of safety would be much reduced. The total number of entrants to an unregulated industry would not be large, and they would have to have relatively ample financing.

tition with good surface travel is of doubtful worth. The Board no longer gets much internal subsidy for its trouble, and so the traditional objective of extending the network of air routes could be achieved by maintaining subsidy for the local-service airlines and throwing the trunk routes open to market forces. This study has emphasized throughout the interrelation of different controls used by the Board. This was particularly pronounced when all carriers received subsidy, but it still exists. If entry is blockaded by public policy, regulation of maximum fares and minimum quality of service is necessary. If the setting of minimum fares is used to guarantee profits that sometimes run higher than normal for part or all of the industry, the control of entry must be used to prevent bothersome fluctuations in the number of firms in operation. This is why, today, the only promising reforms are the minor ones of permitting more experimentation in pricing and service and of trying to get a longer-range perspective on the consequences of particular decisions.

We have already seen that the air-transport industry has characteristics of market structure that would bring market performance of reasonable quality without any economic regulation. How could public policy move, without serious transitional difficulties, from the present system to one of relatively free competition? [15] A first step would be for the Civil Aeronautics Board to sort the network of air routes into three parts. Class 1 would be the city-pair routes large enough to sustain more than one carrier with entry unrestricted. Class 2 would be those local-service cities or routes that probably could not be served without subsidy. Class 3 would be a residual of cities or city-pair markets that would be profitable for a single carrier. The critical first step would be to open the class of large city-pair markets to all certified carriers not receiving subsidy.[16] If this were done at a time when the airlines were running normal load factors, and if the trunks still retained their obligation to provide service in Class 3 markets, the effect apart from some transitional sparring

15. I do not distinguish between changes that would require amending the Federal Aviation Act and those that would affect only the policies of the Board.

16. Local-service carriers could participate, too, if the method for calculating their subsidy could be set to keep the government from subsidizing their entry into open trunk markets. Including them would be desirable, since they would be well equipped for providing commuter service in dense short-haul markets.

would be to encourage airlines to rearrange their market territories in order to use their current aircraft and facilities more efficiently and to reduce problems of seasonal traffic fluctuations. At this same time, possibly even earlier, the Board could use its power to set minimum and maximum fares by placing the legal limits 10 percent above or below the currently prevailing fare for any given class, and by removing restrictions on creating new classes of service. The second step would be to eliminate restrictions on entry of new carriers to city-pair markets in Class 1. This would probably bring no great influx of new airlines, but there would be a few specialists that would enter to operate relatively compact route networks. Both the maximum and minimum limits on legal air fares should be removed. The net result after these measures would probably be that some of the certified trunks will have disappeared by merger or have consolidated and rationalized their route networks. The industry would move toward the pattern suggested previously: a few large carriers with networks serving nearly all major cities, perhaps some similar but smaller regional carriers, and some carriers offering specialized services in limited numbers of markets. A final step, once the situation had again stabilized reasonably, would be to consolidate the first and third classes of markets, leaving only subsidized local-service routes subject to separate regulation. If necessary and desirable, new classes of experimentally certified air services could still be created. The remaining role of the Civil Aeronautics Board would be strictly promotional.

A nation must make a political choice about how many of its industries will be subject to intensive public regulation. The economist can provide two kinds of information useful in making this decision. One is an evaluation of the market performance that is likely to come from any particular industry with or without such regulation. Another is a ranking of industries according to the likelihood that public regulation will improve their performance. Thus, this study has found that the airlines have a market structure which makes them more workably competitive than some unregulated industries in the economy. There are certain goals that can be achieved by airline regulation, but some sacrifices are necessary to achieve them. An economist may feel that the sacrifices are hardly worth the gains, but the decision is ultimately a political one and his role is only to inform.

PART SIX   The Reasons and Results
in Natural Gas
Field Price Regulation

The Rationale for Regulation of
Gas Field Prices

PAUL W. MAC AVOY

This essay seeks the reasons for new regulation of natural gas field prices by the Federal Power Commission and to determine whether these reasons have any validity. It is a condensed version of the first and last chapters of the book Price Formation in Natural Gas Fields *(1962), and relies heavily on the statistical evidence on sales concentration and price behavior contained therein.*

THE CENTRAL QUESTION OF public policy in the gas industry in recent years has been whether producers' sales to interstate pipelines should be regulated. Before 1954, the producers were free of price control. In 1954 a Supreme Court decision, Phillips Petroleum Company v. Wisconsin, found that the Federal Power Commission had jurisdiction to determine whether prices and sales conditions were "reasonable" on gas sold in interstate commerce.[1] Since then, discussion on the necessity of price control has been continuous but inconclusive. In the United States Congress, representatives and senators argued the case for and against legislation to exempt the producers from the Phillips-imposed regulation. The most successful bill was the Harris-Fulbright Bill which proposed to amend the Natural Gas Act so as to exempt producers from any regulation; it carried a majority

1. Cf. Phillips Petroleum Co. v. Wisconsin, 347 U.S. 622; jurisdiction followed under the Natural Gas Act, U.S.C. 717.52 Stat. 821 (1938).

1955 IKE ?

of both houses but was vetoed by the president.[2] Meanwhile, the commission has considered a method of regulation which itself questions the need for any regulation. In Champlin Oil and Refining Co., et al.,[3] the gas producers proposed that only those prices which were not "fair field prices" be regulated. "Fair field prices" were defined as those following from competitive market forces. They would be allowed automatically; other prices would be regulated by the commission. This meant that, if all prices were fair field prices, the commission would do no price regulating. By considering this method of regulation, the commission in effect considered the need and reasons for any regulation.

MONOPOLY AS THE REASON FOR REGULATION

In the Phillips case, in the Congressional bills, and in the commission hearings a number of reasons were given for regulating gas producers' prices. The most persistent, and effective, said that prices were not being determined in a competitive manner. It was argued that there was monopoly control of the in-ground gas and that the pipeline buyer paid higher-than-competitive prices for restricted total amounts of gas. It was said that monopolistic pricing in gas fields should be controlled, as monopolistic electricity rates or rail freight rates were controlled.

Rationale for Regulation in the Phillips Case · Testimony in Phillips Petroleum Co. v. Wisconsin (when not concerned with defining a "natural gas company") was concerned with producers' power to control prices. At one point, counsel for Wisconsin consumers stated: "We want to buy your gas, we want to pay a fair price, but we feel you have a monopoly . . . we don't think you are justified in assuming the Federal Power Commission will not give you a fair price and we don't think we should be subject to the arbitrary whim of some company not even

2. The Harris-Fulbright Bill S. 1853 of the 84th Congress (1955) was vetoed because some industry personnel had exerted "extraordinary" pressure on some members of Congress. It was followed by the Harris-O'Hara "Compromise" Bill, and others that were not reported out of committee in 1956 and 1957.

3. Federal Power Commission Docket G-9277, the "Omnibus" hearings on regulatory methods, 1957–59.

subject to [state] Commission [control], as to the price at which it sells."[4] The Phillips Company disputed the assertion that prices were monopolistic. Its brief stated: "The advocates of federal regulation rely heavily upon the assertion that regulation is necessary to protect consumers against excessive prices. This assertion has no basis in fact. . . . There is sufficient evidence in the record to negate any assertion that Phillips' prices are now excessive or exorbitant. The nature of the business is such as to be carried on by a large number of business units. In 1946 and 1947 approximately 2,300 independent producers or gatherers sold gas directly to natural gas companies [pipelines]."[5] This implied that the monopoly power to set prices, so far from being used to set "excessive" prices, did not in fact exist. The Supreme Court ignored the Phillips' position and stated: "The rates charged [by producers] may have a direct and substantial effect upon the price paid by the ultimate consumers. Protection of consumers against exploitation at the hands of the natural gas companies was the primary aim of the Natural Gas Act."[6]

Rationale for Regulation in Senate Hearings · In the Senate hearings and debate on the Harris-Fulbright Bill, the economic reason given for exempting producers from regulation was that gas field markets were competitive.[7] After a lengthy analysis of current gas deliveries, Dr. John Boatwright, of Standard Oil of Indiana, concluded for the producers. "The producing phase of the industry represents over 8,000 operators. There is a wide diversification of ownership, with present producers daily inviting new men and capital to enter the field. There is no evidence of monopolistic control based on concentration of ownership on a national, regional, state, or producing area basis."[8] Dr. Boatwright found evidence for competition in market behavior as well as in structural conditions. "We have supplied the normal tests of competitive behavior on the supply side of the market

4. 347 U.S. 672, Testimony, pp. 3667–70.
5. "Brief for Petitioner Phillips Petroleum Company," no. 280 *Records*, 347 U.S. 672 (1954), pp. 85, 89, 90–91.
6. 347 U.S. 672 (1954) at 685.
7. There were "noneconomic" reasons, of course, including political and legal considerations.
8. "Consumer Interest in Natural Gas Competition," statement of John W. Boatwright in support, cf. S. 1853 before the Senate Committee on Interstate and Foreign Commerce, p. 110.

. . . prices vary through time, have the flexibility characteristic of lack of control . . . have not gone up with competitive fuels or with the general cost of living . . . prices vary among fields and react to variations of supply resulting from new discoveries. Each and every one of these tests has indicated price behavior typical of that expected in a competitive market. Therefore . . . there is no evidence to indicate monopolistic control on the part of producers." [9] His strongest conclusion was, "The facts here reviewed have established that the consumer inevitably receives his greatest protection from competitive activity . . . and [given the costs of the regulation, expected inefficiencies, etc.] there can be no question but that under regulation the long-run prices paid by the consumer would be higher than if the producing phase were unregulated." [10]

Some members of Congress disagreed with Dr. Boatwright's analysis and conclusion. One in particular, Senator Paul H. Douglas of Illinois (formerly professor of economics at the University of Chicago), took issue with the analysis, point by point, in a lengthy speech on the pending Harris-Fulbright Bill. He said, "Competition is limited by the domination of supply and reserves by a very few major companies . . . by the need [of the pipelines] for huge long-term supplies which only dominant producers can provide . . . by the fact that pipelines can pass high prices on the consumer . . . and the system of Favored Nations clauses makes these artificially high prices the new dominant or average prices." [11] In other words, if the pipelines do not have the incentive to bargain for the lowest (or competitive) prices, and if the larger producers control the major part of the gas supply, then the "public utility" nature of gas pipelining, and the "large" relative shares of production he saw coming from a "few" sellers in some field areas. He concluded, "As the consumer is the captive of the industry, he will get it in the neck if the Federal Power Commission is denied jurisdiction over the sales for resale of natural gas in interstate commerce." [12]

The differences between Dr. Boatwright and Senator Douglas

9. *Ibid.*, p. 104.
10. *Ibid.*, p. 110.
11. The speech has been summarized by Senator Douglas as "The Case for the Consumer of Natural Gas," 44 *Georgetown Law Journal* 566. The quotation is from page 589.
12. *Ibid.*, p. 577.

were not resolved. The Harris-Fulbright Bill was voted by the Senate, so that Dr. Boatwright's arguments, and others like them, were apparently the views of the majority. But the discussion of competition, its existence, and effectiveness continued nevertheless.

Rationale for Regulation in the Commission Hearings · In the Champlin Oil hearings, Professor M. A. Adelman testified, "Natural gas is produced under conditions of low concentration, lower than 75–85 percent of manufactured products. Buyers of gas operate in what is fast becoming a national market . . . they are large, able to review all offers, and have strong inducements to make even small savings." [13] Observation of price differences and price levels led Professor Adelman to conclude, "Variations in prices may be normally expected to exist . . . based on considerations above [i.e., differences in demand for different sales contracts] it is my conclusion that the production of gas is a competitive industry." [14] It was argued that, with the industry *generally* competitive, attention of the Federal Power Commission may be centered upon regulating only the few sales that might not be competitive because of isolated location, and the like. All competitive prices—fair field prices—should be allowed to stand. For "when regulation is based upon [competitive] market prices, the ends if not the means are simple, and they make economic sense." [15]

The proposal to regulate only those prices that were not fair field prices raised immediate objections. Witnesses for pipeline and retail gas distributors denied the proposal's usefulness since the industry was not "generally competitive." Professor Alfred E. Kahn presented a lengthy analysis of seller concentration, of price behavior over a period of time, and of prices from sale to sale at a given time. When asked, "Would you characterize the market for natural gas in the field as ineffectively competitive or monopolistic?" [16] he answered, "I have avoided reference to such characterizations thus far for two reasons. First of all . . . it is not the simple single firm monopoly you find in traditional

13. Before the Federal Power Commission, Champlin Oil and Refining Co., *et al.*, Docket G-9277, p. 458 L.C.

14. *Ibid.*, p. 458 L.C.

15. *Ibid.*, p. 461 L.C.

16. *Ibid.*, p. 4896 L.C.

public utilities. In my judgment however there are peculiar characteristics of these markets that make it impossible for me to call the industry workably competitive—characteristics indeed that introduce the possibility of significant monopoly exploitation." [17] Professor Kahn found that price behavior in existing markets had adverse effects upon income distribution, by favoring producers' returns while not providing incentives for further additions to the supply of reserves. This followed from the ineffectiveness of competition and from "questionable aspects having nothing to do with the effectiveness of competition . . . [but which] may justify price regulation." [18]

Professors Adelman and Kahn disagreed fundamentally upon the extent and effects of competition in gas markets. Their disagreement was similar to that found in the Phillips hearings and in the debate on the Harris-Fulbright Bill; it led to similar contradictory proposals for regulatory policy. In each set of discussions, a conclusion that markets were competitive implied that regulation of gas field sales should be abandoned; a conclusion that markets exhibited monopoly-type behavior implied that prices should be controlled. In fact, price formation in the West Texas, Gulf Coast, and Mid-Continent regions would seem to have followed at times from monopsony, at times from competition in sales of new reserves. Monopsony prevailed in each of the three producing regions at some time, but pricing was generally becoming most competitive during the later 1950s.

MONOPSONY

Conditions in which one buyer controlled field purchases have been present at some time in all three regions. One transporter controlled purchases (with some exceptions) in West Texas–New Mexico at least until 1958. The three original pipelines into the Gulf Coast had the opportunity to control prices there in the late 1940s, and remnants of this control were present in the 1950s at isolated inland fields. Each one of three transporters—buyers in the central Kansas–Oklahoma fields—had control of prices in separate parts of this region in the late 1950s.

When there was control by the buyer, prices were set in the

17. *Ibid.*, p. 4896 L.C.
18. *Ibid.*, p. 4896 L.C.

monopsony manner. Actual prices followed a pattern of preset uniformity. There was remarkably little variation in price; the standard deviation of prices for a reasonably comprehensive sample of contracts was between .916 cents and 1.97 cents per mcf (thousand cubic feet). The volume of reserves, the term-length of the contract, over which gas was to be delivered to the pipelines, and the distance from wellhead to the final consumers, had little effect upon contract price.

This is not as expected from competition among buyers of gas. Those with capacity to take larger volumes (and those with lower transportation costs), and with shorter distances to final users, and with the demand for longer time-lengths of production, should be willing to pay more. Competition on the demand side would establish the necessity for potentially higher demand prices becoming actual higher prices. The contract prices should generally follow the pattern $[P = \alpha + \beta_1 V + \beta_2 D + \beta_3 T]$ with β_1, $\beta_3 > O$ and $\beta_2 < O$ while the presence of monopsony should make it possible *not* to pay more for volume and distance so that β_1; $\beta_2 \sim O$ (and $\beta_3 > O$ only if it *costs* more to produce under long term arrangements).[19]

Uniform monopsony prices and low levels of average prices were found together. This is best indicated by differences in prices on contracts from the same general region, taking some contracts from fields in which there was one buyer, and others from fields containing a number of buyers. Sales prices were significantly greater in the fields where there was buyer's competition. In the farther Louisiana fields there were a number of buyers during 1951–54, while the closer fields in North Louisiana generally had one buyer each. Price levels were greater in the farther fields (since the "regression equation" price was between .578 and .674 cents per mcf greater for each additional one hundred miles traveled by the buyer). A contract price in North Louisiana was on the average 1.50 cents per ncf less than the price on a similar sale in South Louisiana. Similarly, there were large numbers of buyers in the Mid-Continent fields near the Pan-

19. These β in regressions fitted to the sample contracts separately did not have statistically significant effect, and together they explained little more than 25 percent of the variation in prices in the contracts. Cf. P. MacAvoy *Price Formation in Natural Gas Fields* (Yale 1962), pp. 244 *et. seq.*

handle-Hugoton, while any field in central Kansas and Oklahoma had no more than one or two potential buyers. The first group of fields was farther away from points of resale than the second.[20] Prices were much higher in the farther fields: The "regression equation" price indicates that a contract on the border of the Panhandle had a price more than 4.20 cents per mcf higher than that for the same contract in the central Kansas-Oklahoma fields (two hundred miles closer).[21]

COMPETITION

But monopsony was not pervasive, by any means. There had been a number of buyers in the Panhandle-Hugoton fields of the Mid-Continent since the beginning of development of this area. Shares of purchases and changes in shares of purchases indicate that these lines had not been able jointly to control demand. There were sufficient transporters along the Texas Gulf Coast by the early 1950s to have prevented any one of them, or a few of them, from controlling prices there. By the later 1950s, buyer's competition had broken out in West Texas–New Mexico with the entry of Transwestern Pipeline Company.

Price formation, where there were large numbers of buyers, was in contrast to behavior where there was one buyer. When pipelines sought the same reserves, superior contracts brought a price premium. Reserves closest to points of resale and reserves of larger size were preferred by the buyer, as were contracts of longer term. Contracts for reserves one hundred miles closer had prices from .47 cents to 1.74 cents per mcf higher. Those for larger reserves had prices from .19 to 2.11 cents per mcf higher for each additional fifty billion cubic feet, while

20. Similar cases of higher prices at farther points were found in West Texas–New Mexico when a new pipeline entered the exclusive domain of El Paso Natural Gas Pipeline. (Cf. discussion of price offered by Transwestern Pipeline Company in Chapter 5 in P. MacAvoy, *Price Formation, op. cit.*)

21. Competitive prices at farther points should have been *lower* than in closer fields because of additional transportation costs. Allowing for this, prices under competition should have been *lower* in South Louisiana and in fields closer to the Panhandle. The monopsony-competitive price difference in closer monopsony fields should have been the observed difference *plus* an amount for advantageous location.

contracts for longer term had prices from .30 to 4.22 cents per mcf higher for each additional five years. Competition among pipelines seems to have forced the successful bidders to pay higher prices for the preferred new purchases.[22]

In the last years of the 1950s, more of the new fields were in competitive markets. There was buyer's competition for new reserves throughout the Gulf Coast and Louisiana. The entry of Transwestern Pipeline into West Texas–New Mexico provided extensive potential competition in demand there. The Panhandle–Hugoton region of the Mid-Continent long had been competitive in supply and demand. Only the isolated central fields of Kansas and Oklahoma each had one pipeline buyer.

The effects of increasing competition upon pricing patterns were very apparent. New prices in the Gulf Coast and in the Panhandle–Hugoton were greater, the more desirable the contract terms (these terms being dictated by contract volume, time length, and trap distance). There was considerable resemblance between the theoretical competitive pattern and the observed regression patterns in these two regions. Price formation in West Texas–New Mexico showed some similarity to that expected from competition; El Paso Gas Transmission Company found it necessary to pay higher prices for larger volumes, and the level of prices on all Transwestern Gas Pipeline Company contracts was considerably higher than for comparable El Paso contracts. But the absence of systematic price variation with distance and term indicates a lack of buyer's competition throughout West Texas. New prices in the central fields of Kansas and Oklahoma continued to vary with the extent of potential pipeline competition. Higher prices were paid for reserves in the farther Panhandle and Hugoton fields where there were two or more buyers.

Extensive competition in the Gulf Coast and the Panhandle, emerging competition in West Texas, but little buyer's competition in the central Kansas–Oklahoma fields were the legacy from market organization in the 1950s. The question remaining is what should be the nature of Federal Commission regulation in this diverse group of markets.

22. For details on these regression coefficients, and the "goodness of fit" of the regression equations, cf. P. MacAvoy, *op. cit.*, pp. 247–250.

THE PROPER AMOUNT OF REGULATION

[handwritten: 1954]

The Federal Power Commission received a mandate from the *[handwritten: Fed Power]* Supreme Court in 1954 to regulate field prices in order to prevent *[handwritten: Com]* monopoly "extortion of consumers."[23] According to this mandate, prices in the later 1950s should have been regulated to *[handwritten: mandate to price]* prevent realization by producers of monopoly profits. In the Gulf Coast, West Texas, and Mid-Continent regions the commission need not have *set prices* in order to have prevented monopoly, given the predominant presence of competition or monopsony. Perhaps prices should have been regulated in some specific fields where there was one seller and where small buyers had no access to other fields.[24] But these would have been the exception to the rule, where the rule required no price control when there was no monopoly power.

The independent regulatory commission that regulates "best" (i.e., efficiently completes its assigned task) by *not* setting price is bound to be questioned on the necessity for its existence. Regulation is generally conceded to be of doubtful propriety if the reasons for imposition of control were fallacious. Regulation was advocated in the courts and Congress to prevent monopoly prices in the Southwest. Studies of most field and supply markets in Texas, Louisiana, Oklahoma, etc., indicate the presence of systematic competition or monopsony throughout the period in which regulation was proposed.[25] The problem to be solved by regulation seem not to have existed, so that the court mandate *[handwritten: Necessity]* was given for "wrong" reasons. The necessity for Federal Power *[handwritten: Doubtful]* Commission regulation is doubtful.

But perhaps it was the right policy that was followed, even if for wrong reasons. The Federal Power Commission's newly established methods of regulation may yet have desirable net social effects not anticipated at the time of the Phillips decision. These results may warrant continuation of regulation, even in competi-

23. Cf. discussion of Phillips Petroleum Company *v.* Wisconsin 347 US 672 (1954) above.

24. This would no doubt have required regulation of a group of contracts for gas for resale within one state. The Federal Power Commission jurisdiction of "sales for resale in interstate commerce" would not have been applicable.

25. Cf. P. MacAvoy, *op. cit.*, Chapters 5, 6, 7.

tive and monopsonistic markets.

Current methods of regulation are the result of years spent searching for criteria to justify a "freeze" in the level of field prices. The Federal Power Commission refused to review initial price on a new contract (while issuing a "certificate of necessity and convenience" to a producer), but it did review price later, under Section 4 of the Natural Gas Act, when a price increase was requested. This left producers and buyers free to sell new reserves for unregulated prices, since control of price increases could be avoided by paying a higher initial price. In 1959, the Power Commission review procedure was declared to be insufficient by the Supreme Court "where the proposed [initial] price is not in keeping with the public interest." Instead, it was suggested that "the Commission in the exercise of its discretion might attach such conditions [to the certificate] as it believes necessary." [26]

The Federal Power Commission, as a result, proposed the "establishment of price standards to be applied in determining the acceptability of initial price." [27] The price standards in 1960 were "area prices" for each of twenty-three producing regions, and each producer was left free to agree to a contract for a price less than or equal to the "area price" applicable to his region. Any producer seeking certification at a higher price would bear the burden of proving its "necessity and convenience," according to unspecified criteria.

Up to the present, maximum "area prices" have followed pricing patterns observed for 1956–58. The highest regulated "area prices" have been set where there had previously been buyer's competition; the lowest prices have been required where there had previously been one buyer. The "area prices" have been set slightly higher than the regression price for 1958 on a contract for some 50 billion cu. ft.[28] But unregulated new contract prices

26. Atlantic Refining Company v. Public Service Commission, 360 U.S. 328 (1959).

27. *Federal Power Commission Statement of General Policy No. 61–1* (Sept. 28, 1959).

28. Prices from the 1958 regression equations, for a contract of 50 billion cu. ft. of twenty-year term, were:

$$\text{Gulf Coast} = 16.75 \pm 2.50 \text{ cents}$$
$$\text{West Texas} = 13.43 \pm 2.14$$
$$\text{Panhandle-Hugoton} = 13.69 \pm 1.76$$
$$\text{Central Kansas and Oklahoma} = 12.25 \pm 1.75$$

in earlier markets had increased over time where there was buyer's competition, and particularly where monopsony was in decline. The presumed effect of these "area prices" will be to prevent further price increases accompanying the establishment of systematic competition in West Texas–New Mexico and central Kansas–Oklahoma.

Are the effects of a price freeze beneficial? These effects include changes in the amounts of reserves sold, in the distribution of production, and in returns to consumers (as opposed to producers). All such changes are not likely to increase general economic well-being. Holding down the level of price clearly benefits some consumers. Maintaining the 1958 price P_0 given regional (predicted) demand D and supply S of known reserves in 1960–65 will result in excess demand as shown in Fig. 1. The quantity Q_0 will have to be rationed among buyers seeking Q'_0, probably by allowing sales to the established or closest transporter (given present Federal Power Commission certification policies). The exclusion of new pipelines or pipelines located farther from reserves will allow completion of actual sales to consumers included in demand D'. These consumers will receive an increased "consumer's surplus" equal to the shaded area in the diagram, by paying P_0 rather than P_1.[29]

That this group of consumers will gain from the "area price" P_0 is not enough to make regulation generally beneficial. Other groups will lose by such an imposition. The producers will lose economic rents equal to the shaded area, plus the triangle ABC (rents composed of net returns over and above short-run development costs for discovered reserves). Their loss will be greater than the increase in the actual purchaser's surplus by the amount ABC, so there will be a net social loss. Freezing price at the level P_0 will have the effect of lowering earnings at the margin

---

These estimates, computed from the regression equations in P. MacAvoy, *op. cit.*, Table 8:4, can be compared with the initial prices on new contracts on the "area prices" map on p. 254 of the same volume. They are less than the area prices (by more than the standard errors of estimates, shown as the amount after the regression price).

29. "Consumer's surplus" is the excess satisfaction gained from paying a price for all units equal only to the utility of the marginal unit (or to the marginal rate of substitution between this and other goods). In money terms, consumer's surplus is the amount buyers would pay for Q_0 over and above $(P_0 \cdot Q_0)$ rather than be deprived of purchases altogether.

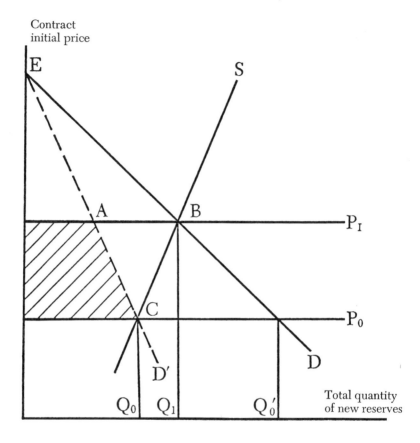

FIG. 1. *Maximum "Area Price" P_0 in a Competitive Market*

Contract
initial price

E

S

A

B

P_I

C

P_0

D'

D

Q_0 Q_1 Q_0'

Total quantity
of new reserves

of sales as well, so that production of new reserves is decreased from Q_1 to O_0.

A review of those effects in detail will show who loses and who gains. Quantity of output O_0 is clearly less than optimal, since an increment to output costs less than marginal consumers would be willing to pay (as indicated by the difference between supply and demand prices for any output between Q_0 and Q_1). Yet some consumers receive more gas for a lower price, and redistribution of income to consumers from producers has long been a central goal of regulation, from the Granger laws setting ceiling prices for rail transport of grain in the 1860s to Professor Kahn's statement, "When changes in [gas field] demand are so great, and supply so apparently inelastic, as to double the basic real price . . . conferring large economic rents and possibly monopoly profits on those who have managed to appropriate a part of our national resources, I am skeptical that economics can be said to dictate a policy of laissez faire." [30] But the excluded potential consumers incur a considerable loss of "consumer's surplus" as well. This loss of surplus, represented by the area AEB in Fig. 1, has to be regarded as a direct effect of the actual purchasers' gain in surplus. For there to be an improvement for all consumers, through regulation, the excluded buyers must be compensated for their loss by the actual buyers and the latter left with a net gain. [31] A net gain is not likely, given that the surplus from the first units of consumption for excluded purchasers is likely to be quite large. It is yet to be acknowledged that such compensation is necessary, so that this established regulation is not a rationalized system of control.

Over the next few years, these matters pertinent for justifying regulation should become more apparent. The choice between low-priced gas for some consumers while others have none, as contrasted with sufficient gas to serve all at a higher price, will be made in a most striking fashion in regions served by new reserves from fields in newly competitive supply areas. "Area prices" in fields emerging from monopsony will involve a differential of at least 35 percent between competitive and regulated price (if the regulated price is at the monopsony level after the new pipelines have entered, as seems likely in West Texas and in central Kansas and Oklahoma). Excess demand at this low "area price" is likely to be apparent both to consumers and the commission. The consumers necessarily excluded from gas service will be the customer of the entering lines creating the competition. The buyer will be much more willing to sell

30. A. E. Kahn, "Economic Issues in Regulating the Field Price of Natural Gas," 50 *American Economic Review* 507 (May 1960).
31. "Before we can say that 'welfare' increases . . . we must know [whether] the gainer by the change can profitably compensate the loser, or bribe him into accepting it; and the loser cannot bribe the gainer into rejecting it." J. DeV. Graaf, *Theoretical Welfare Economics* (Cambridge, Cambridge University Press, 1957), p. 87.

to the established transporter able to begin taking gas immediately, *given* the uniform area price. With a large number of unsatisfied customers in one consuming state, there is likely to be demand for "equitable" distribution of reserves.

Even more important will be the effects of "area prices" upon the amount of new reserves. Not only will there be some effect, such as $Q_1—Q_0$, upon the sale of *known* reserves in any given supply market, but also there should be an effect upon the discovery of new reserves. In simplest terms, the expectation of higher future prices provides incentives for larger exploration investments. Given a priori probabilities of success in finding dry-gas reserves, the larger investment results in larger discovery. The more intensive exploration accompanying higher prices might be related to the supply of new reserves S, the less intensive exploration to supply S' in Fig. 2. In the long run, the surplus of excluded buyers would be greater (the area $A'EB$ rather than AEB). Producer's economic rents for new reserves would have been decreased, and rates of sale of reserves would have fallen by the additional amount $Q_1—Q_0$.

The decrease in output is likely to be large. To begin with, "if we compare new gas reserves with new contract prices . . . same-year prices would indicate that for every cent of increase in price, about 750 billion cubic feet of additional reserves are found per year; previous-year prices would make it about an even trillion." [32] That is, experience during the 1950s points to the long-run supply of known reserves being represented by the straight lines:

$$Q_T = 1,672 + 767\ P_T$$
$$Q_{T+1} = 230 + 965\ P_T$$

where P_T = average initial price on new contracts in cents per mcf, Q_T = billions of cubic feet of newly discovered reserves in year T.[33] If this experience continues, while market price rises 1.0 cents per mcf per year, then actual sales some five years hence

32. Cf. M. A. Adelman, *The Supply and Price of Natural Gas* (Basil Blackwell, 1962), pp. 69, 71. Professor Adelman discusses the limitations of the estimation procedure utilized in reaching this conclusion in pages 69–80. These limitations would not seem to be extensive enough to require abandonment of these "rules-of-thumb."

33. Adelman, p. 75a. The long-run supply curve is the locus of the intersection points of supply S and demand D (such as points B and C' in Fig. 2) and is computed by the least-squares regression technique with time-series data.

FIG. 2. *Maximum "Area Price" P₀ and*
Long-Run Market Conditions

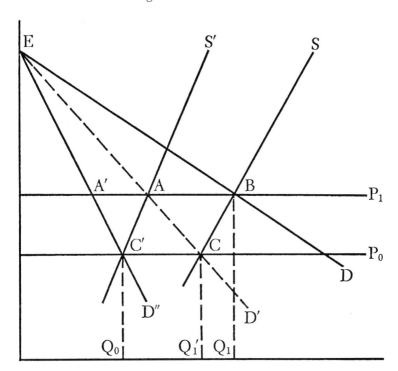

might well be five trillion cubic feet less as a result of maintaining area prices.[34] Consumers as a group may end up with 20 percent "fewer reserves" for purchase.

Demands for "distributive justice," and for more intensive exploration of dry-gas reserves, may make these results from price control obvious. At that point, an attempt to justify the presence of regulation should be made. It has been argued here that the original reason for regulation—i.e., that producer's monopolizing activities need be prevented—has no substance.

34. Professor Adelman also expects the supply curve to shift to the left in the future because of increases in the real costs of finding gas (cf. Adelman, pp. 77–78). If this is the case, the foregone annual volumes of new reserves would be smaller than five trillion cubic feet.

Regulation of competitive and monopsonistic markets can be considered "right," for this "wrong" reason, only if it can be shown that the loss in discovery of new reserves should be ignored. Where the first rationale for regulation is not possible, the second is scarcely probable.

A FINAL REVIEW

As suggested by price formation in the 1950s, gas markets are diverse in structure and behavior, but are generally competitive or changing from monopsony toward competition. Markets with such characteristics need not be regulated by the Federal Power Commission to prevent monopoly pricing. Nor, at present, is it easy to justify regulation on the other grounds, given the undesirable effects on excluded consumers and the rate of discovery and sale of reserves. By and large, the strongest suggestion arising from this study of competition, monopsony, and regulation in the 1950s is that there should be more of the first.

Regulation of the Field Market for Natural Gas by the Federal Power Commission

While the previous essay deals with the reasons for gas field price regulation, E. W. Kitch's investigates the effect of the ceiling prices on gas decreed by the Federal Power Commission. The paper deals with the effectiveness of the controls, as well as their efficiency. Professor Kitch is a lawyer and a member of the faculty of the University of Chicago Law School. He published this paper in the October 1968 Journal of Law and Economics.

THE FIELD MARKET for natural gas is now subject to formal price control regulation administered by the Federal Power Commission. Over the past eight years the Federal Power Commission, with the active encouragement of the Supreme Court, has undertaken to convert a regulatory statute designed to impose traditional rate of return utility regulation into a device for freezing the field price of natural gas at the 1959–60 level. That effort has successfully culminated in the Supreme Court's affirmance of the commission's *Permian Basin* decision this last term. . . .

The Federal Power Commission, in September 1960, announced its intention to abandon the individual cost of service method for regulating producers and adopt an area price method.[1] Under the area price method a uniform selling price is determined for each field. Along with its announcement of the shift to area price regulation, the commission issued two area price "guidelines" for each of the major producing areas.[2] One price was the price above which the commission would not certify new sales. The other was the price above which the commission would not approve applications for price increases. In each area, the first price was set at the level of the highest price at

1. Phillips Petroleum Co., 24 FPC 537, 542–48 (1960).
2. Statement of General Policy No. 61-1, 24 FPC 818 (1960), *as amended*, 18 C.F.R. § 2.56 (1967).

which a sale in the area had been previously certified;[3] the second at the average price for all sales in the area.[4] The guidelines apply until the area rate proceedings are completed. The result is that maximum price for new gas supplies are frozen at 1959–60 levels and that all price increases on old supplies above the guideline must be collected subject to refund. As the Federal Power Commission said proudly in 1963 of a decision to deny rate increases in the southern Louisiana and Mississippi fields, "the decision . . . demonstrated [the commission's] . . . determination *to hold the line against increases in natural gas prices.*"[5]

An examination of the area price proceedings shows that they will, when completed, continue to carry out this price freeze policy.[6]

IMPLEMENTATION OF THE PRICE FREEZE

The court's in-line price doctrine and the commission's guidelines appear to have had an important impact on the field market for natural gas. The steady increase of the average field price between 1953 and 1961 has subsequently leveled off. The interpretation of this leveling off is difficult. The coincidence between the date of the guidelines and the break in the upward trend in prices suggests that the regulation is responsible. But there are several factors which suggest that the market, not the regulation, has been responsible for the price stability.

Most important, price stability was achieved too quickly to be attributable to the regulation. The in-line price doctrine and the guidelines froze the price at the 1959–60 levels. The price statistics are averages. Because of the long term upward price trend, gas flowing under older contracts is lower priced. Each year the percentage of gas flowing under contracts entered into since 1959–60 increases. Therefore the average price of gas should have continued to increase after the price freeze. The fact that the average has been stable suggests that the price for new gas has declined.

3. See the comparisons in Appendix B, Brief of Petitioner Wisconsin, *Wisconsin v. FPC,* 373 U.S. 294 (1963).
4. Brief of Petitioner Wisconsin at 31, *Id.*
5. 43 FPC Ann. Rep. 15 (1964). Italics added.
6. Edmund W. Kitch, "The Permian Basin Area Rate Cases and the Regulatory Determination of Price," 116 *U. Pa. L. Rev.* 191, 206–13 (1967).

The existence of a decline is suggested by two factors. First is the large quantities of gas which have been developed during the 1960s. Although they are inconclusive, the additions to reserves during the 1960s are indeed impressive.[7] Second, there is the increasing competition from electricity and coal. Natural gas has been faced with significant technological changes in both of its major competing energy sources. The rapid development of air conditioning during the 1950s shifted the electric peak load from winter to summer. The electric companies, now faced with surplus capacity in the winter, have for the first time become a factor in the heating market. The cost of coal has steadily declined as the result of automation.[8]

These competitive pressures can best be seen in the market for electric power generation. Power plants have been an important growth segment for natural gas. The percentage of natural gas used in electric power generation has increased from 12.7 percent in 1955 to 15.2 percent in 1966. Between 1955 and 1964 the percentage of electricity generated from natural gas increased from 17.9 percent to 23.2 percent.

But coal for electric power has become increasingly competitive with the development of unit train hauling and mine mouth power plants. In 1958 gas was cheaper than coal for power generation in every area of the country except East South Central and Mountain. The average cost of coal per million Btu (British thermal unit) was 27.4 cents, of gas 19.5. In 1964 coal was cheaper than gas in all regions except West North Central and Pacific, where coal was not a market factor. The national average cost per million Btu of coal had fallen to 24.6, gas had risen to 25.3.

The hypothesis that there has been a decline in the field market price is further supported by the data on the average price realized by the interstate pipelines. The average price realized by the pipelines rose until 1961, then stabilized, and fell slightly in 1964. This pattern might be attributed not to the market, but

7. In 1960 additions to reserve were 13,969,849,000 Mcf, net production: 13,090,450,000. In 1963, 18,380,908,000 and 14,762,266,000. In 1965, 21,319,279,000 and 16,252,293,000. Bureau of Mines.
8. The decline dates from 1957. 1960 Bureau of Mines II 20 Table 16. On an index treating the 1957–59 average price as 100, the wholesale price of bituminous coal has declined from 99.7 in 1958 to 96.5 in 1965. 1963 Bureau of Mines II 29 Table 27; 1965 Id. at 25 Table 29.

to the pipeline regulation. However, it is confirmed not only by the over-all averages, but by the average revenue from unregulated direct sales. This nationwide data is inconclusive, however, because changes in the average might result not from a change in the market for natural gas but simply from a change in the average distance that the pipelines transport the gas. Indeed an increase in the average distance between the point of production and the point of consumption appears to account for a substantial part of the roughly 30 percent increase in average pipeline revenues per mcf between 1955 and 1961. But by 1961 almost all areas of the country were served with natural gas and the rapid geographical expansion of the pipeline system that was characteristic of the 1950s had ended. A similar price pattern emerges from the average revenue data of the Bureau of Mines for the major northern consuming states. The price series from sample states in both the Middle Atlantic and East North Central regions seem to indicate a drop in the consumer price for gas, particularly in the industrial sector of the market, between 1961 and 1964. Most striking is the price data for New Jersey, New York, Michigan, and Wisconsin. The data for Illinois and Pennsylvania is less clear, but suggests a slight decline in price. A decline in the prices received by the pipelines should have been reflected in a decline in field prices.

The magnitude of the decline has apparently been small. Given the relatively small volumes of gas flowing under the older contracts, a small decline in the price would counteract the percentage increase in gas flowing under the new contracts and stabilize the average. The decline is at least small enough so that without field price data correlated with information about contract dates, delivery points, gas quality, and pressure it is impossible to prove conclusively. The data suggest that the market declined slightly below the ceiling between 1961 and 1963, broke rather sharply in 1964, and then recovered slightly.

Even though the market declined slightly, substantial incentives for producers to avoid the price control remained. As a result, significant technical problems in the enforcement of price control under the Natural Gas Act have already been revealed.

The first set of problems arises from three major jurisdictional gaps in the Natural Gas Act. The design of the act was to limit the return on some, but not all, of the activities involved in the production and distribution of natural gas. The commission has had to use its ingenuity to reach transactions not covered by the act in order to prevent effective evasion of the price freeze. This task has been made relatively simple by the Supreme Court which in every case to come before it has construed the act so as to make a price-freeze policy effective.

The first evasive device to come before the commission and the court was based on the fact that the act does not apply to sales not "sales for resale." A large consumer of natural gas could enter into a sale not for resale by purchasing reserves in the field and then contracting with the interstate pipeline simply for transportation. Since the reserves are sold to the consumer, the sale of the gas itself would not be subject to the act. However, the pipeline would have to be granted a certificate of public convenience and necessity for the *transportation* of the gas. In 1959 the commission was presented with such an arrangement in Transcontinental Gas Pipe Line Corp.[9] The Consolidated Edison Company of New York had entered into contracts for the delivery of 50,000 mcf daily with producers in Texas. Edison contracted with Transco for transportation of the gas to a generating plant in mid-town Manhattan. The commission denied Transco a certificate for the transportation partly because of the adverse impact of the arrangement on the field price for natural gas. The commission stated that if such transactions were permitted there would be increased competition for gas reserves, and indicated a clear preference for monopsony.

The impact of large demand on relatively limited supply is certain enough to raise rates and field prices if only one bidder is bringing that demand to bear on the supply. How much more serious is that impact when it is in the form of multiple bidders, each attempting to reserve to itself a firm supply. Inevitably, there would be upward pressure on rate levels in the fields.[10]

Before the Supreme Court Consolidated Edison and Transco argued that the commission was in effect outlawing a form of transaction which was perfectly legitimate under the statute. The court answered:

9. 21 FPC 138 (1959).
10. *Id.* at 141.

[T]he Commission did not exalt form over substance in an attempt to aggrandize the scope of its jurisdiction; rather, whenever the Commission discussed the nonjurisdictional nature of this sale, it tied this discussion into an analysis of one or the other of the substantive evils it was seeking to prevent.[11]

This is to say, whenever the commission exceeded its jurisdiction it did so because it was necessary to make the regulation effective. Although the commission's opinion had been written before CATCO, the court brought the CATCO in-line doctrine to its support.[12] The court's turgid discussion concluded that the commission was properly concerned with the field price because it is "a problem that is not, by its very nature, one with which state regulatory commissions can be expected to deal." [13] Apparently the Court meant that the states were unlikely to hold the price in line.

Five months after the commission had considered the *Transco* case, it was faced with another effort to evade the regulation.[14] The act applies to sales of gas. Suppose a sale of gas was converted into a sale of a leasehold? Would it then be outside the act so that the commission would have no control over the price? In 1949 the Supreme Court had held that sale of a leasehold interest was not a transaction subject to the act.[15]

Four producers in the Rayne Field of southern Louisiana had sought certificates of public convenience and necessity for the sale of gas at 22.4 cents per mcf plus production taxes to Texas Eastern Transmission Corp. The applications were approved by the hearing examiner, but while the case was pending before the commission the Court of Appeals for the District of Columbia decided *CATCO*.[16] The applicants, sensing the in-line doctrine just around the corner, withdrew their applications and restructured the transaction. Texas Eastern, through a subsidiary corporation, agreed to purchase the leases. The subsidiary gave long term notes for the leases which provided for acceleration if production exceeded specified amounts. One of the producers

11. FPC *v.* Transcontinental Gas Pipe Line Corp., 365 U.S. 1, 24–25 (1961).

12. *Id.* at 29.

13. *Id.*

14. Texas E. Transmission Corp., 21 F.P.C. 860 (1959).

15. FPC *v.* Panhandle Pipe Line Co., 337 U.S. 498 (1949).

16. Public Serv. Comm'n *v.* FPC, 257 F.2d 717 (3d Cir. 1958).

agreed to manage the production.
The commission approved the new arrangement.[17] The Court
of Appeals for the District of Columbia reversed.[18] The court
noted that although the commission did not have jurisdiction
over the sale, it did have jurisdiction over Texas Eastern and
a duty to determine whether the cost of the purchase was justified. Since the court thought the commission in its opinion had
approved the cost of the purchase without supporting evidence,
it remanded for further consideration. On remand the commission decided that it did have jurisdiction over the sale.

Any other result would exalt form over substance, would give greater
weight to the technicalities of contract draftsmanship than to the
achievement of the purposes of the Natural Gas Act, and would im-
pair our ability to control the price received for gas sold to the pipelines in interstate commerce to the detriment of the ultimate consumer.[19]

The Supreme Court affirmed.

[I]t is perfectly clear that the sales of these leases in Rayne Field, a
proven and substantially developed field, accomplished the transfer
of large amounts of natural gas to an interstate pipeline company for
resale in other States. That is the significant and determinative economic
fact. To ignore it would substantially undercut *Phillips*, and because
of it the Commission . . . acted properly in treating these sales of
leasehold interests as sales of natural gas within the meaning of the
Natural Gas Act.[20]

The third jurisdictional gap in the act is that it does not, and
probably could not, apply to sales by Canadian producers to
international pipelines for export to the United States. In 1954
the commission took the position that it could not authorize
importation of Canadian gas as the sole source of supply for the
Pacific Northwest because of its inability to protect American
consumers from unreasonable prices.[21] It felt its jurisdictional
inadequacy so strongly, in fact, that it decreed that the Pacific
Northwest should be supplied with gas from southwestern fields

17. 21 FPC 860 (1959).
18. Public Serv. Comm'n v. FPC, 287 F.2d 143 (D.C. Cir. 1960).
19. Texas E. Transmission Corp., 29 F.P.C. 249, 256 (1963).
20. United Gas Improvement Co. v. Continental Oil Co., 381 U.S. 392,
401 (1965).
21. Northwest Natural Gas Co., 13 FPC 221, 235–36 (1954).

over one thousand miles away rather than with Alberta natural gas less than five hundred miles away. But when the successful American applicants applied to import the same gas from the rejected Canadians, the commission approved without comment.[22] The commission first faced the problem of what it could do to "protect" the American consumer on gas imported from Canada in 1960. In Pacific Gas Transmission Co.[23] pipelines owned by Pacific Gas and Electric Company proposed to transport gas from the Alberta–British Columbia border to northern California. The gas was obtained by means of contracts with the Alberta producers who would receive prices higher than the prevailing prices in American fields [24] even though they were farther from the major points of consumption. The examiner imposed additional conditions on the project.

Blanket authorization might imply . . . acceptance during the life of the gas fields of the paradoxical economic preference of Canadian producers in respect of their ability to charge what the market will bear, over American producers restricted by regulation in the consumer interest.[25]

The examiner required the parties to report on the field price of the natural gas which they acquired and to reserve "the possibility that, after completion of the project, the Canadian producers and the Canadian companies may be subjected, despite their existing contracts, to such further regulations as may be evolved for the protection of American consumers." [26] The commission reversed the examiner and approved the project without conditions. The commission did so because it found that the Canadian regulation was sufficiently broad to provide protection of the public interest. The commission was particularly impressed by the provision giving the Alberta Board of Public Utility Commissioners broad powers over field prices and giving them broad discretion to use any reasonable method in arriving at a price.[27]

The commission chose to overlook, however, the fact that the

22. Pacific Northwest Pipeline Corp., 14 FPC 157, 164–67 (1955).
23. Pacific Gas Transmission Co., 24 F.P.C. 134 (1960).
24. See initial decision, Id. at 160–67.
25. Id. at 167.
26. Id. at 168.
27. Id. at 137–38.

public interest of Alberta as a major gas exporting province is different from the interest of the United States, as a gas importer. Alberta's interest is the same as that of an American producing state—to obtain a high price for its exports. The only way in which the commission could have effectively dealt with the problem would have been to extend the in-line pricing doctrine to the Canadian border. It is not clear why the commission did not do so at the time the in-line doctrine was applied to the American fields. One problem was that the occasional history of Canadian import transactions, occurring in single transactions involving large volumes at a point in the distribution system after gathering had taken place, made it difficult to extrapolate an "in-line" price. The commission might also have feared an adverse reaction from a Canadian government hesitant to see its wealth of natural gas reserves largely dedicated to American consumption.[28]

In 1967 the commission changed its hands-off position and applied a new version of the in-line pricing doctrine to a new proposal for additional imports from Canada to the Pacific Northwest.[29] The commission limited the import price to a price equivalent to that charged by the exporter to large Canadian consumers.[30] This version of the in-line doctrine is not designed to put Canadian producers on the same basis as American producers. Rather, it is designed to prevent the development of a price differential between the Canadian domestic and export markets. As we have seen, the American exporting states early attempted to reserve for themselves a large part of their reserves and thereby enjoy the consequence of a lower domestic price. Canada's National Energy Board has been following the same policy for Canada.[31] The efforts of the producing states were nullified by the interstate commerce clause; but Canada is not a

28. First Report of the Canadian Royal Commission on Energy to the Governor in Council 10 (1958): "The Commission is of the opinion that, if the granting of an export license would in any way interfere with the supply of the reasonably foreseeable natural gas requirements of those parts of Canada within economic reach of the producing provinces, permission to export should be withheld."

29. El Paso Natural Gas Co., FPC Opinion No. 526 (Aug. 10, 1967).

30. Id. at 9–11.

31. See Trans-Canada Pipe Lines Ltd., Canadian National Energy Board Report to the Governor in Council (mimeo March 1960); Alberta & S. Gas Co. Ltd., Id. (mimeo July 1965).

member of our federal union. Ironically, the Natural Gas Act has achieved in part the objective of the producing states. Since interstate sales in the field are subject to regulation and while intrastate sales are not, the intrastate sales involve fewer costs and are therefore made at a lower price.[32] But the Federal Power Commission has not yet insisted that all interstate sales should be made at the same price as intrastate sales. At this writing the National Energy Board of Canada has refused to accept the commission's price limitations.

[A]pproval of this [export] application would seem to carry with it, despite any protestations we might make, a de facto acceptance of the in-line method of pricing our gas exports, with its implication that the only way to improve export prices in future would be to increase prices charged by the transmission company to its Canadian distributor customers.[33]

The second area of difficulty in enforcing the price-freeze policy has been the fact that although the price of a contract may be in compliance with the regulation, other non-price terms of the contract may have been altered so as to substantially enhance the value of the sale to the producer. The principal weakness of both the in-line price doctrine and the guidelines is that they specified nothing about the terms of the contract other than price. In such a situation, the simplest way to avoid the regulation was simply to tie sales of high quality gas to sales of inferior gas and sell the entire package for the ceiling price. The commission has become sensitive to this problem and in its Permian Basin area rate decision made the area price subject to adjustments for energy content, pressure, and impurities. But the commission has done nothing about two other factors which are important determinants of the value of the gas—location and the size of the reserves available from each well. Pipelines can to some extent increase the "price" by moving the delivery point closer to the well and taking on more of the costs of production. It should be possible to partly nullify the area price regulation by tying sales of gas from small wells far from the principal market with sales of gas from large wells closer to the market.

32. See Robert W. Gerwig, Natural Gas Production: A Study of Costs of Regulation, 5 J. Law & Econ. 69 (1962).

33. Westcoast Transmission Co., Canadian National Energy Board Reasons for Decision 8–26 (mimeo December 1967).

Beyond the desirability of the gas itself, there are other factors which affect the value of a contract. Most important are the terms of payment. For instance, if the pipelines agree to make payments in advance, that is equivalent to offering a higher price. Or the purchaser may offer the seller a guarantee as to the regularity of the payments he will receive. In the industry these are known as "take or pay" contracts and assure the seller that he will receive at least a minimum payment under the sales contract no matter how much gas is actually taken. In 1961 the commission became concerned about the prepayment situation of some pipelines. It issued a notice of proposed rule making designed to limit the use of terms of this type.[34] The rule was finally issued in 1967, and when issued it was relatively innocuous, providing only that the pipeline under such a contract must be given a five-year period to actually take the gas without any additional charge.[35] The commission explained its action on the ground that the prepayment situation had substantially improved.

While we maintain concern over the potential harm which could be caused by an undue burden of excess prepayment balances, we are cognizant of the fact that there are but a limited number of pipeline companies who currently have made prepayments to the same degree as that prevalent in earlier years. Most companies have been able to reduce their prepayment burdens. One major contribution to the alleviation of the burden has been our relaxation of the 12-year deliverability requirement for pipeline companies.[36]

The improvement in the prepayment situation is probably due to the decline in the field market price. If the market price rises, the commission's rule will not prevent the use of prepayment to minimum payment provisions as a device for evading the price ceiling.

34. 26 Fed. Reg. 4615 (1961). The proposed rule limited payments to be made for gas not taken to 80 percent of the contract volume and limited the daily contract volume to one mcf for each 8,000 mcf of reserves under the contract.

35. FPC Order 334, 32 Fed. Ref. 865 (1967), as amended. 18 C.F.R. § 154.103 (1968).

36. FPC Order 334, 32 Fed. Reg. 865 (1967). The relaxation of the twelve-year average deliverability requirement was made in FPC Order 279, 29 Fed. Reg. 4873 (1964). The relaxation of this requirement could not have had any more than a short-term impact on the field market.

Another problem results from the fact that a producer sale of natural gas often involves a sale of two things: pipeline gas and the extractable liquids. Customarily the producer is paid a price for the gas plus a share of the revenues obtained by the pipeline from the liquids. But in some cases a guarantee has been given that the producer's share of the liquid revenues will be at least a designated minimum. But payments ostensibly made for liquids can in fact be hidden payments for natural gas.

One answer to the problem would be to forbid any separate payment for the liquids and treat the total payment under the contract as the controlling price. Such an approach, however, would result in the same price for gas of greatly different worth. Another approach would be to ascertain the actual value of the liquids and require that the payment for the liquids could not exceed their value. But this would be a difficult and complex rule to administer because the value of the liquids would have to be calculated from their value when extracted less the costs of extraction.

In 1963 the commission confronted the problem in *El Paso Natural Gas Co.*[37] Its solution was rather arbitrary. It held that it had no objection to arrangements which provided for sharing liquid revenues but that it did object to any flat minimum guarantee for the liquids. "To permit [the one cent minimum] . . . would be tantamount to a flat allowance of 18 cents per mcf in an area in which the in-line price is no more than 17 cents per mcf."[38] The commission in 1967 relaxed its position to hold that such a one cent minimum guarantee in a contract was not objectionable, as long as it was not actually utilized because the revenues under the sharing agreement exceeded the minimum.[39] The result is that as long as the liquids revenue to the producer exceeds one cent, the contract is all right; but when they fall below one cent the one cent minimum is invalidated if it makes the total price greater than the ceiling. This approach still leaves the possibility that the sharing percentages can be manipulated to favor the producer, although the commission would probably intervene where the producer's share was unusually high. It

37. 29 FPC 1175 (1963).
38. *Id.* at 1184.
39. Union Texas Petroleum, FPC Order Granting Waiver, 1965 Util. L. Rep. ¶ 10,891 (Dec. 7, 1967).

does, however, limit the amount of the payments which can be made ostensibly for liquids but in fact for gas, to the actual revenues generated by the sale of the liquids. If and when market prices obtainable in the field move above the price ceilings, even more substantial incentives will exist to evade the regulation. No doubt other means will be developed to accomplish that purpose. The commission will have to be vigilant to ensure that the regulation applies to all sales in the interstate market and that transactions are not rearranged so as to increase the value of the contract package to the producer even though the price complies with the ceiling.

THE FUTURE OF THE REGULATION

For the moment all is well with the Federal Power Commission's regulation of natural gas field prices. The commission can pride itself on having constructed price control regulation out of a traditional regulatory statute; increasing reserves and competition in the consumer fuel market have made its regulation look even more effective than it can possibly be. But what of the day when the market is no longer in equilibrium at the ceiling price? Will the commission's regulation under the Natural Gas Act provide the appropriate response?

In its *Permian Basin* opinion [40] the Commission has fairly well outlined what will happen in such a situation. In the *Permian Basin* opinion the commission established a two price system. The first price, the old gas price (in the Permian Basin area, 14.5 cents), applies to natural gas committed to interstate commerce before January 1, 1961, and all gas produced in association with oil. The new gas price (16.5 cents in the Permian Basin area) applies to all nonassociated gas committed to interstate commerce after January 1, 1961. The commission adopted this two-price system because it found that the supply of new nonassociated gas was "more" responsive to price, while the supply of gas already committed to interstate commerce and gas produced in association with oil was "less" responsive. Therefore, reasoned the commission, there is no need to offer a higher price for the "old" gas because a higher price cannot increase supply.

40. Area Rate Proceeding 61–1 (Permian Basin), 34 FPC 159 (1965).

The January 1, 1961, date was chosen in recognition of the fact that the two-price system carried forward in modified form the dual-pricing system first established in the price guidelines issued in 1960.[41]

These prices are set for the foreseeable future. The gas having been committed to interstate commerce, there is no need to offer a higher price to induce its production. When in the future the new gas price proves insufficient to stimulate the development of adequate supplies, a "new new" gas price will be issued applicable to gas sold after the date of its promulgation.[42]

The most serious problem with this system is the probability that the commission will not permit the "new new" gas price to rise at a rate fast enough to assure adequate supply. In the history of natural gas regulation much has been made of the fact that the supply of natural gas is relatively inelastic. The more important fact is that the supply of natural gas is responsive to price. It is true that in the Appalachian gas crisis production declined and prices rose. But the undeniable fact is that because of those higher prices production has continued for more than forty years at a substantial rate. The fact that the supply schedule for gas is relatively inelastic may mean that it is possible to transfer wealth from producers to consumers by means of a price ceilinging with less loss than if it were more elastic. But so what? The loss—the gas left unproduced—remains for all of society. The only fact the history can prove is that supply responds to price. The exact degree of elasticity at any particular time cannot be known, it is constantly shifting as the geological facts and the technology change. In a world of necessary ignorance the safest position for the regulator is not to allow a single large price increase, which would bring criticism from those opposed to higher prices, but a small price increase followed by a wait to see if it will be sufficient to attract the needed supply. If not, then another small increase, followed by a similar wait. The commission's action in the *Permian Basin* case follows this pattern. Gas price ceilings were set at or just barely above the present market.[43] Any further increase will need commission approval.

41. *Id.* at 188–89.
42. *Id.* at 227.
43. *Id.* at 188: "The separate price we fix herein for new gas-well gas in the Permian Basin should serve to furnish a practical test of whether in fact it will result in bringing forth additional supplies."

The ultimate irony is that the effect of this regulatory intervention is to significantly increase the market's unresponsiveness to changing conditions of supply. An increase is slowed by the period needed for regulatory consideration. Because the outcome of the commission's consideration will be based on arbitrary and unpredictable considerations, the industry cannot count on an inevitable increase. Therefore, those involved in the development of additional reserves will have to wait until the increase has actually been allowed before they make commitments based on the expectation of the higher price. The "inelasticity" of political and regulatory mechanisms is responsible for the fact that the last two major adjustments in the field market have been made by means of the market rather than regulation. The Appalachian crisis was followed by regulation of the interstate gas market only after nineteen years. In 1960 the commission clamped a ceiling on the field market only after the upward price trend of the fifties resulting from increased transmission efficiencies and competition had halted. But the next time an upward shift in the field market occurs the commission will be firmly astride the field market. It will respond just as slowly as it has in the past. The tragedy is that the next increase may be another increase in the field price, like the increase of the 1950s, without any corresponding increase in the delivered cost of gas to consumers. In the 1970s many natural gas pipelines will be fully depreciated. The depreciation charges are now running about 8 percent of revenue.[44] Given the fact that the pipelines are in place and most cannot be used for any other purpose, it will be profitable for their owners to transport gas from the field to market at a cost equal to the cost of operation. This decrease in the transmission charge could lend to another substantial field price increase without an increase in the price charged consumers. But the regulation will interfere with the ability of the consumer to use this cost saving as a way of bidding for additional supplies of gas.

In the field market the regulation will only cause the loss of gas which would otherwise be produced. In the consumer markets the possible consequences are even more disturbing. The transportation system is subject to rate base regulation which prevents price increases due to scarcity. Therefore, when and if

44. See FPC, Statistics for Interstate Natural Gas Pipeline Companies 1966 at XII Table 21 (1967).

the price ceiling in the field becomes economically effective, the price ceiling will be transmitted forward to the consuming market. There will be a shortage. We have had experience with two periods of crisis in the gas supply. The first, the Appalachian crisis, was largely handled through the market. Consumers switched one by one from natural to mixed or manufactured gas, or other forms of fuel as the price rose to the point where it was profitable for them to do so. The percentage of industrial use declined steadily and substantially. In World War II, on the other hand, there was effective price control. All customers continued to consume until the system was brought to the brink of collapse, a collapse which was only avoided by the mandatory disruption of a wide range of activities. The gas supply system simply does not lend itself to enforceable rationing. Price control without rationing creates a market crisis which, in the case of natural gas, can literally be disastrous.

These difficulties are compounded by the multiprice system. The pipelines and the distributors of natural gas are subject to regulation which requires average cost pricing. Thus the consumer of natural gas will face a price based upon the average cost of all gas—old, new, and new new—being supplied to his system. This cost will be lower than the actual cost of producing the gas necessary to satisfy that consumer's demand. Thus, to illustrate, the consumer may face a price based upon an average field price of 18 cents plus transportation charges of 60 cents, but acquisition of the supply necessary to satisfy his demand may cost a "new new" price of 26 cents. Since more consumers will be willing to pay 78 cents for the gas than 86 cents, the demand for the "new new" gas will be greater than is actually justified by its economic value to the ultimate consumers. The regulation creates a market in which the amount of gas demanded is in excess of the amount that would be demanded if purchasers were faced with prices based on the actual marginal cost of producing the gas.[45] This excess demand will make the shortage problem more acute.

45. The exact reverse of the situation created by the regulation of the market for milk, where the consumer faces a dual-price system and the producer an average price. In regulated milk markets more milk is produced than would be produced if farmers faced a price based on the marginal value of their production to the consumer. See Reuben A. Kessel, "Economic Effects of Federal Regulation of Milk Markets," 10 *J. Law & Econ.* 51, 58–60 (1967).

These implications of the multiprice system are even more troublesome in the context of imported gas. Eventually the United States will have to turn to foreign sources for significant amounts of its "new new" gas. This gas will probably either come overland from Canada or Mexico, or by undersea pipeline or methane tanker from Venezuela. The Canadian experience suggests that we will not be able to avoid paying the market price for this gas; certainly as the domestic supply decreases our bargaining position will weaken. But it is ironic that the price of domestic gas is held down with the consequence that the demand for foreign gas is increased.

In the field, the multiprice system leads to further waste. The fact is that the supply of "old" and associated gas, although less responsive than the supply of new nonassociated gas, is to some degree responsive to price. In the case of associated gas, the the amount of the income from gas may affect the time when a well is abandoned. Even if the time involved is only a month or so, the gas lost because of an earlier abandonment is lost forever. Old nonassociated gas wells may need further work, or further development of other producing depths covered by the original contract. Whether or not to undertake this work will be determined by the old gas price. The commission has recognized the need for exceptions where wells are not longer profitable to operate.[46] But simply obtaining such exceptions will be complex and time consuming. The gas that would have been produced at the market price is, again, lost forever.

This discussion is premised on the assumption, of course, that the regulation will be effective. But the market for natural gas is of sufficient diversity and complexity so that it is reasonable to question whether or not the price control will be completely effective. This is particularly so in view of the small staff of the commission. One of the principal reasons given for the institution of the area approach in 1960 was that the commission had insufficient staff to deal with rate problems on a producer by producer basis.[47] The shift to an area rate procedure, however, was

46. 34 FPC 226.
47. Phillips Petroleum Co., 24 FPC 537, 545–46 (1960): "Thus, if our present staff were immediately tripled, and if all new employees would be as competent as those we now have, we would not reach a current status in our independent producer rate work until 2043 A.D.—eighty-two and one half years from now."

largely a sleight of hand. It did unify in a single proceeding one question—the permissible price. But it left hidden the need to enforce that price determination on a contract by contract basis. The commission was quite unrealistic about this problem in *Permian Basin,* leaving the resolution of the amount of the quality and pressure discounts on each individual contract to negotiation between the parties.[48] When it is in the interest of both parties to avoid the price ceiling, they cannot be counted on to enforce it. Perhaps when the commission realizes the magnitude of the task of enforcing price control and the public clamor that will follow from a failure to stop widespread evasion, it will realize its own interest in keeping the price ceilings above the market.

48. 34 FPC 225. "[S]hould it be found that evasion or abuse is prevalent, it may be necessary to take measures to fix the precise price variations corresponding to variations in gas quality." *Ibid.*

Part Seven   Regulatory Reform

Reasonable Rules for Rate Regulation: Plausible Policies for an Imperfect World

WILLIAM J. BAUMOL

This essay aptly summarizes the findings in the papers above on results from regulation (although it was not written for that purpose). But it then goes further to make proposals for reform that are imaginative and economic. But, as the author himself asks, will they work? William Baumol is professor of economics at Princeton University and has published important papers in the economics of welfare, mathematical economics, and in most of the applied fields as well.

A CONSIDERABLE PROPORTION of the goods and services supplied by the public utilities (broadly defined) have long been provided under conditions of natural monopoly. Because effective competition in the production of at least some of the firm's products is not a reasonable alternative in most of these cases, the necessity of public regulation of rates and of other aspects of the operation of these firms is widely accepted. Yet despite extensive experience, the regulatory principles that have emerged still seem far from perfect. This paper undertakes the formulation of a set of procedures which have a somewhat firmer foundation in economic analysis. These procedures are designed to deal with the problems which may potentially arise from the monopolistic nature of the firms in question. But it should be recognized that some of the problems discussed may in practice turn out to be unimportant, or they may arise only infrequently. And, because the discussion ignores completely the existing legal framework and regulatory traditions, some of the proposals discussed are of doubtful practical import, but they should at least be of some interest in bringing out the relevant issues.

Economists complain, with some reason, that the criteria employed by regulatory agencies find little justification in economic analysis. Yet a regulatory commissioner can reply with at least equal justice that the economic literature offers little help to those who must decide on policy in our imperfect world. For the economists' tests, in all their subtlety and sophistication, break down completely when arrangements in the remainder of the economy do not accord with the underlying premises of his models. Welfare economics tells us that there is much to be said for a system of pricing in which *every* rate in the economy is equal to the marginal cost incurred in supplying the service. And from this a number of investigators have jumped to the conclusion that the resulting rule is a good guide for pricing in a nationalized industry. Presumably such an approach has not been advocated widely for public utilities operated as private enterprises only because of the financial loss which it would in many cases impose and the political problems that must inevitably accompany such deficits. Yet it does not require the mathematical elaboration of the Lipsey-Lancaster second-best theorem for us to see that if other products in the economy are not priced at marginal cost, the use of marginal-cost pricing by a few nationalized firms can easily lead to a misallocation of resources. By making relatively cheap the few services supplied by these firms demand is apt to be distorted and activity in the nationalized sector overexpanded.

The theory of the second best tells us, in principle, how such a situation should be dealt with. In formal terms it goes through the mathematical calculations that determine the best that can be done under these conditions. But no one, least of all the authors of the theorem, has ever pretended that this is a practical alternative. To carry out such a procedure one must be able to specify explicitly all the economy's imperfections, employing them as constraints in the optimality calculations. This and the other information requirements of such a procedure place it well beyond the realm of practicality.

What then is the alternative? Two approaches seem possible, each of which is used at some points in this paper. First, one can simply proceed on grounds of plausibility; one can describe a set of procedures which, taking into account all that economic analysis has told us, seem likely as a matter of subjective judgment to lead to results that promote the public welfare as well as might reasonably be expected in the circumstances. Second, one can formulate a set of desiderata—a set of minimal objectives which we feel a public policy must accomplish before it is considered acceptable. Thereupon one can proceed to design policies that satisfy these minimal acceptability criteria.[1]

What this paper attempts, then, is to provide a set of basic rules for the regulation of public utility rates, principles which seem to accord roughly with the spirit of the results derived by more rigorous analysis for the idealized circumstances that are analytically tractable. In doing so the discussion takes no account of any existing procedures and traditions of regulatory policy. It assumes, in effect, that it is possible to clean the slate and start all over again.

SOME DESIDERATA OF UTILITY RATE REGULATION

To the economist two goals of regulatory policy are obvious. First, while one wishes to permit the firm to earn a reasonable rate of return, pure monopoly profits, however defined, should be prevented. Second, one desires to minimize the misallocation of input that results because prices do not generally reflect the real resources used up in supplying a unit of output to a consumer. However, there are a number of other desiderata which are somewhat less obvious, some of which arise out of the nature of the regulatory approach normally employed.

A sensible procedure for the prevention of monopoly profits, and one that is widely utilized, imposes some sort of ceiling on over-all company earnings, a ceiling normally expressed as a maximal rate of return on investment (the "rate base"). But, while treating one problem, the arrangement creates a host of other difficulties. Where, as seems frequently to be the case, the demand for some services of a public utility is inelastic over the relevant range, the maximal permitted earnings rate and the

---

1. This approach has honorable antecedents in economic theory; it is, for example, the basis of Kenneth Arrow's analysis in his *Social Choice and Individual Values* (New York: 1951). Note also the relationship to Herbert Simon's satisficing concept: the regulatory agency that employs the approach under discussion satisfices (it makes sure that is policies meet the minimum conditions required for them to be considered satisfactory) but gives up any pretense of *maximizing* the social walfare.

actual rate of return are most unlikely to diverge substantially. For if the company's returns threaten to fall short of the ceiling, it need merely raise its rates for its inelastic demand services by a suitable amount, and the short-fall will be eliminated. This means that with any reasonable degree of efficiency and in the absence of any serious shortage in demand, such a company is virtually guaranteed its permitted earnings level. However, there is only one way open to the company for increasing its total earnings: an expansion of its rate base.

Several unfortunate consequences may then follow, consequences whose prevention may reasonably be considered an appropriate objective of public policy.

1. The company may lose much or all of its incentive for operating efficiency and innovation. For if the firm is virtually certain of earning x dollars, no more and no less, whatever its cost outlays—if it can make up for any rise in cost by a suitable increase in rates for its inelastic demand services, there is little motivation to keep down expenditures. Waste becomes costless to the company, and if the management's motivation includes empire building as an objective in addition to profitability,[2] it may not resist the temptation to hire unnecessary staff and to increase salary rates beyond the levels they would ordinarily attain. What is really remarkable, then, is the rather high degree of efficiency that seems to characterize the operations of many public utilities in practice.

2. The obvious avenue for an increase in rate base is an investment outlay. And for our regulated company the usual profitability criteria for an investment decision do not automatically apply. If an increase in investment means that the firm is permitted a corresponding rise in its overall earnings *which can, if need be, be obtained by raising rates on inelastic demand services*, the new investment will necessarily produce the usual rate of profit, whether or not it is utilized effectively and serves an economic purpose.

3. Investment, whether useless or useful, is not the only way to augment the rate base. If the rate base is evaluated in terms of replacement or reproduction cost, it is even profitable to have

2. See, e.g., O. E. Williamson, *The Economics of Discretionary Behavior* (Englewood Cliffs, N. J.: 1964).

suppliers of the company's equipment raise their prices! A 10 percent increase in the price of a new machine causes the company no loss in profits (for it will still obtain its permitted r percent rate of return) and in addition *its older machines may then automatically be revalued* at their increased replacement cost so that the corresponding portion of the rate base will go up 10 percent![3]

4. Destructive pricing may be defined as the temporary lowering of rates in order to drive out a competitor and thus clear the field for monopoly pricing and monopoly profits. While the typical public utility supplies some of its services under monopoly conditions, often it faces competitors in the market for a number of its other products. Regulatory agencies have for a considerable time sought to prevent destructive pricing in these markets. But with limitation of rate of return, the deliberate elimination of a competitor may serve yet another purpose; it may clear the way for expansion of the offending firm, as a means to increase its investment and hence its rate base.[4]

Most of the practices that have just been described (some of which are perhaps hypothetical) would involve the misuse of society's resources through the promotion of relatively useless investment, inefficient operation, etc., and might clearly have adverse effects on the company's competitors. It is only a little less obvious that the interests of one other class of individuals are likely to be served badly. For the cost of any type of inefficiency in the production of an item, particularly one whose demand is elastic, may well fall on the consumer of some other service or services of the firm. If inefficiencies are paid for by increases in the prices of items whose demand is inelastic, the cost will be shifted directly to the purchasers of these other services.

In sum, attempts to regulate away one sort of problem are all too likely to give rise to other difficulties. It is this list of difficulties which this paper takes to constitute the basic assignment of the regulatory agency. A good program of regulation of utility

3. This possibility was apparently first pointed out by Westfield. See F. M. Westfield "Regulation and Conspiracy," *American Economic Review,* Vol. 55, (June 1965).

4. See H. Averch and L. L. Johnson, "Behavior of the Firm under Regulatory Constraint," *American Economic Review,* Vol. 52, (Dec. 1962), pp. 1057–1059.

rates, then, is required to accomplish at least the following:

1. The prevention of monopoly profits without at the same time precluding the profitable operation of the company.
2. The reduction as far as can reasonably be expected of the misallocation of resources and the distortion of demand patterns resulting from the administratively determined rates for the various company services.
3. The provision of some strong motivation for operating efficiency and innovation.
4. The prevention of predatory competition in those product lines which are not provided under monopolistic conditions.
5. The protection of the consumers of company services whose demands are inelastic from the burden of inefficiencies in other portions of the company's operations.
6. The elimination of the motivation for uneconomic investment as a means of expanding the rate base.
7. The preclusion of the use of other socially undesirable means to expand the rate base—of methods such as the encouragement of price rises by equipment suppliers and the elimination of competitors as means of providing new investment opportunities.

The remainder of this paper, then, undertakes to describe some regulatory policies which are responsive to these criteria. It is to be emphasized that since they are all untested, any one of these measures may well lead to unanticipated side effects that are politically unpalatable. In any event, there is no reason to believe that this is the only set of measures capable of doing the job, or that it will do the job more effectively than any substitute proposal. I suggest only that these policies seem to meet the minimum conditions of acceptability which have just been set out. It must also be emphasized that if some of the regulatory problems that have just been listed turn out to be unimportant in practice, prudence and economy may recommend that the corresponding regulatory proposals be dropped from consideration. If it can be shown that some anticipated problem is virtually nonexistent, it would be folly to devote effort and resources to its prevention.

PROFIT CEILINGS AND THE ENCOURAGEMENT OF
OPERATING EFFICIENCY

Short of providing some effective competitors—a possibility which in most cases is patently ludicrous—there unfortunately appears to be no substitute for a ceiling over company earnings as a means to prevent monopoly profit. Moreover, it makes economic sense to proportion these permitted earnings to the company's level of investment, in effect producing a limit, not to total earnings, but on rate of return for investment.

Though it is likely to rub an economist the wrong way, there is also some rough justice in the contention that the rate base— the calculated volume of investment to which the ceiling rate of return on investment is applied—should be based on historical or sunk costs rather than on reproduction or replacement cost. The economist, who is normally concerned with efficiency rather than with considerations of justice, usually wishes to determine the consequences of a course of action currently under consideration. And for this purpose, sunk cost is a piece of ancient history over which no one any longer has any influence. But where equity is involved one may argue persuasively that matters go the other way. A ceiling on earnings precludes for the investor any windfall gains. It seems only fair that as compensation he should also be provided some protection against windfall losses. This means that the earnings he is offered ought not to depend on the valuation which subsequent fortuitous events have imposed on his investment. Rather, it should be based on the investment outlays he actually incurred in the past. On this line of reasoning, original cost data require only depreciation and price-level corrections in the calculation of the value of the rate base. Price-change adjustments are appropriate, for without them, in a world of secular inflation, the investor is not protected effectively from windfall loss. The r per cent earnings permitted to him he will receive in relatively debased dollars in compensation for an investment which was paid for in far more valuable monetary units. This suggests that an appropriate price index for this purpose might be the consumer price index or some other index in the family which measures changes in the purchasing power of the security-holder's funds. However, as usual there is no unique index for the job.

There is another reason that favors an original cost evaluation of the investment base, corrected only for price-level changes and depreciation. For this arrangement eliminates any possibility of tacit or explicit conspiracy between a utility and its equipment-suppliers to increase the utility's rate base through a rise in the price of new equipment. If the rate base is evaluated in terms of original equipment outlays, a change in replacement cost simply will leave the rate base unaffected and so the utility will have no motivation to encourage such price moves.

It is appropriate to include a few comments on the choice of the number that is to constitute the r percent rate of return permitted to the company. Ideally this should be what in the literature of corporation finance is called the cost of capital for the company's risk class. Roughly, it is the rate of earnings on capital (current market value of total company equity and debt) which is presently received by other firms whose stockholders are subject to comparable risks. A company which is not permitted such a rate of earnings will have difficulty in obtaining the funds required for its growth, since it will find itself at a direct disadvantage in comparison with the other firms with which it competes for financing.

The cost-of-capital figure to which the company's rate of return should be equated is not the same as the rate of interest which the company pays for its borrowings. As is clear from the literature of corporation finance, the company's bond interest rate is merely a nominal capital cost which fails to take into account the risk that added debt imposes on the stockholder.[5] It is to be expected, then, that the cost of capital will be higher, and typically substantially higher, than the interest return on company debt.

With such an earnings ceiling, how can one motivate the firm to watch its outlays, to combat waste, and to seek actively to

5. See, e.g., E. Solomon, *The Theory of Financial Management* (New York: 1963), pp. 71–88. The main argument in the Averch and Johnson article (n. 4, p. 111) seems to rest on a confusion between the interest cost of borrowing and the cost of capital. These authors argue, correctly, that if the regulatory ceiling on company earnings were higher than its cost of capital the company would be led to overexpansion and to an inefficiently large utilization of capital as a substitute for other inputs. However, they seem clearly wrong in contending that the difference between the permitted rate of return and the interest cost of borrowed funds indicates the presence of this problem.

institute cost-saving innovations? The answer is to be found in the workings of the competitive process for which the regulatory mechanism is presumably intended to serve as a substitute. As Schumpeter showed many years ago,[6] while competition tends to eliminate "above-normal" profits in the long run, the excess profits which it permits in the short run are essential for economic progress. The motivation for a firm to innovate is the unusual but temporary profits which the innovation permits. Of course, once competitors learn about the new idea and its effectiveness they will be led to imitate it, and so the profits will ultimately disappear. But in the meantime these profits will have done their job— they will have induced management to adopt the innovation, a process which will not subsequently be reversed when earnings have returned to their normal level.

This immediately suggests an analogous arrangement for the regulation of returns to a utility. Suppose rates are subject to regulatory re-examination only at periodic intervals; as an illustration, say that they are reconsidered every three years. At such a re-examination date these rates could be set to provide the company currently no more than the r percent rate of return on historical investment that is considered justified. Suppose, however, that the company is permitted to retain all the earnings it makes during the three-year interval before the next review date, *whatever the level of these earnings*. In doing so the company would be permitted to lower its rates wherever it chose to do so subject only to the several proposed rate-reduction regulations which will be described presently. However, it would not be allowed any interim rate raises except under most unusual circumstances.[7]

6. J. A. Schumpeter, *The Theory of Economic Development*, translated by R. Opie (Cambridge, Mass.: 1936).

7. Thus, if there were an unanticipated inflationary upsurge in prices generally a review by the regulatory commission at the request of the company might determine that some increase in rates is required for the viability of company operations.

It may be objected that the proposed regulatory principle would in practice give most companies more than the r percent return that is considered socially desirable. But experience should soon permit regulation to prevent excessive profits from this source. The initially permitted r percent rate of return would just have to be adjusted downward sufficiently. If it were found that rates initially yielding r percent typically yielded kr percent over the three-year period, only an initial rate of return of r/k percent might be allowed, so that in fact an average utility or a given firm would over the

This proposal is thus designed to permit the company to retain the fruits of its cost-saving efforts. It would find it profitable to save money because cost reductions would then lead directly to corresponding though temporary increases in profits.

It is said that in a rough and ready manner such a procedure is already employed, albeit unintentionally, by many regulatory commissions. Because it is simply not practical to review and revise rates constantly, there is usually a regulatory hiatus and a lag in price adjustment which permits the company to increase its profits somewhat when it manages to effect a decline in cost. It is not clear whether more general and more even application of such an approach and the explicit dissemination of information on its workings would yield increases in efficiency sufficient to justify the required upheaval in the mode of operation of the regulatory agencies.

PROTECTING THE CONSUMER OF SERVICES WITH INELASTIC DEMANDS: TESTS OF COMPENSATORY OPERATION

Much of the complexity of the regulatory problem arises from the ability of the regulated firm to shift any relative losses incurred by inefficient portions of its operations onto consumers of services whose demand is inelastic. But once the problem is stated so explicitly, economic analysis readily provides a solution which is straightforward in its outlines, even if its details do involve a number of complications.

A service can be defined as compensatory (its provision under current arrangements is justified by economic considerations) if its availability affects adversely neither the interests of the stock-

---

long run average r percent on its investment and only companies whose efficiency rose to an unusual extent would do better than this. Note also, in accord with the comment of the preceding paragraph, that in an inflationary period k might prove to be less than unity (actual earnings tending to less than r percent) so that the adjusted initial return, r/k, would exceed r.

Professor Bonbright has suggested that a three-year review period (which is used in this paper merely as an illustrative figure) is a very short interval for the purpose. But he also notes that managements might be tempted to bunch their price-reducing inducements right after each rate-setting period. For just this reason a short review period (or a review period of random length) may have something to be said for it.

Incidentally, Professor Bonbright credits public yardstick rates and cost comparisons among private companies as effective influences toward efficiency in public utilities.

holders nor the consumers of alternative company services. In most cases we would of course expect somewhat more than this —the provision of a service on terms that are compensatory should in fact normally provide real benefits to at least one of these groups. In other words, given its current mode of operation, a service is compensatory if its elimination would redound to the net disadvantage of stockholders or of the consumers of other company output.

The nature of the appropriate criterion of compensatory operation should now be obvious; a service is compensatory if its revenues exceed what Professor Lewis terms its "escapable costs" [8]—the costs that would in the long run be avoided if the company were to terminate the provision of the service in question. For if this condition is met, without an effective ceiling on profits, stockholders are clearly better off with the provision of the service than without it. On the other hand, if because of regulatory restrictions the rate of return would remain the same whether or not the service were available, provision of a service that is compensatory must reduce the amount of profit obtained from the consumers of other company services—with services whose demand is inelastic this would necessarily require lower rates than those which would prevail in the absence of our compensatory service.

It follows that many of the problems of rate regulation could be solved by requiring regulated companies to submit evidence (either periodically or on request) showing that each of their services is supplied on a compensatory basis, and by requiring them to make corrective adjustments whenever this test is not passed. The nature of the appropriate corrective adjustments is not always obvious, but it raises no serious problems in principle. It may, of course, involve an increase in rates for a service that is noncompensatory. But if demand for the service is highly elastic a decrease in rates may be what is needed to put the service on a compensatory basis. It is also conceivable that no adjustment will

8. W. A. Lewis, *Overhead Costs* (London: 1949), pp. 9ff. Sometimes it is not obvious how a particular service should be defined. For example, in supplying gas, is the commercial supply to be considered different from the domestic supply even though they employ common distribution mains? In principle *any* service or combination of services, however defined, should be subject to a test of compensatory operation, but, of course, simpler rules of reason would have to be used in practice.

prove capable of rendering the service compensatory. In that case, in the absence of marked external benefits sufficient to justify a public subsidy, provision of the service should be discontinued altogether.

In principle, then, the test of compensation can prevent three of the major difficulties of utility rate regulation: the exploitation of the consumers of other company services, the recourse to uneconomic investments undertaken only as a means to expand the rate base, and, in particular, the attempt to eliminate competitors as a means to clear the way for expansion of the rate base, Of course, it might still be possible for our company to outcompete a rival firm by providing a service more cheaply. But if the service is supplied on a compensatory basis, economic efficiency is clearly served by competition of this variety. Even if the competitor is unable to survive, he will have been driven from the field only by his inability to supply his output without an excessive use of resources. It may be that our regulated company is the more efficient supplier of the service only because he can provide it jointly with some other services, which together offer substantial economies of scale. But this is still a matter of real economic efficiency—it makes the firm that has been driven from the field no less a casualty of economic progress. Its exit is the normal price exacted for growth in economic productivity, the elimination of the inefficient suppliers.

While the test of compensatory operation promises to help considerably with the regulatory problems, its appropriate utilization does involve several complicating caveats:

(a) The pertinent information is that reporting *long-run* escapable costs. That is, it must include the present value of all future outlays required to keep the service in operation (unless the company plans to terminate provision of the service in the foreseeable future).[9] For a service is not compensatory if the present value of the stream of its expected revenues falls short of the discounted stream of costs to which it commits the company.

(b) The test of compensatory operation does not tell us

9. Of course, to this figure one must add the value of the firm's current equipment and inventory in their best alternative use, for if the service were discontinued, its assets would presumably be transferred to the most profitable employment open to them. Thus such opportunity cost would then also be avoided.

whether the terms on which the service is provided are optimal either from the point of view of the company or from that of society. Thus a company may wish to change the price or the rate of growth of supply of even a compensatory service. But then the test must be administered anew; indeed, it may be desirable that this be done frequently when market conditions or the nature of company operations change. For the fact that an activity is compensatory under one set of circumstances does not guarantee that it will be so under other conditions.

(c) If the rate base is calculated in terms of historical "imbedded" cost of the company's capital, then, strictly speaking, a double test of compensatory operation is called for. First one must see whether escapable cost is covered, evaluating equipment in terms of its prospective replacement costs and its current opportunity value, in the manner already described. In addition, however, it is necessary to determine whether the service yields at least the r percent return legally permitted the company on the portion of the historical rate base which could be eliminated under current legal and accounting practices by sale or scrapping of equipment or any other appropriate means if the service were discontinued. Suppose the company were permitted r percent earnings on its rate base and, if the service were eliminated, the resulting reduction in rate base and expected net revenues were ΔB and ΔR respectively. Then if $(\Delta R/\Delta B) < r$, consumers of the company's other services would not have to provide so large a contribution as before to yield the r percent rate of return on the remainder of the rate base.[10] Thus provision of the service must in these circumstances impose a burden on the consumers of other company services, i.e., provision of our service would not be compensatory in the sense we have defined it. However, this is a matter of the conventions of the rate-base

10. Let $B + \Delta B$ and $R + \Delta R$ be the total initial rate base and the total initial net revenues respectively, where
$$(R + \Delta R)/(B + \Delta B) = r.$$
Let R' be the revenue required to yield an overall r percent return to the company after elimination of the service, so that
$$(R'/B) = r.$$
Since $(\Delta R/\Delta B) < r$ it follows that $R/B > r$ and so $R' < R$, as asserted in the text. Note, incidentally, that the legal and accounting conventions might sometimes prevent any reduction in the rate base on elimination of a service, i.e., we would have $\Delta B = 0$ so that our second test would automatically be passed.

calculation and there are no purely economic criteria to determine the rules of this second test of compensatory operation.

(d) In all this it should be remembered that statistical calculation of escapable costs runs into the many difficulties that beset the determination of marginal cost figures, so that one can expect to obtain no more than approximate but defensible escapable cost figures, and these are likely to require substantial outlays for data gathering.

PREVENTION OF DESTRUCTIVE PRICING

Destructive pricing may be described as the temporary reduction of rates undertaken to eliminate competitors in order to clear the way for monopoly prices in the future. The regulatory program which has so far been outlined goes at least part of the way toward meeting this danger. For the effective way to prevent destructive pricing is to eliminate its profit yield. If the firm is limited in its overall rate of return, it cannot at a later date expect arbitrarily to raise its rates unless there is a simultaneous increase in the company's rate base. The proposals of the following section, if adopted, would also appear to eliminate any danger of destructive pricing, as will be shown presently.

However, an alternative, or perhaps a supplementary, provision would operate by putting firms on notice that once they lower rates they will not be permitted to raise them again after competition has been eliminated, unless the firm can show that some unexpected and unavoidable increase in costs has subsequently occurred. The fact that the service has been supplied at a certain price while competition was present would constitute prima facie evidence that the company can afford to supply at that price when it no longer has rivals to contend with. And, if technological progress makes for a secular decline in the company's costs, it might in the future even be appropriate to require it to reduce its rates correspondingly.

It may be felt that the sort of guarantees which have just been described constitute a desirable supplement to the ceiling on a company's overall rate of return, because it is always possible that a firm will wish to eliminate a competitor not in order to raise its rates immediately but as a matter of insurance—as a means to shift a service from the elastic to the inelastic demand categories so that if at some future date the company falls on harder times, it will have another string to its bow—it will have another service which can be used to provide the profits it is legally permitted. With the restriction on future rate increases just described, the elimination of competitors would no longer offer this attraction.

However, the proposals discussed in the following section would also serve this purpose, in addition to the objective they are primarily designed to achieve.

RELATIVE PRICING AND IMPROVED RESOURCE ALLOCATION

We come finally to what may well be the most questionable among the set of proposals offered in this paper: the rules suggested for the determination of relative rates for different company services. Two systematic approaches have been proposed elsewhere for the purpose: (1) "full-cost pricing," and (2) a mixed arrangement in which prices for services whose demands are elastic are set so as to maximize the net profits flowing from each such service and in which the remaining rates are determined residually by these profit flows and the ceiling on overall company earnings imposed by regulation. There is no need to recapitulate in detail the economist's objection to "full-cost pricing"—its arbitrary allocation of joint costs, the likelihood that it will yield results deleterious to the general welfare by discouraging the consumption of decreasing-cost output, etc. Surely our profession should be able to design a pricing arrangement which is at least superior to that based on a "fully allocated cost" calculation.

The second approach, while somewhat more attractive, itself differs in two respects from an abstract ideal. First, there is no basis in terms of the perfect competition model which we use as a criterion in much of our pure theory for such a differentiated treatment of inelastic and elastic demand commodities. The only justification usually offered for the distinction accorded the two classes of output is the fact that the profit-maximizing price is likely to be more or less reasonable where demand is elastic, while with inelastic demand the sky is the limit—the higher the price the greater the profit. In addition, this approach leaves some degree of ambiguity in the calculation. If a company provides only one service whose demand is inelastic, the r percent limitation on overall company earnings does automatically fix its price. Since the profits of this service rise monotonically with its price, there will be exactly one price at which total company profits (including the maximal yields from the elastic demand services) add up to r percent of the rate base. However, if the company offers m different inelastic demand services, this rule can only be used to determine some sort of average price. It will not select the m individual prices. It offers us only one equation to determine m variable values. Given the prices of the elastic demand output, if total profits are represented by $T = f(p_1, \ldots, p_m)$ where p_i is the price of the ith inelastic demand service, then the condition

$$f(p_1, \ldots, p_m) = rB \text{ (B = rate base)}$$

is obviously insufficient to determine the value of $p_1, p_2, \ldots, p_m$.

The literature does suggest that, where two such services are substitutes, there is something to be said for setting their relative prices equal to the ratio of the marginal costs, for the consumer is likely to compare directly their advantages and disadvantages in choosing between two substitutable goods, and a price reflecting their relative resources cost will guide the consumer to allocate resources optimally between them.[11]

But precisely the same considerations would seem to suggest that it would be desirable for *all* public utility prices to be set so that they are proportional to marginal costs. Since utilities are typically decreasing-cost operations, obtaining the legally permitted rate of return on the rate base would normally require all rates to exceed marginal costs. However, under this proposal they would all exceed marginal costs by the same percentage.[12]

11. It has also been suggested that in some cases it is instead desirable to set prices so that the difference in the prices of the two services is equal to the difference between their marginal costs. Suppose, for example, that one service is the same as another except that the former contains some supplementary features (e.g., a newspaper provided at a newsstand *vs.* a newspaper delivered to one's door, or a trip on a train with a dining car *vs.* a trip on a train without one). Then it has been proposed that the choice between acceptance and rejection of the supplementary service feature is least distorted by a price that is actually equal to the marginal cost incurred in its provision. In that case the difference between the prices of, e.g., a delivered and an undelivered newspaper would be the marginal home delivery cost.

12. It has been known for some time that such an arrangement will not lead to an optimal allocation of resources, even if *every* seller priced at the

Under this arrangement, then, in a rough and ready way the consumer would at least receive the right price (cost) signals for a rational choice among the alternatives provided by the company. Prices would, in principal, be perfectly determinate, subject only to the obvious difficulties involved in calculating marginal costs *not as fixed scalars but as functions of the quantities supplied.* For the choice of prices will surely affect quantities purchased and hence marginal costs. Thus, if we write the marginal cost function for commodity i as $mc_i = g_i(p_1, \ldots, p_n)$ the prices of the company's n services (this time including both the items whose demands are elastic and those which are inelastic) would normally be determined by the n—1 relative price conditions,

$$p_i/p_n = g_i(p_1, \ldots, p_n)/g_n(p_1, \ldots, p_n)$$

and the total profit constraint $f(p_1, \ldots, p_n) = rB$. If, as seems plausible, these equations are consistent and independent, the prices of all items of company output would be uniquely specified.

As a practical matter, of course, this proposal is even less straightforward then it may seem at first glance. It would certainly not be easy to keep the calculation up to date. And while it is hard enough to obtain current marginal-cost figures, even these are not the data that the computation requires. For the relevant marginal costs to which prices should be proportioned are the hypothetical marginal costs which would apply after the change in output and demand caused by the required price revisions—marginal-costs figures whose calculation would require us to know in some detail the demand functions for each item of the company's output!

It might, moreover, be necessary to make a few modifications in the prices of some of the elastic demand services. For it is

same percentage markup over marginal cost. For example, McKenzie has pointed out that if a commodity serves both as a consumer's good and as input to another process (coal), a k percent markup on that good will result in a more than k percent markup on resources cost for the commodity that utilizes our good as input. For in the process a second k percent will be added on the coal—the coal-mining firm will have added k percent in extracting the coal, and the steel firm that uses the coal will apply k percent to its own input costs, which include the coal purchase price. See L. McKenzie, "Ideal Output and the Interdependence of Firms," *Economic Journal,* Vol. 61, (Dec. 1951). Since in our world it is not even true that all firms apply the same markup to marginal costs, one is left with very little presumption that the proposal will lead to an optimal allocation of resources or even to a second-best allocation.

possible that prices set in accord with the principles just described would result in noncompensatory operation of a number
of company services. In such a case, readjustment of the corresponding prices would be required, but in every case the
price modification permitted should be as small as possible—the
price should vary from proportionality with marginal cost by
the minimal amount needed to permit the service to pass our
tests of compensatory operation.

The justification for such "discriminatory pricing" is the fact
that a good sold on compensatory terms must yield a positive
consumers' surplus. For if at some price consumers in total
are willing to pay for a service an amount greater than its real
escapable cost, provision of the service must be definition yield
a positive net benefit to society.

Since the price of each service presumably affects the revenues obtainable from the others, instead of minimizing the adjustments in the prices of the services one item at a time, it
might be more desirable to minimize some sort of weighted-
average-price adjustment. In that case prices would be determined as follows:

Let p_1^*, . . . , p_n^* be the prices satisfying $p_1^*/p_n^* = mc_1/mc_n$,
$i = 1, . . . , n$—1 and $f(p_1^*, . . . , p_n^*) = rB$. Then the final
prices p_i might be those which minimize the variance of prices
(the weighted average of their squared deviations from the prices
that are proportional to the marginal costs). That is, letting Q_i
be the quantity sold of item i and $E_1(p_1, . . . , p_n)$ be the
escapable cost incurred by service i, the p_i would be those that
minimize.

$$\Sigma_i Q_i(p_i - p_i^*)^2/\Sigma Q_i$$

subject to

$$f(p_1, . . . , p_n) = rB \text{ (the legal profit ceiling)}$$

and which pass the test of compensatory operation:

$$p_i Q_i \geq E_i(p_1, . . . , p_n)$$

and where, of course, all $Q_i \geq O$.

Of course this calculation probably involves refinements too far
beyond what can be achieved in practice. It does offer the
advantage, perhaps not always negligible, of precluding destructive pricing. For under the suggested pricing rules the
discretion required in order to price destructively—the ability to

cut prices temporarily as a means to drive out a competitor and then to raise price again—would simply be denied to the firm.

However, we can achieve this result and determine prices in a manner more firmly based in economic analysis with the aid of a theorem originally derived by Manne and subsequently rediscovered by Flemming, Boiteux and others.[13] The theorem asserts the following: Suppose a firm is required to meet some prestated profit requirement, e.g., it is required to cover all of its costs including its cost of capital. If this result if not attained by prices equal to marginal costs, then consumers' surplus from the consumption of the outputs in question will be maximized if, for any two of the firm's outputs i and j, prices are set so that the ratio between $(p_i—mc_i)/p_i$ and $(p_j—mc_j/p_1)$ is equal to the inverse ratio of the elasticities of demand of the two items.

The theorem is particularly interesting because it takes into account not only costs but also consumers' relative preference patterns. Moreover, it is not simply a plausible rule of thumb, but it derived from explicit consideration of consumers' surplus (or Hicksian compensating variation) so that it does in fact arise out of an analysis of the requisites of welfare maximization. Moreover, the theorem, whose logic may at first seem obscure, has a simple intuitive explanation. For if we consider as a distortion in demand any departure in demand patterns from those that result from prices set at marginal costs then, if it is necessary in order to meet a revenue requirement to vary prices from marginal costs, the least distortion will be caused if the largest price changes fall on those items whose demand is inelastic, i.e., those items whose demand will not change markedly in response to a departure from marginal cost pricing.

13. See Alan S. Manne, "Multiple-Purpose Public Enterprises—Criteria for Pricing," *Economica*, N. S. Vol. 19, August 1952, pp. 322–326. See also Marcus Flemming, "Optimal Production with Fixed Profits," *Economica*, N. S. Vol. 20, August 1953, pp. 215–236, and Marcel Boiteux, "Sur la gestion des Monopoles Public astreints à l'équilibre bugétaire," *Econometrica*, Vol. 24, No. 1, January 1956, pp. 22–40. For simple proofs of the theorem see Manne and Boiteux. Professor Bradford and the present author have extended the result to cover the influence of cross elasticities and to derive the result in terms of the concept of compensating variation. This and other related results will be published elsewhere.

CONCLUDING COMMENT

By and large the proposals presented in this paper are in line with the precepts of economic analysis and seem to be the logical means to deal with the issues that have been posed. They would provide for compensatory operation of the firm, motivation for efficiency and innovation, and should serve effectively to discourage deliberate rate-base inflation and destructive competition. It would be visionary to expect that regulatory procedures will march abruptly in the directions that have been outlined. The main practical impact of the discussion is perhaps its systematic account of the shortcomings of current regulatory practice. Yet there are some indications, just barely discernible, suggesting that regulatory procedures are beginning to move slowly toward some of the broader patterns suggested by the paper.

Controlling the Rate of Return on Investment: A Suggested Plan

E. W. CLEMENS

E. W. Clemens, of the University of Maryland, made the following proposals for regulating reform in his Economics of Public Utilities *(1950). They have been promulgated by others since then and persist as "ideas" if not "policies."*

THE MOST significant test of a fair return is whether it will attract capital. What rate of return, with due regard to risk and uncertainty, will attract the investor? Utilities, like competitive industries, must compete for capital. By this test they are drawn into the competitive economic system where they can function with a minimum of arbitrary and dictatorial control. It is not necessary or desirable that a perfect parallel with competitive industry be attained. The indispensable nature of utility service gives the public a compelling interest in creating conditions of stability so that a utility's credit is not endangered, whatever conditions in competitive and less essential industries may be. In short, the elements of both competition and stability must be blended in a workable concept of the rate of return.

Consistency does not require those who argue for a stable rate base to argue likewise for a stable rate of return. The troublesome rule of Smyth *v.* Ames may be rejected for administrative reasons alone, while a certain correspondence to competitive conditions may be attained by a rate of return which fluctuates moderately with the cost of capital.

Let us formulate a policy more specifically.

Partly as a result of the administrative latitude created for commissions by the Hope Natural Gas case there has been a growing tendency to base the rate of return upon the actual past cost of debt capital and upon the present market cost of equity capital. In the writer's mind this is good policy. Since the bondholders receive a contractual return, any change in the market rate of interest would not change the cost of debt capital to the company. Interest would virtually become an operating expense. In the long run the cost of debt capital might be lowered slightly as a result of this consistent policy. The dividend requirements of preferred stock would be handled in the same manner. On the other hand, the risk-taking stockholders might well expect to receive a variable return, based upon the market return from similar securities. Earnings-price and dividends-price ratios would furnish the measure of the cost of equity capital.

The fairness of the return might be measured by the market reaction of the stock of the utility under consideration. Assume for example a utility with common stock representing a prudent investment of $1,000,000 and earning $60,000 after interest charges and preferred dividends. A market value of $1,200,00 for this stock would indicate an earnings-price ratio of 5 percent. The going rate of 5 percent would then be applied to the $1,000,000 to indicate a fair return of $50,000 and a downward adjustment of earnings of $10,000. The value of the stock would presumably be depressed to approximately $1,000,000. A decline in earnings to $45,000 would probably be matched by a decline in the value of the stock to $900,000. An upward adjustment of earnings to $50,000 would bring a rise in the value of the stock to $1,000,000. If, due to investment conditions, the market value of the stock should now fall to $900,000 while earnings held at $50,000, the earnings-price ratio would rise to 5.55 percent. Earnings of $55,500 would be justified on the $1,000,-000 investment. These earnings would normally be justified in comparison with those of other industries.

In other terms, the objective of this formula would be to maintain the market value of common stock by varying the rate of earnings. Certain of the risks incident to the possible depreciation in the market value of capital investments would be eliminated and a somewhat lower cost of equity capital would probably result. At the same time, the overall rate of return as well as the return on common stock would reflect conditions of the investment capital market at all times.

Control on this basis would require either the control of dividend policies or some modification of the earnings-price ratio in respect to the dividends-price ratio. Otherwise a utility could earn a higher rate of return by merely omitting dividends and depressing the market value of its stock. The control of dividend policies and restrictions upon ploughing back profits or internal financing might be desirable for still other reasons.

Control of the rate of return must be premised upon the control of the capital structure. A prudent investment rate base is assumed. The progress made by the SEC, FPC, and the various state commissions gives reason to believe that this objective will be attainable in the near future.

Possible Alternatives to Direct Regulation

EDWARD RENSHAW

These proposals center on changing the profit-making motivations of the public utility companies rather than on curbing profits directly. Edward Renshaw, professor of economics at the State University of New York (Albany), first presented these proposals in an article entitled "Utility Regulation: A Re-Examination" in the Journal of Business of October 1958.

AS AN ALTERNATIVE TO the direct regulation of price, quantity, and the rate of return, society might well consider the possibility of adopting institutional changes that will insure an identification of management's interest with that of the public. Rational behavior on the part of management would then be to strive toward marginal cost pricing rather than to maximize monopoly profits. The following ways in which this identification might be achieved are meant to be illustrative of possibilities; no attempt is made to refine or make operational any one of them.

(a) Consumers might be granted a voting interest in all firms designated to be utilities as a matter of law. To facilitate an efficient operation, important actions by management or the board of directors could be referred to the consumer via municipal elections [1] or the consumer's controlling interest might be delegated to a group of responsible citizens who would form a voting trust.[2]

(b) Consumers could be granted the right to buy the common stock of a utility at a certain price above par. The conversion privilege [3] would serve to put an effective limit on the extent to which it would pay the board of directors to pay out excess profits in the form of dividends. Any time that consumers in

---

1. Oregon statutes grant to municipalities the power to determine service standards required of local utilities and to the voters of municipalities the power, within certain limits, to determine the rates to be charged (see Ralph C. Hoeber, "Role of the Courts in Public Utility Regulation as Exemplified in Oregon," *Land Economics*, XXXIII [February, 1957], 44).

2. For a discussion of voting trusts see Dewing, *op. cit.*, pp. 107–22.

3. For a discussion of conversion privileges see *ibid.*, pp. 256–74.

general felt exploited, they would have the option of recouping losses via stock purchase at a fair price.

(c) Consumers might be given the common stock of all firms designated to be utilities. In order to compensate the holders of outstanding common stock, provision would be made to convert old common stock into bonds and preferred stock yielding a limited return. On first blush, a financial plan involving zero original cost on the part of equity owners may seem radical. Actually, the security of bonds and preferred stock is directly related to earning power,[4] which is a function of the stability and inelasticity of consumer demand. Other things being equal, the greater the degree of monopoly. The more likely it will be that a utility can finance itself completely by means of debt, transferring to the consumer the rewards and costs of risk-bearing. As added protection to bond and preferred stockholders, provisions could be made for the gradual accumulation of equity by the board of directors on behalf of consumers, the returns from equity accumulation to be paid out eventually in the form of dividends or preferably in the form of lower prices.[5]

4. *Ibid.*, pp. 168–255.
5. From time to time it has been suggested by economists that many utilities are subject to decreasing costs. In the case of decreasing-cost industries, it has been pointed out that society might be made better off in the sense that aggregate welfare would be maximized if firms were subsidized to permit marginal cost pricing or allowed to use discriminatory pricing. The interpersonal comparisons involved in subsidization and danger of a monopoly return being exacted if price discrimination were permitted have been deterrents to the actual attainment of marginal cost pricing in decreasing-cost industries. These difficulties would be avoided if consumers were permitted to accumulate equity in decreasing-cost industries, since the returns from equity accumulation could then be distributed in the form of lower prices rather than dividends. For a recent critique of marginal cost pricing see Robert W. Harbeson, "A Critique of Marginal Cost Pricing," *Land Economics*, XXXI (1955), 54–74.

Suggested Further Readings

Averch, H. and L. L. Johnson, "Behavior of the Firm under Regulatory Constraint", *American Economic Review* (December, 1962).

Bernstein, Marver, *Regulating Business by Independent Commission* (Princeton, N.J.: Princeton Univ. Press, 1955).

Bonbright, James, *Principles of Public Utility Rates* (New York: Columbia Univ. Press, 1961).

Caves, Richard, *Air Transport and Its Regulators* (Cambridge, Mass.: Harvard Univ. Press, 1962).

———, "Direct Regulation and Market Performance in the American Economy," *American Economic Review* (May, 1964).

Clemens, Eli W., *Economics and Public Utilities* (New York: Appleton-Century-Crofts, 1950).

———, "Marginal Cost Pricing: A Comparison of French and American Power Rates", *Land Economics* (November, 1964).

Coase, Ronald, "The Federal Communications Commission," *The Journal of Law and Economics* (October, 1959).

Cramton, R. C., "The Effectiveness of Economic Regulation: A Legal View," *American Economic Review* (May, 1964).

Davidson, R. K., *Price Discrimination in Selling Gas and Electricity* (Baltimore, Md.: Johns Hopkins, 1955).

Fulda, C. H., *Competition in the Regulated Industries: Transportation* (New York: Little, Brown and Company, 1961).

Friendly, H. J., *The Federal Administrative Agencies: The Need for Better Definition of Standards* (Cambridge, Mass.: Harvard Univ. Press, 1962).

Garfield, P. and W. Lovejoy, *Public Utility Economics* (Englewood Cliffs, N.J.: Prentice Hall, 1964).

Gerwig, Robert, "Natural Gas Production: A Study of Costs of Regulation," *The Journal of Law and Economics* (1962).

Henderson, A., "The Pricing of Public Utility Undertakings," *The Manchester School Economic Studies* (1947).

Hilton, George, "The Consistency of the Interstate Commerce Act," *The Journal of Law and Economics* (1966).

Hughes, W. R., "Short-Run Efficiency and the Organization of the Electric Power Industry," *Quarterly Journal of Economics* (November, 1962).

Johnson, L. L., "Joint Cost and Price Discrimination: The Case of Communications Satellites," *The Journal of Business of the University of Chicago* (January, 1964).

Jones, W. K., *Cases on Regulated Industries* (The Foundation Press, 1967).

Kahn, A. E., "Economic Issues in Regulating the Field Price of Natural Gas," *American Economic Review* (May, 1960).

Keyes, L. S., *Federal Control of Entry into Air Transportation* (Cambridge, Mass.: Harvard Univ. Press, 1951).

Kolko, G., *Railroads and Regulation 1877–1916* (Princeton, N.J.: Princeton Univ. Press, 1965).

Levin, H. J., "Federal Control of Entry in the Broadcast Industry," *The Journal of Law and Economics* (October, 1962).

———, "Economic Effects of Broadcast Licensing," *The Journal of Political Economy* (April, 1964).

Lewis, B. W., "Ambivalence in Public Policy toward Regulated Industries," *The American Economic Review* (May, 1963).

MacAvoy, P. W., *The Economic Effects of Regulation: The Trunkline Railroad Cartels and the I.C.C. before 1900* (Cambridge, Mass.: M.I.T. Press, 1962).

———, *Price Formation in Natural Gas Fields* (New Haven, Conn.: Yale Univ. Press, 1962).

———, and James Sloss, *Regulation of Transport Innovation: The I.C.C. and Unit Coal Trains to the East Coast* (New York: Random House, 1967).

Meek, R. L., "An Application of Marginal Cost Pricing: The Green Tariff in Theory and Practice," *The Journal of Industrial Economics* (July, November 1963).

Meyer, J., M. Peck, J. Stenason, and C. Zwick, *The Economics of Competition in the Transportation Industries* (Cambridge, Mass.: Harvard Univ. Press, 1959).

Nelson, J. R., "Practical Applications of Marginal Cost Pricing in the Public Utility Field," *The American Economic Review* (May, 1963).

Phillips, Charles F., Jr., *The Economics of Regulation* (Homewood, Ill.: Irwin, 1965).

Troxel, E., *The Economics of Transport* (Homewood, Ill.: Irwin, 1965).

Turvey, R., "Marginal Cost Pricing and Practice," *Economica* (November, 1964).

Westfield, F., "Regulation and Conspiracy," *The American Economic Review* (June, 1965).

Wellisz, S., "Regulation of Natural Gas Pipeline Companies: An Economic Analysis," *The Journal of Political Economy* (February, 1963).

Wiles, P., "Pilkington and the Theory of Value," *The Economic Journal* (June, 1963).

Wilson, George, *Essays on Some Unsettled Questions in the Economics of Transportation* (Bloomington: Indiana Univ Press, 1962).